SINFULNESS

OF

AMERICAN SLAVERY:

PROVED FROM

ITS EVIL SOURCES; ITS INJUSTICE; ITS WRONGS; ITS CONTRARIETY TO MANY SCRIPTURAL COMMANDS, PROHIBITIONS, AND PRINCIPLES, AND TO THE CHRISTIAN SPIRIT; AND FROM ITS EVIL EFFECTS;

TOGETHER WITH OBSERVATIONS ON EMANCIPATION, AND THE DUTIES OF AMERICAN CITIZENS IN REGARD TO SLAVERY.

BY

REV. CHARLES ELLIOTT, D. D.

EDITED BY

REV. B. F. TEFFT, D. D.

"Thou shalt not steal."—EIGHTH COMMANDMENT.

"He that stealeth a man and selleth him, or if he be found in his hand, he shall surely be put to death."—EXODUS XXI, 16.

"The law is made . . for men-stealers."—1 TIMOTHY I, 9, 10.

"Hominum fures, qui vel servos vel liberos abducunt, retinent, vendunt, vel emunt." [Those are *men-stealers* who abduct, keep, sell, or buy slaves or freemen.]—POOL'S SYNOPSIS ON 1 TIMOTHY I, 9, 10.

"Every American who loves his country, should dedicate his whole life, and every faculty of his soul, to efface the foul stain [of slavery] from its character."—EDINBURG REVIEW, NO. LXI, P. 146.

IN TWO VOLUMES.

VOLUME II.

Cincinnati:

PUBLISHED BY L. SWORMSTEDT & J. H. POWER,

FOR THE METHODIST EPISCOPAL CHURCH, AT THE WESTERN BOOK CONCERN, CORNER OF MAIN AND EIGHTH STREETS.

R. P. THOMPSON, PRINTER.

1850.

CONTENTS.

PART V.

EFFECTS ON THE SLAVE, THE MASTER, AND COMMUNITY.

CHAPTER I.

EFFECTS ON THE SLAVE.

CHAPTER II.

EFFECTS OF SLAVERY ON THE FREE PEOPLE OF COLOR IN THE UNITED STATES.

CHAPTER III.

EFFECTS ON THE MASTERS.

CHAPTER VI.

EFFECTS OF SLAVERY ON THE STATE.

CHAPTER VII.

WITNESSES.

CHAPTER VIII.

OBJECTIONS AGAINST THE FOREGOING VIEWS STATED, CONSIDERED, AND CONFUTED.

CHAPTER IV.

CONCLUDING AND PRACTICAL REFLECTIONS.

PART V.

EFFECTS ON THE SLAVE, THE MASTER, AND COMMUNITY.

SINFULNESS

OF

AMERICAN SLAVERY.

CHAPTER I.

EFFECTS ON THE SLAVE.

ONE of the plainest tests in the world is that declaration of our Lord, in reference to false teachers, as well as to all good and evil persons or things: "By their fruits ye shall know them."

In reference to the false prophets, our Lord declares: "Beware of false prophets, which come to you in sheep's clothing, but inwardly they are ravening wolves. Ye shall know them by their fruits. Do men gather grapes of thorns, or figs of thistles? Even so every good tree bringeth forth good fruit; but a corrupt tree bringeth forth evil fruit. A good tree can not bring forth evil fruit, neither can a corrupt tree bring forth good fruit. Every tree that bringeth not forth good fruit is hewn down, and cast into the fire. Wherefore, by their fruits ye shall know them," Matt. vii, 15–20.

Our Savior, in order to show the real character of the wicked Jews, who spoke blasphemously of his ministry and acts, declares: "For a good tree bringeth not forth corrupt fruit, neither doth a corrupt tree bring forth good fruit," etc., Luke vi, 43–45.

The plain common-sense truth is here brought up, that a bad tree will produce bad fruit; and a good tree, good fruit. And the character of the tree, whether good or bad, is easily *known* by its fruits; that is, the *effect* will always be similar to its *cause*. The good heart is the good treasury, and the treasure in it is the love of God and man, or holy principles, and all the benevolent affections, and right acts toward men. The bad heart is the bad treasury, and its treasure is the carnal mind, which is enmity against God, and *ill-will* to man; and this heart is a receptacle charged with error, prejudice, sensuality, irreligion, envy, hatred, malice, and all uncharitableness.

What is true of individuals, is also, in this respect, true of bodies of men, whether of nations, Churches, or any collection of men, under any influences which act on them as bodies. Slavery is a system which influences greatly the slaves themselves, the masters who own and treat them as slaves, as well as the slave community, whether of white non-slaveholders, or colored persons not slaves. On the part of the slave, he is deprived of what are called natural rights, as the right to himself, his labor, property, his wife, children, liberty, and personal security. Slavery utterly neglects or opposes his intellectual, moral, and religious instruction; slavery annuls marriage, authorizes the licentious and indecent treatment of females; it permits excesses and barbarities in punishment, with the perversion of those laws which profess to restrain such abuses; and all the hardships under which the slave labors, in point of law and practice, from his liability to be sold apart, the rejection of his evidence, the impediments to his acquisition of freedom, and its insecurity when obtained.

On the part of the master, slavery, besides its prostration of all human rights, and its contempt of all Divine obligations, leaves to the uncontrolled and uncontrollable direction of masters and managers, the food, the clothing, the general treatment, the continuity, and the intensity of the compulsory labor of the slaves, and of the means by which that labor shall be enforced; and leaves also to the masters the enjoyments of the slaves, with all the unnumbered comforts and charities of their social and domestic life.

Now, if slavery be good and right, its effects will be good on the master and the slave, and the community. But we maintain the contrary; for, when God made men, he made them not to be slaves. So when men are actuated by the best dispositions and feelings, they can not frame a system of slave laws which would prevent injustice, oppression, and the most flagrant breach of God's laws. Slavery has never existed in the world, or in any quarter of it, either before or after the Christian era, in which the vices of the slaves, and the vices of the master in his conduct toward the slaves, have not formed prominent and characteristic features of the history of the times which were polluted by its prevalence. We will take occasion to consider the effects of slavery on the slave, on the master, and on the slave community. And, in the first place, we will notice the effects of slavery on the slaves.

1. We will commence with a few preliminary remarks.

While exaggerations on this topic should be avoided, humanity requires that the whole truth should be honestly spoken.

In treating of the *effects* of slavery, we will speak of its *general*, not universal, effects. There are natural differences among the bond as well as the free; and there is great diversity in the circumstances in which they are placed. The house slave is in circumstances far superior to those of the field hands. The mechanics, too, hold a medium above the field hands, and below the house slaves. But these varieties do not determine the general character of the institution. It has general characteristics, founded on its very nature, and which predominate wherever slavery exists.

There are certain principles which operate on every man in his natural condition of freedom, which restrain his vicious propensities, and greatly regulate his conduct.

Among these may be placed, personal liberty, personal security, the right to property, to one's family, etc. Where these rights are enjoyed, the happiness and welfare of communities are promoted. Wherever these rights are taken away, those who are despoiled of them sink down into creatures of appetite and passion. They approach the level of the beast, and can be moved only by such influences as move beasts. This is the condition to which slavery reduces the great mass which wears its brutalizing yoke. Its effects on the soul are worse than its effects upon the body. Character, property, family respectability, are all withdrawn from the slave. Thus slavery deranges and ruins the moral powers of man.

2. The effects of slavery on the development and training of the intellectual powers may be placed among its evil first-fruits.

South Carolina long ago decided, by several penal sanctions, that it was highly criminal for slaves to do any thing at "mental improvement," and any one who aided slaves to read, write, or keep accounts, was by law considered criminal. And in 1834 the same state, in amending former laws, continues the barbarous vandalism of a former age. The act makes it a crime "to teach or aid any slave to read or write, or cause or procure any slave to be taught to read or write." No slave or free person of color can be employed as "clerk, or salesman." (See for the act Anti-slavery Record, vol. i, p. 157.) Such is law or custom in every slave state. The synod of Kentucky, in 1835, say of Kentucky: "Throughout our whole land, so far as we can learn, there is but one school in which, during the week, slaves can be taught. The light of three or four Sabbath schools is seen glimmering through the darkness that covers the black population of a whole state. Here and there a family is found, where humanity and religion impel the master, mistress, or children, to the laborious task of private instruction. But, after all, what is the utmost amount of instruction given to slaves? Those who enjoy the most of it, are fed but with the crumbs of knowledge which fall from their master's table."

Such is the state of education among slaves in the most privileged slave state of the Union. And, indeed, it is much worse in the states further south. In every country where slavery has existed, either penal laws, or custom, or other causes, have stood in direct opposition to the mental improvement of the slaves. In the West Indies, the grossest ignorance prevailed during the reign of slavery.

Slaveholders are aware that knowledge is power. They know, too, that to instruct the slaves in common school learning, would be to emancipate them. Hence, the true spirit and practice of slaveholders are to fetter the mind, as well as the body, and that, too, in direct opposition to the Gospel and the proclamation of it, which brings light to the intellect and the conscience.

The synod of Kentucky, on this point, says all that can be said on the subject; and, as they testify what they have seen, we will rely on their declarations on the subject. Speaking of the want of education among the slaves, the synod says: "*Nor is it to be expected that this state of things will become better, unless it is determined that slavery shall cease.* The impression is almost universal, that intellectual elevation unfits men for servitude, and renders it impossible to retain them in this condition. This impression is unquestionably correct. The weakness and ignorance of their victims is the only safe foundation on which injustice and oppression can rest. And the effort to keep in bondage men to whom knowledge has imparted power, would be like the insane attempt of the Persian tyrants to chain the waves of the sea, and whip its boisterous waters into submission. We may as soon expect to fetter the winds, seal up the clouds, or extinguish the fires of the volcanoes, as to prevent enlightened minds from recovering their natural condition of freedom. Hence, in some of our states laws have been enacted prohibiting, under severe penalties, the instruction of the blacks; and even where such laws do not exist, there are formidable numbers who oppose, with deep hostility, every effort to enlighten the mind of the negro. These men are determined that slavery shall be perpetuated, and they know that their universal education must be followed by their universal emancipation. They are then acting wisely, according to the wisdom of this world, when they deny education to slaves; they are adopting a measure necessary to secure their determined purpose. Its policy, however, is akin to that which once induced the ruffian violators of female chastity to cut out the tongue and cut off the hands of their victim, to disable her from uttering or writing their names. She has to be maimed, or they would be brought to justice. It is just such policy as the robber exhibits, who silences in death the voices that might expose him, and buries in the grave the witnesses of his crime. He is determined to pursue his occupation, and his safety in it requires that he should not indulge in the weakness of keeping a conscience. How horrible must be that system, which, in the opinion of even its strongest advocate, demands, as the necessary condition of its existence, that knowledge should be shut out from the minds of those who live under it; that they should be reduced as nearly as possible to the level of brutes or living machines; that the powers of their souls should be crushed! Let each one of us ask, Can such a system be aided, or even tolerated, without deep criminality?" (Address of the Synod of Kentucky, pp. 8 and 9.)

The defenders and apologists of slavery are greatly puzzled, when called upon to defend and explain the want of intellectual and moral cultivation of the slaves. Dr. Fuller labors hard at this oar. He says, (Letters, p. 140:) "The words 'moral cultivation' signify, I presume, improvement in holiness. Now, suppose a slave to have the word of God, and to enjoy all the means of grace: why should his moral improvement be impossible, because he labors for my benefit? Then, again, as to intellectual cultivation: the laboring population in all countries have but little taste or time for literature; but if our slaves were taught to read, I know no class of people, employed in manual industry, who would have more leisure for books." Again, p. 157, Dr. Fuller says: "You must already have perceived, that, speaking abstractedly of slavery, I do not consider its perpetration proper, even if it be possible. My sole business now is with present duty. That duty is not the emancipation, but the instruction, moral and intellectual, of the slave; just as, in a despotism, the duty is not granting a free constitution, but improving the subjects." Did not Dr. Fuller know that the slaves have not the word of God, and, if they had, they could not read it? Nor have they the means of grace, seeing this liberty depends on the will of the despotic masters. So Mr. Fuller, p. 158, concedes: "Upon no two plantations is our servitude the same thing. In some instances there may be all the injustice and heartlessness you so well describe." So the treatment varies according to the will of the master; yet, in *some instances*, great cruelties are perpetrated; and this entirely confutes all the pleas that can be rendered for the good treatment of even the many masters—by the way, a very doubtful thing.

3. Let us see what provision slavery makes to supply the bodily wants of the slave. The great principle of slavery is, to make the slave as *profitable* as possible to his master; and to make him a profitable article of property, his bodily powers and wants are to be attended to. As much *profitable labor* as possible is to be exacted from him, and as little expense as is consistent with his availability is to be incurred, in supplying him with food, clothing, house, and medical

attendance. A principle of slavery, then, is, to make the most of his labor, at the least possible expense of food, clothing, housing, and nursing. This alone is treating human beings in direct opposition to the law of God, which teaches that the chief end of man is to glorify God, in improving and exercising his intellectual and moral powers, and doing good to his fellow-men.

The *labor* of slaves is entirely forced, and not voluntary. The problem for the slaveholder is, what is the greatest amount of labor which he can extract from all, male and female, young and old, consistently with his own interests. In the sugar plantations of the West Indies the average labor of the year was about fourteen or sixteen hours a day. In the sugar plantations of the south the amount is probably near the same. This forced labor is calculated to imbrute the man, as the intellectual or moral powers have no proper sphere of exercise.

The *habitations* of the slaves, being generally cold and comfortless, without separate apartments for the sexes, or furniture, have the effect of degrading the inmates to no small degree; while the *food* of the slave is either scanty, or of inferior quality, or partaken of as the offals of the master's table. Hence, when in quantity and quality the food is sufficient, the servile manner in which it is received is calculated to degrade and brutalize the slave.

Nor can the apologists for slavery make out their case, if they can establish the fact, that the slaves are well clothed and fed, and when their labor is not greater than their bodily constitution enables them to endure, or, in short, when the slave has the ordinary sufficiency of comfort for one of inferior species—for a mere brute animal. Our opponents forget that the slave is a being formed for immortality—that God has given him mental faculties like our own—that he has given him human dispositions and feelings, hopes and joys, and social propensities. They forget the right of the slave to Christian marriage, and to instruct and train his children in the nurture and admonition of the Lord. Their claim, too, to education and religious instruction is forgotten. All these rights are denied and withheld by the system of slavery; and it has been held by those who defend the system, that the slave, like his fellow-brute, should be contented if he has a sufficiency of food and clothing, and is secured from the inclemencies of the weather, and has due medical care.

4. The moral effects of slavery on the slave are of the most ruinous kind.

There is necessarily a great want of *moral obligation* on the part of the slave. For what sense of moral obligation can he be expected to possess who is shackled in every action and purpose, and is scarcely dealt with as an accountable being? Will the man, for example, whose testimony is rejected with scorn, be solicitous to establish a character for veracity? Will those who are treated as cattle be taught thereby to restrain those natural appetites which they possess in common with their fellow-laborers of the team? or will women be prepared for the due performance of domestic and maternal duties by being refused the connubial tie, or by being led to regard prostitution to their owner or his representative as the most honorable distinction to which they can aspire? From slavery proceeds that moral degradation which sinks its victim to the level of the brute, with this farther disadvantage, that not being wholly irrational, he is capable of inspiring greater degrees of terror, resentment, and aversion, and will, therefore, seem to his owner to require and to justify severer measures of coercion. Let us enumerate a few particulars in which the demoralizing influences of slavery on the slave will be plainly manifested.

(1.) Slavery leads to licentiousness among the slaves.

This has been the result of it in every country. Just

look at it in the West Indies. Dr. Williamson, who resided in Jamaica fourteen years—from 1798 to 1812—and a steady advocate for slavery, in his Medical and Miscellaneous Observations says: "A stranger is much surprised to observe the domestic attachments which many of the most respectable white inhabitants form with females of color. Among the negroes licentious appetites are promiscuously gratified, and the truth requires that it should not be concealed. The whites on estates follow the same habits, on many occasions, to a greater extent. Black or brown mistresses are considered necessary appendages to every establishment: even a young book-keeper, coming from Europe, is generally instructed to provide himself; and however repugnant may seem the idea at first, his scruples are overcome, and he conforms to general custom." (Vol. ii, pp. 42–49.) "That unrestrained habit of promiscuous intercourse, which almost universally prevails in Jamaica, is, in itself, an insuperable bar to population. Negro women, in that unrestrained and corrupt line of conduct they are apt to pursue, on arriving at puberty, contract habits inimical to all decency, and particularly adverse to all probability of increasing numbers on the estate. . . . An unlucky habit of debasement has established itself, by long custom on estates, of book-keepers attaching themselves to mistresses, slaves on the estate."

In the United States the same system of slavery prevails as in the West Indies, and with the same consequences. The total disregard of marriage by the slave system, which leaves the female slaves entirely in the power of their masters, produces licentiousness, among the colored people, of the most corrupting kind; and this is the inseparable concomitant of slavery, according to all impartial witnesses. The synod of Kentucky declare: "Slavery produces general licentiousness among the slaves." It were needless to make quotations from the host of witnesses which could be produced on this revolting topic. Suffice it to say, that slavery has always been, is now, and ever must be, the cause of unbounded licentiousness. This is inseparable from its very nature. It is, therefore, sinful, because it produces, *per se* and inevitably, this sinful and demoralizing result.

(2.) The slave is a *liar*, because he is a slave. His state of subjugation makes him a hypocrite. The business of his life is to deceive his master. While he is cursing him in his heart, he avows strong affection for him. He pretends sickness to avoid labor. He lies at every turn, to conceal the faults for which he dreads the lash of the overseer or driver.

Indeed, southern law brands the slave as a liar, whose testimony is to be received in no case where a white party is concerned; and, indeed, Chief Justice Henderson, of South Carolina, so decides, in a case where the testimony of a slave was offered. He says: "The master has an almost absolute control over the body and mind of the slave. The master's will is the slave's will. All his acts, all his sayings are made with a view to propitiate his master. *His confessions are made, not from a love of truth, not from a sense of duty, not to speak falsehood, but to please his master;* and it is vain that his master tells him to speak the truth, and conceals from him how he wished the question answered. The slave will ascertain, or, which is the same thing, think that he has ascertained the wishes of his master, and mold his answer accordingly. We, therefore, more often get the wishes of the master, or the slave's belief of his wishes, than the truth. And this is so often the case, that the public justice of the country requires, that they should be altogether excluded. Confessions made to propitiate the good opinion of the jailer, or to avert harsh treatment, are excluded on the same principle. I think the case of master and slave much stronger. The power of the jailer is temporary and limited, that of the master permanent and almost unlimited." (See Sixth Annual Report of Antislavery Society for 1839.)

(3.) He is a *thief*, because he is a slave. This is proverbial. The slave considers theft as merely some recompense for the robbery of his wages. To make up for the quantity and quality of his food, he purloins not only from his master, but from the neighbors of his master.

And indeed theft, especially petty theft, and the knavery connected with it, have always been the effect of slavery in every country. The Anglo-Saxon word *knave* was at first used to designate a *serving man* or *slave*. But, as most slaves became purloiners of their masters' goods, the word *knave* became the name of an unprincipled servant or slave. The name *fur*, which signifies a *thief* in Latin, became synonymous with slave:

> "*Quid domini facient, audent cum talia* FURES?"
>
> (Virgil, Eclog. iii, 16.)

"When servants [*thieves*] do such things, what may not be expected from their masters?"

So Plautus, (Aulul. ii, 46,) says, "*Homo es trium literarum*"—"Thou art a man of three letters," that is, FUR, a THIEF. Theft is, therefore, a legitimate and unfailing consequence of slavery. The example of the original theft committed on the slave, and the continual robbery which he endures, teach him to do likewise. And the daily thefts of slaves generally are no more than imitations, on a small scale, of the felonious theft or robbery practiced by the master on the slave, in depriving him of the fruits of his labor and appropriating them to himself. The master, both by *precept* and *example*, teaches the slave to be a thief. He teaches him by *precept*, when he affirms that slavery is right or it is the best for the slave, under the circumstances, or he has bought him, or inherited him, or the like. The master teaches the slave by *example* to be a thief, in the daily wrongs inflicted on him, and the rights of which he is divested. When the master, openly, daringly, and constantly breaks the commandment, "Thou shalt not steal," on the person of the slave and the labor of his hands, is it marvelous that the slave should imitate his example, and steal food when he is hungry, or any thing else which would, even in part, recompense him for the robbery which he suffers?

(4.) He is a *Sabbath-breaker,* because he is a slave. To say nothing of slavery in heathen countries, its effect has been to violate the Sabbath. In the West Indies, Sabbath markets and Sabbath work became generally established, and the practice was continued till slavery was destroyed. In the United States, where work is not required on the Sabbath, this day is the common day of recreation to the slaves, when they are not compelled by necessity to cultivate their gardens for food, or make and mend their clothes, or attend market and visit their friends. And in proportion as the Sabbath is violated, the manners of the people are vicious, regardless of every commendable principle, and afford examples of human depravity which corrupt society.

(5.) He is a *murderer,* because he is a slave. He *hates* his oppressor. His bosom is actuated with a spirit of *revenge.* All slaves are not guilty of these sins habitually, which lead to murder. But the *tendency* of slavery is to lead its victims to hatred and revenge, and then to murder. The system has *murdered* the slaves, and, by the law of retaliation, the slave in his turn approaches the master with the same evil design. And the various insurrections of slaves, and the murders which have arisen from them, are nothing more than the natural workings of the system of slavery.

(6.) He is *indolent,* because he is a slave. Having no motives to urge him to industry, arising from the support of himself and family, or benevolent enterprise, and as the fruit of all his labor goes to his owner, the slave, in the absence of all adequate motives to industry, works as little as he can. The whip and its fear are the only stimulants to action; and these are evaded as much as possible.

5. Slavery, in its mildest form, is an *unwarrantable degradation of human beings.* Man was created in the image of God, and placed over the animate and inanimate creation. He is formed to seek happiness, perform duties, to scatter blessings in his sphere. Slavery dethrones him, places him in society with brutes, and subjects him to a condition for which he was not made, and to which he is not adapted—where he can not act himself, and where little that is human is left, except a capacity to suffer. The degradation of man to an article of *property* is not an *accident* of slavery; it is the very essence of the thing, and which must enter into a system of servitude to constitute slavery. Without this there could be no slave. A deprivation of self-ownership, is the unwarrantable degradation of man; and this is inseparable from slavery—it is slavery itself. He is branded as a liar by the laws of the system, in being refused the right of bearing testimony. He can not be a party to a civil suit in any equitable way. He is doomed to ignorance by being deprived of education. The means of moral and religious instruction are not granted to the slave; on the contrary, the efforts of the religious to supply these wants are either forbidden or discountenanced by law. The slave, too, must submit to the master. The penal codes bear much more heavily on the slave than on the free man. They are prosecuted and tried upon criminal accusations in a manner inconsistent with the rights of humanity and the spirit and precepts of religion. Let us just glance at a few of those degrading and inhuman indignities to which the slave is constantly exposed, and to which he is reduced.

The very name of SLAVE, and its derivatives, *slavish, servile, bondage,* etc., show the degradation of the man. We can say nothing more insulting or disparaging of another, than that he is *servile* or *slavish*. And to possess the spirit and feeling and occupy the place of a slave, is to have sunk to the lowest depth of degradation and dishonor. No punishment except death is more dreaded than slavery, and to avoid it many have suffered death. The processes by which the spirit is broken to slavery are among the most inhuman that can well be enumerated.

The heir to slavery, since the theft and robbery of the African slave-trade have ceased, is seized upon at birth, in helpless infancy, and is degraded into a thing and vendible property, without either intellectual, moral, or religious training. And if humanity can succeed in teaching and elevating in any degree the slave, it receives neither encouragement nor help in this work, but, on the other hand, discouragement and almost insuperable hinderances.

Look at the practice of *selling slaves*, the practice of having *markets* for men as for cattle, of examining the limbs and bodies of men and women as of a brute, putting human beings under the hammer of an auctioneer, and delivering them, like other articles of traffic, to the highest bidder, the separation of families, with a thousand other indignities and degradations, that pen can not write and tongue can not utter; the doings only of the slave market can utter such atrocities of sin and degradation of the human species.

Look at the degradation of the *whip*, and the *fear* which it inspires. The motive to labor, on the part of the slave, is the fear of the whip, or other corporeal punishments. Take away the whip, and the slave, as a matter of course, would be idle, because his labor hath neither dignity nor reward. His labor brings no new comforts to his wife or children. The motive which sways him is necessarily a base and degrading one. To work in sight of the whip, under the terror of blows, is to be exposed to perpetual insult and degrading influences. The disgrace of the whip is itself a dishonor, which sinks its victim to the grade of a brute.

Nor has slavery spared woman in its tortures. In the West Indies, the flogging of women on the naked back and hips, while in a prostrate condition, was customary, and never could be broken up by a thousand enactments, and by all the shame and dishonor connected with it. When the Legislature of St. Christopher refused to abolish female flogging, they decided, however, that women, for the future, should have the privilege of being flogged "on the *shoulders*," instead of the "*hips*." A benevolent slave apologist, Mr. Huskisson, however, hoped the Legislature of the island would consent "entirely to abolish a mode of punishment so destructive of self-respect, and so calculated to debase the female character." But he was disappointed in his pious wish.

The flogging of women in the United States presents the most revolting picture of degradation. And, although the cases of flogging women on the bare back, while prostrate on their face on the ground, may not be of general use, the occurrence of *one such case*, unwhipped by the severest stripes of justice, is a sin and disgrace to any nation, sufficient to stamp them with one of the worst traits of barbarism and cruelty. Suspending women by the hands, or in any other manner confining them, and inflicting on their bare backs the incisions of the whip, is a common mode of correcting slaves, and sufficient to bring the wrath of Heaven on the perpetrators of such inhumanity—on those who enact the laws, or can silently remain subject to such laws, without using every means in their power to annul them. Yet, this could not be done while slavery exists; for while it exists the whip and female whipping on the bare back form part and parcel of the very system, and an indispensable part of it, too.

And then look at their common implements of torture,

confinement, correction, and, certainly, the most revolting degradation is inseparable from them. Here are the large *chains*, to which the ranks of emigrating or transported slaves are attached, with the small side chains and handcuffs, to complete their apparatus of migration; and then, the *branding irons*, and *iron collars*, and the like, too ignominious for the most degraded felons and murderers sent to our penitentiaries or sentenced to the gallows! and all these in open daylight exposure, to say nothing of the private modes of degrading punishment and treatment, brutalizing to those who are punished and those who inflict the punishment.

The slaves are more degraded than the Africans. However humiliating the statement may be, it is nevertheless true, that, low in point of morals as the Africans may have been in their own country, their descendants in this country are lower still. Such, at least, are the accounts that some travelers give of the Africans, before they were corrupted by the European slave-traders.

6. We might bring to view a variety of facts to show, that the degradation of the slaves, morally, intellectually, and in their modes of life, is of the lowest kind, and that this is owing to slavery; but it seems unnecessary to add any thing to what we have already given on this point, in previous pages.

7. Nor can the kindness of masters do away the evils of slavery. It is readily admitted, that the kindness of masters does much for the mitigation of slavery. Were it possible to render it innocent, the efforts of some masters would accomplish the object. Slavery itself is evil, corrupt, and sinful, not merely through any singular corruption in slaveholders, but from its own intrinsic nature, and in spite of all efforts to make it good. It is incapable of reform or of essential mitigation. It is radically wrong, and can never be made right; and meliorations, to do away its leading, moral wrongs, would proceed from step to step, till

they would reach the master wrong—the root of all others—the making man a slave at all, or, in other words, making him property and a chattel, or, as the civil law terms it, making him a *quadruped,* or beast. Slavery itself is a corrupt fountain, which sends forth bitter waters. It is a bad tree, which brings forth bad fruit.

8. Nor can slave laws be resorted to as an apology or release from the sins or bad effects of slavery. The legal constitution of slavery has been written in characters of blood, and hung round with all those attributes of cruelty and revenge which jealousy, contempt, and terror could suggest; and should it be pleaded, that the present race of slaveholders are not so much in fault as the *system* in which they are involuntarily connected, yet slavery is, in itself, an atrocious crime; and every man, who loves his country, should do his utmost, in all righteous ways, to do it away.

CHAPTER II.

EFFECTS OF SLAVERY ON THE FREE PEOPLE OF COLOR IN THE UNITED STATES.

1. THE diversities of men, as to color, stature, and a variety of other circumstances, are numerous and striking, although all are derived from one common stock—Adam and Eve.

The known influence of natural causes is sufficient to account for the diversities which characterize the inhabitants of different continents.

The influence of heat over all material substances is almost omnipotent, in changing their form, magnitude, and color. Vegetable plants removed to a climate or soil different from their own, manifest a wonderful power of adapting their conformation and habits to the circumstances around them. Several of the annual herbs of the polar regions, when transferred to a temperate clime, become perennial shrubs; and our shrubs, in the torrid zones, become stately trees. Some trees, covered in their wild state with thorns, when cultivated become smooth and harmless. All the different kinds of *apples* are derived from the same original, and owe their peculiarities, to their various climates, soils, situation, and culture.

The diversities in man are not greater than those found among vegetables or animals. Quadrupeds of the same family, in the state of nature, are generally of one color; but they become of various colors by domestication; and so of animals in general.

In the different climes of Europe, Asia, Africa, and America there are men of all shades of color, from white to black, and of various sizes. There have been reckoned five races of men; but fifty might as well be enumerated as five. The Portuguese colony settled at Mitomba have become perfect negroes. The Foulahs, by their mode of life, neat dress, cleanliness of person, have preserved their elegance of form and delicacy of features, though dwelling among the naked and deformed aboriginals of Guinea. In America the grades of color among the aboriginals are less than among other nations, owing, doubtless, to similarity in their modes of life; and the great equality of climate, owing to the contiguity to the great seas, as well as other causes. In Europe the complexion becomes darker as the climate becomes warmer. The English and the more northern Europeans are fairer than the Germans and French, while those on the southern verge of Europe are darker than those who dwell north of them. In short, in the process of time the descendants of negroes have acquired the very same complexion which the descendants of Europeans have acquired by residing, for successive generations, in the same climate.

2. We have sufficient proofs of the high intellectual character of portions of the African race, to place them on the same general footing with the people of other countries.

If Africa now ranks low in civilization, there was a time when she ranked high. Before imperial Rome was known, even by name, Thebes, the wealthy and the great, was celebrated in song by Homer; and Memphis was renowned in power and magnificence when Greece was in a state of barbarism. Egypt excelled in science, in population, wealth, and power, and gave letters to Greece. Carthage was long the rival of Rome in wealth, in arms, in power, and knowledge. Other nations of northern Africa contended long and stoutly with the mistress of the world. Origen, Tertullian, Cyprian, and Augustine were all Africans. At a later period the Moors were distinguished for their learning and genius.

Among modern Africans even those who have been chained in mind as well as in body, by the crushing influence of slavery, we find men who will advantageously compare with those of the Anglo-Saxon race. Time would not allow us to give a list of them, much less to give a description of their characters. (See, for this, "Tribute to the Negro," which will give a detailed account of the talents and characters of many Africans.)

Many nations, who were once considered as deficient in mental capacity, have reached the highest pitch in the scale of empire; while the very nations, which at one time contemned them, have sunk into a state of degeneracy. The Romans could have found an image of their own ancestors in the representation they have given of ours, in their description of the ancient Gauls, English, Germans, and Spaniards; and we may see a very exact picture of our early ancestors, in the condition of the African and Indian tribes. Cicero, in one of his letters to Atticus, says: "The result of the British war may now be looked for. It appears that the entrances to the island are fortified with wonderful barricades. It is now known that there is not a particle of silver in that island, nor any hope of prey, except in slaves; and I suppose that you will not expect that any of these slaves are instructed either in music or in letters." (Epist. ad Atticum, lib. iv, ep. 16.) The ancient Britons went nearly without clothing, painted their bodies in a fantastic manner, offered up human victims to rude idols, and lived in hollow trees or the rudest habitations. Cicero informs us, that the ugliest and the most stupid slaves came from England; and he urges his friend Atticus "not to buy slaves from Britain, on account of their stupidity, and their inaptitude to learn music and other accomplishments. Cæsar describes the British, generally, as a nation of very barbarous manners. "Most of the people in the interior," he says, "never sow corn, but live upon milk and flesh, and are clothed with skins." In another place he remarks: "In their domestic and social habits the British are as degraded as the most savage nations. They are clothed with skins, wear the hair of their heads unshaven and long, but shave the rest of their bodies, except their upper lip, and stain themselves a blue color with wood, which gives them a horrible appearance in battle." We would be surprised if, from these circumstances, Cicero, Cæsar, Tacitus, and Pliny, would argue that the present descendants of the Britons should be slaves; yet this is both the law, the practice, the argument, and the judicial decision in the United States.

3. Among those colored people who are free in the United States, the effects or operations of slavery are visible, injurious, and unjust.

In the early part of the government of the United States, the slaves were mostly colored persons. Free colored persons were, therefore, the object of hate to slaveholders. In 1790 they drove Congress into a most barbarous policy, in excluding all colored foreigners from being naturalized. In 1792 an act was passed prohibiting all colored men from being enrolled in the militia. In 1793 Congress passed the inhuman law by which every foot of soil in the north was made legitimate race-ground for the slave-catcher, and making it the duty of every state officer to aid when called on. In 1810 a law was passed that no colored man should carry the mail, or be employed as a *driver* on a coach that carries it, under a penalty of $50.

"In some of the states, if a free man of color is accused of crime, he is denied the benefit of those forms of trial which the common law has established for the protection of innocence. Thus, in South Carolina, it is thought quite unnecessary to give a grand and petit jury the trouble of inquiring into his case; he can be hung without so much ceremony. But who is a *colored* man? We answer, the fairest man in Carolina, if it can be proved that a drop of negro blood flowed in the veins of his mother.

"The following extract, from a late Charleston paper,

gives us a curious instance of the administration of criminal justice in a Christian country, in the nineteenth century:

"'*Trial for Murder.*—William Tann, a free colored man, was tried on Friday last, at John's Island, for the *murder* of Moses, the slave of Joseph D. Jenkins, Esq., of that place. The *court* consisted of William H. Inglesby and Alexander H. Brown, Esqrs., judicial magistrates, (justices of the peace,) of this city, together with *five freeholders.* The murder was committed at John's Island, on the fourth of July, 1832, Tann shooting down Moses with a musket loaded with buckshot. Tann was at that time *overseer* for a Mr. Murray, and from the *fairness of his complexion was thought to be and passed for a* WHITE MAN. He was *accordingly* bound over to answer for this offense to the COURT OF SESSIONS, but it having been decided on an *issue* ordered and tried at Walterboro, for the purpose of ascertaining his *caste,* that he was of MIXED BLOOD, he was *turned over* by the court, to the jurisdiction of *magistrates and freeholders.* The court found him guilty, and sentenced him to be hung on Friday next, April 24, 1835.' (Charleston Courier.)

"In South Carolina, if a free negro 'entertains' a runaway slave, he forfeits ten pounds, and if unable to pay the fine, which must be the case ninety-nine times in a hundred, he is to be sold as a slave for life. In 1827 a *free woman and her three children* were thus sold, for harboring two slave children.

"In Mississippi, every negro or mulatto, not being able to *prove* himself free, may be sold as a slave. Should the certificate of his manumission, or the evidence of his parents' freedom, be lost, or stolen, he is reduced to hopeless bondage. This provision extends to most of the slave states, and is in full operation in the District of Columbia.

"In South Carolina, any assembly of free negroes, even in the presence of white persons, 'in a confined or secret place, for the purpose of *mental instruction*,' is an unlawful assembly, and may be dispersed by a magistrate, who is authorized to inflict twenty lashes on each free negro attending the meeting.

"In the city of Savannah, *any person* who teaches a free negro to read or write, incurs a penalty of thirty dollars. Of course, a father may not instruct his own children.

"In Maryland, a justice of the peace may order a free negro's ears to be cut off for striking a *white* man. In Kentucky, for the same offense, he is to receive thirty lashes, 'well laid on.' The law of Louisiana declares, 'Free people of color ought never to insult or strike *white* people, nor presume to conceive themselves equal to the whites; but, on the contrary, *they ought to yield to them on every occasion*, and never speak or answer them but with respect, under the penalty of imprisonment, according to the nature of the case.'

"The corporation of Georgetown, in the District of Columbia, passed an ordinance, making it penal for any free negro *to receive from the post-office, have in his possession*, or circulate, any publication or writing whatsoever of a *seditious* character.

"In North Carolina, the law prohibits a free colored man, whatever may be his attainments or ecclesiastical authority, to preach the Gospel.

"In Georgia, a white man is liable to a fine of *five hundred dollars* for teaching a free negro to read or write. If one free negro teach another, he is to be *fined* and *whipped* at the discretion of the court! Should a free negro presume to preach to, or exhort his companions, he may be seized without warrant, and whipped thirty-nine lashes, and the same number of lashes may be applied to each one of his congregation.

"In Virginia, should free negroes or their children assemble at a school to learn reading and writing, any justice of the peace may dismiss the school, with twenty stripes on the back of each pupil.

"In some states, free negroes may not assemble together for any purpose, to a greater number than *seven*. In North Carolina, free negroes may not trade, buy, or sell, out of the cities or towns in which they reside, under the penalty of forfeiting their goods, and receiving in lieu thereof thirty-nine lashes.

"By a late law of Maryland, a free negro coming into the state, is liable to a fine of fifty dollars for every week he remains in it. If he can not pay the fine, he is SOLD.

"In Louisiana, the penalty for instructing a free black in a *Sunday school*, is, for the first offense, five hundred dollars; for the second offense, DEATH!

"Such, in a greater or less degree, is the situation of three hundred thousand of our fellow-citizens." (Jay's Inquiry.)

The laws of some free states have largely partaken of the spirit and character of those of the slave states in reference to free colored people. But this is no other than the element of slavery at work even in the very bosom of freedom. In Ohio, these odious laws have been repealed, and we trust the same will take place in every state where they now exist.

4. The power of slavery, so constantly associated with color, has been and is now severely felt by the free colored people throughout the Union, especially in the slave states. The mere acquisition or exercise of political official power, though of itself of great value, is not always necessary for every individual in society, in order to secure and enjoy the rights of justice, as is the case with minors, women, and aliens, and others. Of these advantages we need not speak just now; nor will our treatise afford room to discuss the subject of political rights. We refer to the common privileges of right and wrong, of justice and injustice; and

we must maintain, that slavery, apart from color, has entailed on the free colored people the infliction of great wrongs, as well as deprived them of many just and equitable rights. The quotation from Jay, given above, presents, in part, the serious wrongs which the free colored man suffers in every part of the United States. We can give here no more than some limited views of the practical operations of this disfranchisement of personal rights.

Take an example. The Rev. Jabez P. Campbell, pastor of the African Methodist Episcopal Church, for the cities of Boston and Providence, was traveling from the latter city to Philadelphia, in March, 1843. He went to the office of the Jersey City Railroad Company and purchased a ticket, paid as others paid, on the condition that he should have, without molestation, a comfortable seat. After he had got on his way till the second conductor entered the cars, he was ordered out of the car, although he had purposely seated himself in a corner, to be as inoffensive as possible. On his refusal to go, the conductor, assisted by others, beat him unmercifully, and conveyed him to a baggage or lumber car.

When Mr. Douglass, a colored man, paid his passage from Liverpool to New York, on board the Cunard steamer line, on the condition of equal privileges, he was, on the passage, deprived of this right, and compelled to occupy a room by himself.

But the instances of injustice toward free colored persons would fill volumes, and we can not enlarge on the subject. Indeed, this is not necessary, as the most careless observers must have noticed these things.

5. As to the present state of moral and intellectual improvement of the free people of color in the United States, especially in the free states, some remarks may be made here.

According to the census of 1840, the number of free persons of color in the United States was three hundred and eighty-six thousand, two hundred and thirty-five, amounting now, we suppose, to about four hundred thousand; and as the slaves amount to about three millions, the free colored people are about one-eighth part of the entire colored people. In the free states, and in some of the slave states, the religious and intellectual improvement of the free colored people is very considerable, taking into view their great disadvantages. Although shut out generally from the schools and colleges of the whites, they are providing for themselves, by patronizing schools, academies, and even colleges of their own. Their religious movements, too, are such as to give great promise for the future. And although their progress, as yet, is far behind that of their more fortunate neighbors, yet their advancement is such as to afford guarantee that they are rapidly, on the whole, approximating to a state which will be hazardous to the existence of slavery. They have several weekly papers, conducted by colored persons. Those who, raised in slavery, could not read, are learning; and every free man, woman, and child, who can read ever so imperfectly, apply themselves constantly in reading books and papers, of all descriptions. With the power of the press in their own hands, and the doors of knowledge considerably open to them, their advancement, in the next and succeeding generations, will be such as to show a wonderful improvement that will shake the very foundations of slavery, if, indeed, slavery can live to see two or three generations of its further existence in the United States.

6. Yet the colored free population are very little in love with a northern climate. In Ohio they mostly live, by choice, in the southern portions of the state. The same remark will apply to the free states generally. The colored people shun the cold, and strongly incline to the warmer regions. Even the free population of the slave states are slow to move north, and, indeed, prefer the greater disabili-

ties in connection with a slave population to the greater advantages connected with their color in the free states.

Nor is Canada an exception, only that the miserable fugitive, pursued in the slave states by the blood-hounds and the man-catchers, and through the free states by the iron hand of unjust laws, and unprincipled hireling man-stealers, finds that legal security from unjust laws under the mane of the British lion, which he could not enjoy under the soar of the American eagle. In 1848, in Canada West, according to the census taken, the entire number of colored persons was ten thousand. About three thousand, three hundred and forty-two, or *one-third*, are natives of the United States. The increase for the previous five years was one thousand, four hundred and four, or about two hundred and eighty-one per year. The number in all Canada was considered, in 1840, to be about fifteen thousand. Yet Canada is far from being the genial home of the colored people. Nor do they, as some suppose, enjoy even there equal political privileges. (See proceedings of the World's Convention, for 1840, pp. 302–314, and p. 285.)

The free people of color in Virginia are now sixty thousand; in 1900 they will be about two hundred and forty thousand; and in 1950—one hundred years from now—they will be one million. A similar progress will be the result in other slave states.

7. *Colored people under the British government.*—It is asserted, however, with great confidence, that the colored people under the British flag are treated in all respects as British subjects, and as white men are treated in England. This, we are persuaded, is an error of considerable magnitude, as well as of injurious consequences to those whom it is intended to favor. It is most true, that in the colored provinces of the British empire, the colored man is now free, and on the highway to progress. It is also true, that when colored diplomatists visit Britain they are treated

in character. It is also true, that colored visitants to England, as public persons, are for the time being admitted into the best British society. But then the privileges end just there. In social relations, the unofficial colored man, in the heart of England, is not a whit better in his social advantages than he is in the free states of America. And, as a demonstration of the matter, no persons in America are more unwilling to form any kind of association with colored people, than the English, Irish, Scotch, and German emigrants; and this same prejudice—or call it what you please—they carry with them from the very bosom of England, Scotland, and Germany.

Mr. Walsham, an English author, in his admirable "Essay on Colonization," in speaking of the condition of the colored people of London about the year 1840, says, "The blacks living in London are generally profligate, because uninstructed, and vitiated by slavery, for many of them were once slaves of the most worthless description; namely, the idle and superfluous domestic, and the gamblers and thieves who infest the towns in the West Indies. Some come to attend children and sick persons on board, and others are brought by their masters by way of parade. In London, *being friendless* and *despised on account of their complexion*, and too many of them being incapable of any useful occupation, they sink into abject poverty." (See Tribute to the Negro, p. 112.)

8. *British colonization of colored people.*—Many colored persons, embracing slaves and free persons, at the Revolutionary war, adhered to the British government. These, for the most part, settled in Nova Scotia. Some went to England. The rigid climate and the disabilities of color barred their prosperity. Those who went to England found no genial home in the social relations of England, from which they were excluded. Although those in Nova Scotia were settled there as a reward for their services by the British

government, their condition was miserable. Mr. Clarkson, brother to Thomas Clarkson, who was intrusted with this matter, took over eleven hundred persons of them to Sierra Leone, in fifteen vessels, and formed there a colony, about the year 1790. Others, from time to time, were sent there from England, and captured slaves were added to the colony. Notwithstanding the various vicissitudes of this colony, Mr. T. Clarkson, in 1840, speaks of it in the following encouraging terms:

"It is pleasing, however, to reflect, that, though the object of the institution, as far as mercantile profit was concerned, thus failed, the other objects belonging to it were promoted. Schools, places of worship, agriculture, and the habits of civilized life were established. Sierra Leone, therefore, now presents itself as the medium of civilization for Africa. And, in this latter point of view, it is worth all the treasure which has been lost in supporting it; for the slave-trade, which was the great obstacle to this civilization, being now happily abolished, there is a metropolis, consisting of some hundreds of persons, from which may issue the seeds of reformation to this injured continent; and which, when sown, may be expected to grow fruit without interruption. New schools may be transplanted from thence into the interior. Teachers, and travelers on discovery, may be sent from thence to various directions, who may return to it occasionally as to their homes. The natives, too, able now to travel in safety, may resort to it from various parts. They may see the improvements which are going on from time to time. They may send their children to it for education; and thus it may become the medium of great intercourse between England and Africa, to the benefit of each other." (Clarkson's History of the Slave-Trade, pp. 492, 493.)

After the British philanthropists had succeeded in abolishing the slave-trade, and accomplished emancipation in the West Indies, they especially turned their attention to the condition of Africa, and the relief of those free persons of color who remained among the whites. Accordingly, Mr. Buxton, in 1839, after due consultation, held a meeting of a few friends, consisting of about twenty noblemen and gentlemen, preparatory to the formation of the "African Civilization Society." It was held in Dr. Lushington's house in London. The following is the memorandum prepared by Mr. Buxton for the meeting:

"*April*, 1839.

"The principle has been sufficiently explained: it is the deliverance of Africa, by calling forth her own resources.

"In order to do this, we must, 1. Impede the traffic; 2. Establish commerce; 3. Teach cultivation; 4. Impart education.

"To accomplish the first object, we must increase and concentrate our squadron, and make treaties with coast and land chiefs.

"To accomplish the second, we must settle factories and send out trading ships.

"To accomplish the third, we must obtain by treaty lands for cultivation, and set on foot a company.

"To accomplish the fourth, we must revive African institutions, look out for black agents, etc.

"What, then, is actually to be done now by government? Increase the squadron; obtain Fernando Po; prepare and instruct embassies—or authorize governors; to form treaties, including prevention of traffic; arrangements for trade; grants of land. By us: form a trading company; revive the African institute." (Buxton's Life, p. 380.)

"After all the assistance that could be obtained from white agencies, in order to promote civilization and Christianity in Africa, the managers of the association declare, 'We want black persons for all conceivable situations, from the highest to the lowest, in our African colony, and every one ought to be a real Christian; but a good Providence has prepared these in the West Indies and at Sierra Leone.'" (Ibid., p. 383.)

9. *Colonization of free people of color in the United States, and the American Colonization Society.*—The climate of the United States, especially the northern states, is not congenial to the African constitution. Hence, a climate further south is the object of earnest desire to the colored man. The disabilities of color, also, are in the way, and that, too, independently of slavery, just because black is not white or red. This is a fact, known, and read, and *felt* by all men, both black and white, apart from all moral considerations, and moral principles and actions. Yet, color of any hue is no plea, excuse, or even plausible sophism for injustice or wrong of any kind, much less for the master wrong of slavery. Equality refers to social as well as political and civil life. Social equality must be founded in marriage and the social relations growing out of it. And yet it is an inalienable right of all adults to have one-half of the making of the marriage contract, leaving to the other partner the other half. And such alliances are not likely to take place in the United States very soon. Hence, the want of social equality, between whites and blacks, is felt every-where. And who can force this? Would not laws enforcing this be of the same type with the slave laws themselves? Hence, the most careful observers perceive that the colored people now, or at any early period, if ever, are not likely to stand up in the enjoyment of equal social privileges with white persons in the United States, any more than in England, Ireland, Scotland, or Germany.

There are *four* extensive countries which, as to climate, soil, and productions, are congenial to the constitutional make of the colored man; namely, Africa, the West Indies, Mexico, and South America.

Africa has territory enough to meet the wants of all the colored people of the United States.

The West Indies alone could probably receive them and be ample enough.

And then Mexico, with a colored population, could find room for all of them.

The countries of South America, with its vast savannas, has territory enough for all the colored people of the United States, ten times told.

Thus, God has provided for them ample ground to occupy, much more suitable to their constitutions and habitudes than the United States. And who, that carefully considers the matter, but will come to the conclusion that the colored man will emigrate south, whether the white man will aid him or not? he will seek the warmer climate after his emancipation, as opportunities will offer. At present, Liberia is the most desirable home for the colored freeman. The West Indies, now mostly free, will soon become a point of great attraction, as the white inhabitants of these islands will either return to their mother countries, or be amalgamated with the colored. Thus, the great wave of colored emigration, already commenced, will set in for the south, and will find a safe resting-place there.

The following appeal of William W. Findlay to the colored people of Indiana, will soon, in all probability, be the general sentiment of the free colored people of the United States. Already this opinion is of considerable strength and extent; but it will, doubtless, soon become general. This is in the nature of things—in the inseparable relation of cause and effect. This appeal is extracted from the Western Christian Advocate of April 25, 1849:

"Dear Friends,—The writer being a colored man, it may be supposed that he desires the well-being of his race, not of a part of the colored race, but of the whole race of

Africans, in this land and in Africa. Nor do I consider myself guilty of affectation, when I say, that I ardently desire their elevation, and am willing to contribute all I can to that end. It has long been an inquiry with me, how can our race be elevated? *How can colored men be made truly independent?* After much anxious and painful inquiry, I have concluded, that to be *truly* independent, we must enjoy rights and privileges *as broad* and *as liberal* as those enjoyed by the white citizen of the United States; in other words, have the right of electing our law-makers and our magistrates; and all the offices of state should be accessible to our color; and not only so, but we should be free to move in such circles of society as we may be entitled to by our moral worth, character, and talents; and likewise, free to form alliance with those classes of society. These, in my humble opinion, are the rights and privileges *we must possess* before we can be *independent.*

"But now let us inquire in candor, do we as a people enjoy such independence? Do colored men, in the most liberal of the northern states, enjoy such independence? You all know that they do not. The sad reverse is the case. And will the time soon come, in the history of American society, when the colored man will be permitted to enjoy such independence—independence, not only in civil things, but independence in all the more delicate matters of social equality? I must honestly confess, I think not. And further: I am bold to confess, that any thing short of the above-described independence will not satisfy me; nor should any thing short satisfy the man of an independent spirit.

"But such independence we can not obtain in the United States; therefore, I will seek it outside the United States. *I will seek it where I know I can find it,* and that is in the republic of Liberia, which is the only Christian republic where the colored man can find a quiet and secure home.

Nor do I act dishonorably, in thus escaping from civil and social oppression; for I am only doing what thousands of the first and best settlers in the United States did; and I think it an honor to follow their example, in seeking liberty, though, like them, I be compelled to seek it in a wilderness. And the object of this appeal is, to invite you who love true independence, and are willing to endure some toil to obtain it, to go with us to that land of liberty, where we may likewise aid in the elevation and enlightenment of our whole race, *which duty is more obligatory on us* than upon the white race, many of whom are willing to *sacrifice* their lives and property in the work of converting Africa.

"Some of you may blame us for not staying in this land and contending for all the above rights of man. Our answer to all such complaints is this: we believe that civil slavery in this land will be abolished by divine Providence without the co-operation of the free colored man; he requires not our aid in this work—he can and will in his own way, sweep slavery from the civil institutions of America. But I honestly doubt whether it is the will or order of Providence to grant us perfect social equality *with the white race at this time,* nor am I disposed to strive or quarrel with them for this favor, but would follow the example of Abraham, who disliked the strife that had sprung up between him and Lot, and religiously proposed separation as a remedy for the quarrel, and a means of perpetuating peace; so we should separate from the white race, that we may be free and they enjoy peace; for, doubtless, God has given this land to them. Acting from the above religious and honorable views, we confidently expect that God will bless us in our movements.

"It is the design of the writer and some of his friends, to go out to Liberia about the month of October or November next, and it is desirable to have as many emigrants from Indiana as we can muster. Liberia holds out many attractions for the man of color, but the greatest is that of liberty and independence. Thousands have gone from this land to that, and all who have been industrious have done well; many of them are becoming wealthy, but what is best, *they are all free!* Come, let us go and cast our lot in with them and be free likewise. If any of you have been cherishing the spirit of independence, and long for such freedom as the free republic of Liberia offers, and if you desire a passage to that land, just let your wishes be known to the Agent of the American Colonization Society of this state. Address Rev. J. Mitchell, at Indianapolis, who will be pleased to book your name as an emigrant, and procure for you a passage out, and send you all the information you may want. No time should be lost. *Act now*—act for yourselves, your children, and your race.

"WM. W. FINDLAY.

"*Covington, Ia., April* 6, 1849."

Indeed, the sentiments entertained by Mr. Findlay are such as are inevitable, from the facts in the case. Dr. Bailey, of the National Era, who has so long stoutly opposed the American Colonization Society, positively pleads for colonization, or, in other words, voluntary emigration—the very thing that all true-minded colonizationists plead for, notwithstanding the vast amount of unmerited reproach which has been cast upon them. Mr. Bailey justly says:

"All that we need is faith in God and his wise providence. Let us do what we know to be right; do to the black man as we would wish to be done by; and in the long run, good, and nothing but good, must be the result. We have no doubt but the Creator has ordained laws as well for the distribution of men over the face of the earth, as for their government. Were slavery abolished throughout the whole south to-day, by the voluntary action of the people having the power, those laws would begin to operate, and different races of men would seek the latitudes congenial to their constitutions and habitudes; so that, in process of time, without any violent disturbance or compulsory colonization, they who can labor all the year round in a hot climate, in latitudes whence the white man must exile himself one-half of every year, would be concentrated about the shores of the Gulf of Mexico." (National Era, March 22, 1849.)

10. *The American Colonization Society.*

If any institution on the face of the earth could be destroyed by hard words and fierce denunciation, the overflowing of unmingled hatred and total uncharitableness, then the American Colonization Society must long since have perished. In elaborate essays, in public speeches, in the resolutions of conventional assemblies, in newspapers, pamphlets, and common parlance, it has been accused, condemned, and then hanged, quartered, and burned, with the most determined hostility. If one-thousandth part of what it has been charged with is true, then it should certainly have perished under the stroke of justice.

And what does this Society propose to do? Nothing else, kind reader, except to colonize, on the coast of Africa, the free colored man of the United States, with the consent or at the request of those colonized. This is the whole, except to aid the colored man there to begin the world, form a free government, and thus present a model republic for the benefit of Africa, the colored people of the world, and the good of the human race. This is the avowed object of the Society, and, certainly, the avowed object of the leading men who have conducted its business.

It will be readily admitted, that some, perhaps many, who have engaged in promoting the interests of the Society, have been influenced by unworthy motives. Some may have been colonizationists, in order to send off the surplus free colored persons, so as to strengthen the bonds of slavery. Others, very unworthily, or unwisely, have made colonization the condition of emancipation. This, too, is a *wrong* way to do a *right* thing; and to make colonization the condition of emancipation, is to make transportation its condition; that is, it punishes the emancipated, as the price of his freedom, with the penalty of his manslaughter, or murder in the second degree, as in Britain; or with a place in the penitentiary, as in the United States. The present plan proposed in Kentucky, though called colonization, is not the voluntary colonization of the Colonization Society. It is the transportation penalty of Great Britain imported to this country. It is punishing innocent men as felons, and will never meet with God's blessing; and if we read right the book of God's providence, Kentucky will sooner be the field of the plagues of Egypt, or the destruction of Jerusalem, than that God will permit such unheard-of injustice to succeed, without the severest judgments of his hand. The moral sense of good men in Kentucky will never admit of this outrage on human rights; and, surely, the present Colonization Society could never allow of such a perversion of its fundamental principles, as to become a partner in such wrong.

After all the hard things said about the Colonization Society, it is in a fair way to answer the end of its institution. In 1840 Lieutenant W. T. F. Jackson, of the English blockading squadron, writes thus, respecting colonization in Africa and Liberia:

"Formerly, during Governor Turner's time, we held the sovereignty from Sierra Leone to Gallinas; but, owing to some false economy, we withdrew our protection and lost our authority. I would rather hold up Liberia, as an example to our government, than offer my own remarks; the Americans have established a colony, and from that spread north and south, from Cape Mount to Cape Palmas, between which places slavery is now hardly known. When we look upon this handful of people, unprotected by their own government, alone and unaided, and consider what they have done, I think we may well blush at the futility of our own efforts."

11. The truth is, that the free colored people of the United States and of the West Indies are destined, in the providence of God, in spite of slavery, to be the harbingers of God to the entire colored population of the world. Their growing intelligence will soon enable them to be the pioneers of religion, science, and civilization to all colored countries. The slaves of the United States, state after state, will certainly become free. All who are free will improve, and will find employ wherever they are set free. In process of time they will seek for the *social* and full political equality further south, among those of their own color, which they can never enjoy, by any change of laws, in the present United States, any more than they now do in Canada, England, or in any other country where the white people have such a vast preponderancy.

Besides, it is preposterous to suppose, that insurrections would take place by securing to them liberty, at least the liberty of just and equal rights, to say nothing of mere political equality. Good and just treatment would secure their love, and aids to assist them to emigrate would be all they would ultimately wish or require, if even that. The testimony of General Jackson to the colored soldiers would be the testimony which, no doubt, would be awarded to the three millions of slaves now in the United States, were they made free with as little delay as the mere alteration of constitutions and laws would demand, in order to accomplish the work of general emancipation.

On December 18, 1814, General Jackson issued, in the French language, the following address to the free people of color:

"Soldiers! when on the banks of the Mobile I called you

to take up arms, inviting you to partake the perils and glory of your white fellow-citizens, I expected much from you; for I was not ignorant that you possessed qualities most formidable to an invading enemy. I knew with what fortitude you could endure hunger and thirst, and all the fatigues of a campaign. I knew well how you loved your native country, and that you had, as well as ourselves, to defend what man holds most dear—his parents, relations, wife, children, and property. You have done more than I expected. In addition to the previous qualities I before knew you to possess, I found, moreover, among you a noble enthusiasm, which leads to the performance of great things.

"Soldiers! the President of the United States shall hear how praiseworthy was your conduct in the hour of danger; and the representatives of the American people will, I doubt not, give you the praise your exploits entitle you to. Your General anticipates them, in applauding your noble ardor.

"The enemy approaches; his vessels cover our lakes; our brave citizens are united, and all contention has ceased among them. Their only dispute is, who shall win the prize of valor, or who the most glory—its noblest reward.

"By order, THOMAS BUTLER, *Aiddecamp.*"

CHAPTER III.

EFFECTS ON THE MASTERS.

1. This topic can not, perhaps, be discussed, without giving great offense; yet truth and right demand its consideration. On the most careful examination of this point, it will be found that the effects of slavery on the masters have been evil, and only evil. It can not be allowed for a moment, that the relation of master and servant is a right one, or the proper fulfillment of its reciprocal duties sufficient; for slavery is no relation established by God, but expressly forbidden and punished by him; and it is a total perversion or gross abuse of the relation of master and servant. Still, in regard to a certain class of slaveholders, who are not such by choice, but necessity, the following declaration of Rev. Samuel C. Wilks, in his sermon on slavery, p. 34, preached in London, in 1830, may not be inapplicable. He says: "The present wretched condition of all classes, the master as well as the slave, in our slave dependencies, shows that the blessing of God has not rested on the system. I impute no blame to individuals; some I highly respect, others I pity. I would advocate nothing harsh or personal; many are not involved in slaveholding by any act of their own; it was their patrimony, and they grieve over its evils, and would willingly diminish them; but the system is too direful to be dealt with tenderly; it is incurable; it must be exterminated."

The effects of slavery have always been injurious to those who practice it. It is so opposed to the nature of man, which can not bear, without great moral injury, the exercise of absolute power or absolute subjection. Man can not with safety be the depository of despotic power over individuals, especially over those of the other sex, if protected by no ties of natural affection. The incessant and inhuman cruelties practiced in the system of slavery, necessarily tend to harden the human heart against the tender feelings of humanity in the proprietors of slaves, in their children, in the overseers, in the slaves themselves, and in all who habitually see these cruelties. Now, the eradication, the diminution or weakening of compassion, tenderness, and humanity, is a great depravation of heart, and must be followed by a great depravation of manners. And measures which lead to such depravation of heart and morals can not but be extremely hurtful. The facilities also to low vices which absolute power bestows, it is not in the unregenerate nature of man to resist. Whatever, then, may be the effect on individuals, the community in all slaveholding states is stamped with moral peculiarities, of the most odious character, the direct and inevitable result of the institution.

2. The testimony of the best witnesses might be multiplied to almost any extent, in proof of the deepest degeneracy of morals among masters, in all slaveholding countries. We will adduce a few of these testimonies, out of the great number that could be produced.

The synod of South Carolina and Georgia, in the year 1833, draws the following hideous picture of the *moral* influence of slavery on the masters. "The influence of the negroes upon the moral and religious interests of the whites is destructive in the extreme. We can not go into special detail. It is unnecessary. We make an appeal to universal experience. We are chained to a putrid carcass. It sickens and destroys us. We have a millstone hanging about the neck of our society, to sink us deep in the sea of vice. Our children are corrupting from their infancy, nor can we prevent it. Many an anxious parent, like the missionary in foreign lands, wishes that his children could be brought beyond the reach of the corrupting influence of the depraved heathen. Nor is this influence confined to mere childhood

If that were all, it would be tremendous. But it follows into youth, into manhood, and into old age. And when we directly come into contact with their depravity in the management of them, then come temptations, and provocations, and trials, that unsearchable Grace only can enable us to endure. In all our intercourse with them, we are undergoing a process of intellectual and moral deterioration; and it requires almost superhuman effort to maintain a high standing either for intelligence or piety.

"Those only who have the management of servants, know what the *hardening effect* of it is upon *their own feelings toward them.* There is no necessity to dwell on this point, as all *owners* and *managers* fully understand it. He who commences to manage them with tenderness, and with a willingness to favor them in every way, must be watchful, otherwise he will settle down in *indifference, if not severity.*

"Who would credit it, that in these days of revival and benevolent efforts in this Christian republic, there are OVER TWO MILLION [now three] of human beings in the condition of *heathens,* and, in some respects, in a worse condition? From long-continued and close observation we believe that their moral and religious condition is such that they may justly be considered the *heathen* of this Christian country, and will bear a comparison with heathen in any part of the world. . . . It is universally the fact, throughout the slaveholding states, that either custom or law prohibits them the acquisition of letters, and consequently they have no access to the Scriptures. . . . In the vast field extending from an entire state beyond the Potomac to the Sabine river, and from the Atlantic to the Ohio, there are, to the best of our knowledge, not *twelve* men exclusively devoted to the religious instruction of the negroes. As to the *ministers of their own color,* they are destitute, infinitely, both in point of numbers and qualifications, to say nothing of the fact that such a ministrv is looked upon with distrust, and discountenanced. But do not the negroes have access to the Gospel through the stated ministry of the whites? No. . . . We venture the assertion, that if we take the whole number of ministers in the slaveholding states, *but a very small portion pay any attention to them.* . . . The negroes have no regular and efficient ministry; as a matter of course, NO CHURCHES; neither is there sufficient room in their white churches for their accommodation. We know of but *five* churches in the slaveholding states built expressly for their use. . . . We may now inquire if they enjoy the privilege of the Gospel in private, in their own houses, or on their own plantation? Again we return a negative answer. They have NO BIBLES to read at their own fireside; they have no family altars; and, when in affliction and sickness, or death, they have no minister to address to them the consolation of the Gospel, nor to bury them with solemn and appropriate services."

The remarks of Mr. Jefferson, in his Notes on Virginia, are valuable as the testimony of a slaveholder. He says: "The whole commerce between master and slave is a perpetual exercise of the most boisterous passions; the most unremitting despotism on the one part, and degrading submission on the other. Our children see this, and learn to imitate it; for man is an imitative animal. If a parent had no other motive, either in his own philanthropy or his self-love, for restraining the intemperance of passion toward his slave, it should always be a sufficient one that his child is present. But generally it is not sufficient. The parent storms; the child looks on, catches the lineaments of wrath, puts on the airs in the circle of smaller slaves, gives a loose rein to his worst passions, and thus nursed, and educated, and daily exercised in tyranny, can not but be stamped by it with odious peculiarities."

3. Slavery is the parent of *idleness* to the slaveholder and his family. The slaves are the servile class whose business

it is to do all the labor, and consequently to exempt the masters from manual work. Hence, as labor is confined principally to the slaves, it becomes disgraceful to work. In a country filled with slaves, labor belongs to them only, and a white man is despised in proportion as he applies himself to it. The consequence is that some will nearly starve; others will betake themselves to the most dishonest means to obtain a livelihood. Hence, also, indolence and an aversion to work are necessarily engendered in youth surrounded by a servile class, who are engaged in these pursuits. And even when parents are disposed to raise their children to industry, they find it in all cases very difficult, and in most cases totally impracticable. Children very soon learn that work is the business of slaves, and that for free people to labor is disgraceful. Idleness and an aversion to labor follow, inseparably, the holders of slaves.

4. Prodigality is another effect of slavery. Either accustomed to derive much profit from the toil of slaves, or at least calculating on this, slaveholders have generally been wanting in economy, and wasteful in their outlays. This is the history of slavery in all countries, and in all ages. More bankruptcy and squandered estates prevailed in the West Indies than in any other part of the British dominions. And it is notorious, that where fortunes have been often so easily made, in the southern states, the bankruptcy and prodigal expenditures have far exceeded any thing to be found in the free states.

5. Slavery debilitates the constitutions of slaveholders. Idleness leads to this. Ease and luxury debilitate the body and the mind; and this process of debility is producing in every successive generation a people more feeble than their predecessors. While slavery violates the plan of Heaven, by dooming some to excessive toil, and releases or debars others from healthy labor, it reduces the exempt class to debility, sickness, and premature death.

6. Pride and haughtiness in the masters are among the natural productions of slavery. This is the tendency in all who are in power, wealth, or station considered as above their fellow-men. But it is peculiarly true in regard to slaveholders. The reason is the following, and the proofs of it are found in the actual workings of slavery. The slave is placed in a relative degradation to the master, far below what any other class of men, not slaves, are placed in reference to others. Hence, the pride of elevation on the part of the master is proportionally increased. And the haughtiness of the master to the slave expresses itself in a great variety of ways. The very *names* given to the slaves frequently utter this truth. The terms of disrespect, such as *fellows, dogs,* teach the contempt of the masters toward them. Their treatment, in all the social relations of life, go to the same point. And were we to give specimens of the actual expressions of pride, haughtiness, disdain, etc., on the part of the masters toward the slaves, we could fill volumes with the details. The same pride of the slaveholders manifests itself to all non-slaveholders who labor for their living, and who are called, in the style of slaveholders, "white slaves," "mean whites," and such other designations as show the temper of the man possessing absolute power.

7. But the despotism or tyranny of slavery is one of the most striking characteristics of the system. Indeed, after the first theft or robbery committed on the slaves by the master when he obtains his slaves, whether by purchase or *receiving* as heir the stolen property, despotism is the first and leading element in the character of the slaveholder. The slave is one who is entirely in the power of his master. The master is one who has absolute control over the life, liberty, and the best interests of the slave; for the slave laws that seem to protect the lives and property of the slaves, are, in most cases, perfect nullities. The law which rejects

the testimony of slaves, properly nullifies all laws protecting the life and persons of the slaves. And, as despotism enters largely into the original elements of slaveholding, so the system generates it in all its ramifications, to an enormous extent.

The love of power is one of the strongest passions of the human breast; and the more nearly that power approaches to absolute despotism, the more it is desired and enjoyed. It has been remarked by Tacitus, one of the most shrewd observers of human nature, that there is nothing so sweet to the human heart as the gratification which arises from the consciousness of having the life of a fellow-creature at one's disposal. And power, in the hands of men, is in no case so much subject to abuse as in its exercise over their own species; a circumstance which forms no small argument against slavery. Take an example: When an ordinance was enacted at the Cape of Good Hope, permitting slaves to redeem themselves, a Mr. Cloete, a landholder near Cape Town, was violently declaiming against this ordinance, when a gentleman said to him: "But if any of your slaves obtain the means of paying you the full market price for their freedom, are you not sufficiently compensated?" "No," said the slave-owner; "for their mere *labor* I may be compensated; but what will compensate for the deprivation of the *power* I have over them—the power not merely of a *master*, but of an *owner?*" Man is also a tyrant, it is true, to the inferior animals; but, unrestrained by law, he becomes a wolf to man, and, under the influence of violent passions, liable to be excited by the most trifling circumstances, is not to be intrusted with power over the liberty and life, the soul and body, the happiness or misery of his fellow-man.

8. Another result from slavery is licentiousness among the masters.

To own the persons of females as slaves, is necessarily

fatal to the purity of a people. Females, under the dominion of masters, have no power to resist the violation of their persons. The master may perpetrate on them the most horrid crimes without redress. The slave must, without murmur, give up his wife, daughter, or sister for prostitution, should the master require it. Hence it happens, that in some families it is difficult to distinguish the free children from the slaves. It is often the case that the greater number of the master's own children are born, not of his wife, but of the wives and daughters of his slaves, whom he has basely prostituted as well as enslaved.

In a slave community the loose rein is given to youthful licentiousness. And early licentiousness is fruitful of crime in after life. The early habits of young men in close familiarity with the slaves, continue in exercise in mature life.

A consequence of this criminal connection is, that the same slave mother often becomes the mother of children of which the master and his sons are the fathers. And hence masters, not unfrequently, transmit to perpetual bondage their children and grandchildren. Brothers and sisters are often the slaves of their own natural brothers and sisters. Among the pollutions of heathenism nothing is worse than this. A slave country reeks with licentiousness.

Besides, slavery not merely puts the chastity of the slave in the power of the master and his sons, but, also, exposes it to the attacks of any white man. Slaves can not bear testimony against any who are white; hence, the door is open for the practice both of violence and seduction. The consequence of this is manifest in every slaveholding community, by the constant increase of mulattoes.

In addition to this, in the slave-growing states, which comprise the northern range of slave states, it is an object to have the progeny as nearly white as possible. Hence, the association of the whites and the expected mothers is encouraged or rewarded; and young female slaves, the fruits of such damning admixtures, are held at very high prices by their owners. They are purchased with great readiness by the slave-traders, and sold at enormous prices in the far south to the abandoned white bachelors, who abound in this country.

9. The licentiousness of slave countries has become notorious. Without exception, the abominations of slavery, in this one point alone, are sufficient to stamp it with the greatest sinful criminality that can be conceived. It is, however, an unpleasant task even to refer to such wickedness. We will just make a few quotations, from the published statements concerning the licentiousness of slavery in the West India Islands. The entire identity, in all material respects, between the state of things in the West Indies and this country, is so complete, that a description of the one is a description of the other.

Edwards, in his history of the West Indies, (book iv, chap. 1,) says: "Concubinage is practiced by white men of all ranks or conditions; the fact is too notorious to be concealed or controverted." Dr. Williamson, (vol. i, p. 49,) an apologist for slavery, declares: "And the truth requires that it should not be concealed, the whites follow the same habits, on many occasions, to a greater extent." Mr. Stewart, (Past and Present State of Jamaica, p. 173,) after stating that "the most gross and open licentiousness prevails among all ranks of the whites," declares additionally, "every unmarried white man, and of every class, has his black or brown mistress, with whom he lives openly."

The Rev. Mr. Bickell observes, (West Indies As They Are, pp. 104, 105:) "It is a well-known and notorious fact, that very few of the white men in the West Indies marry, except a few professional men, and some few merchants in the towns, and here and there in the country a proprietor or large attorney. Most of the merchants and shopkeepers in the towns, and the whole of the deputy planters [overseers] in all parts of the country, have what is called a housekeeper, who is their concubine or mistress, and is generally a free woman of color; but the book-keepers, who are too poor and too dependent to have any kind of establishment, generally take some mulatto or black female slave from the estate where they are employed, or live in a more general state of licentiousness. This is so very common a vice, and so far from being accounted scandalous, that it is looked upon by every person as a matter of course; and if a newly-married young man happens to have brought a few moral or religious ideas with him from Great Britain, he is soon deprived of them by taunt or ridicule, and is in a short time unblushingly amalgamated into the common mass of hardened and barefaced licentiousness." (See Godwin's Lectures on Slavery, p. 68.)

The *annual profits* to proprietors in England, from estates in Jamaica, arose in part from the prostitution of the negresses to the book-keepers, mechanics, etc. The following is a specimen of the accounts rendered to the home proprietors: "Hire of Gracey, a mulatto, to Mr. ——, at £50 per annum;" "Hire of Anne Clarke, a mulatto, to Mr. ——, at £16 per annum;" "Hire of Catharine Stewart to Mr. ——, from 5th of June to Dec. 31, at £20 per annum." (See Antislavery Reporter, vol. v, p. 77.)

The licentiousness of Jamaica, in the reign of slavery, almost exceeds belief. Here is a part of the testimony of Mr. Baillie, before the committee of Parliament, replete with information. "Does not much licentious intercourse take place between the white classes and the slave population, whether black or colored? I do not consider that there is any licentious connection between them, if I may be permitted to put this construction upon it: white people are in the habit of having a woman living with them, and, I believe, in most instances in the same way as man and wife do in this country (England)—kept mistresses they are called; but as to any violation of decency, I have not seen it. Can you name any overseer, driver, or other person in authority, who does not keep a mistress? I can not." (See second Letter from Legion, p. 33.)

"It [slavery] produces general licentiousness among the slaves. Marriage, as a civil ordinance, they can not enjoy. Our laws do not recognize this relation as existing among them; and, of course, do not enforce, by any sanction, the observance of its duties. Indeed, till slavery waxeth old and tendeth to decay, there can not be any legal recognition of the marriage rite, or the enforcement of the consequent duties; for all regulations on this subject would limit the master's absolute right of property in his slaves. In his disposal of them, he would no longer be at liberty to consult merely his own interest. He could no longer separate the wife and husband to suit the convenience of the purchaser, no matter how advantageous might be the terms offered. And as the wife and husband do not always belong to the same owner, and are not often wanted by the same purchaser, their duties to each other would thus, if enforced by law, frequently conflict with the interests of the master. Hence, all the marriage that could ever be allowed to them would be a mere contract, voidable at the master's pleasure. Their present quasi marriages are just such contracts, and are continually thus voided. They are, in this way, brought to consider the matrimonial engagement as a thing not binding, and they act accordingly. Many of them are united without even the sham and forceless ceremony which is sometimes used. They, to use their own phraseology, 'take up with each other,' and live together, as long as it suits their mutual convenience or inclination. This wretched system of concubinage inevitably produces revolting licentiousness." (Address of Synod of Kentucky, pp. 13, 14.)

10. One undeniable effect of the licentiousness of the white slaveholders, is the amalgamation of the whites with the blacks. According to the laws of slavery, both ancient and modern, the child must follow the condition of the *mother;* so that if the mother be a slave, her offspring must also be slaves. But if the contrary were true, and children would follow the condition of the father, a large portion of those who are now slaves, under the operation of such a law, would become free; and in a few generations all would be free, provided no new cargoes of slaves would be smuggled from Africa. A mixture of color is rapidly increasing by means of illicit connections, much more so than by lawful marriage. Were the slaves freed, they would improve in moral and religious principles, which would tend to prevent irregular practices. If free, they would no longer be subject to the power of despotic masters, who can, without restraint, compel the female slaves to become their prostitutes when they please. Hence, where the colored people are free and enlightened, we find them living in families, according to the institution of marriage, and forming alliances among their own color. The amalgamation of the races is mostly between the slaves and their masters and other white persons. And where slaves are raised for market, and the whiter the color the higher the prices, a great variety of measures and inducements are resorted to, that the marketable chattels may be enhanced in value by the lightness of their color, and the absence, as far as possible, of the black color. Hence, in the south the process of amalgamation is going on with great rapidity. In slave states where the colored people are few and the whites numerous, very few slave children can claim persons of color for their fathers. For instance, it is positively affirmed, or, rather, it is a matter of fact, that in Kentucky and Missouri most of the colored children are the offspring of white

fathers; the children, in most cases, being a medium color between the white father and the colored mother.

11. The truth is, slavery is a great system of amalgamation, and masters often enslave their own children and other near relatives.

The following advertisements, mere specimens out of thousands, are the testimonials to this, and their own pens, and mouths, and public manifestoes undeniably declare this:

"*One hundred dollars reward* will be given for the apprehension of my negro, Edmund Kenney, alias Roberts. He has *straight* hair, and a complexion so nearly *white* that a stranger would suppose there was no African blood in him. He is so very artful, that in his language it is likely he will deceive those who might suspect him. He was with my boy Dick a short time since in Norfolk, and offered him for sale, and was apprehended, but escaped under the pretense of being a white man. ANDERSON RAWLES,

"*Dentonville Post-office.*

"*January* 6, 1837."

"*One hundred dollars reward.*—Ran away from James Huyhart, Paris, Kentucky, the mulatto boy Norhan, aged about fifteen years, a very bright mulatto, and would be taken for a white boy, if not closely examined; his hair is black and straight.

"*August* 4, 1836."

"Absconded from the subscriber, her negro man, John. He has a very *light complexion*, prominent nose, etc.

"W. J. SANGLAIS."

Another advertisement says: "Sam calls himself Sam Pettigrew; *light sandy hair, blue* eyes, *ruddy* complexion; he is *so white* as easily to pass for a white man."

The following is a case exemplifying the abomination brought to view here:

"On our arrival, Mr. W. purchased a farm, five or six

miles from the city, [St. Louis.] He had no family, but made a housekeeper of one of his female slaves. Poor Cynthia! I knew her well. She was a quadroon, and one of the most beautiful women I ever saw. She was a native of St. Louis, and bore an irreproachable character for virtue and propriety of conduct. Mr. W. bought her for the New Orleans market, and took her down with him on one of the trips I made with him. Never shall I forget the circumstances of that voyage. On the first night that we were on board the steamboat, he directed me to put her into a state-room he had provided for her, apart from the other slaves. I had seen too much of the workings of slavery not to know what this meant. I accordingly watched him into the state-room, and listened to hear what passed between them. I heard him make his base offers, and her reject them. He told her that if she would accept his vile proposals, he would take her back with him to St. Louis, and establish her as his housekeeper, on his farm; but if she persisted in rejecting them, he would sell her as a field hand, on the worst plantation on the river. Neither threats nor bribes prevailed, however, and he retired, disappointed of his prey. The next morning poor Cynthia told me what had passed, and bewailed her sad fate with floods of tears. I comforted and encouraged her all I could; but I foresaw but too well what the result must be. Without entering into any further particulars, suffice it to say that W. performed his part of the contract at that time. He took her back to St. Louis, established her as his mistress and housekeeper at his farm, and before I left had two children by her. But mark the end! Since I have been at the north, I have been credibly informed that W. has been married, and, as a previous measure, sold poor Cynthia and her four children—she having had two more since I came away—into hopeless bondage." (Narrative of the Life of William W. Brown, pp. 45, 46.)

12. The effects of slaves on domestic peace are of the most injurious kind, producing discontent, contention, jealousy, and the constant breach of natural affections. Slaves are generally raised without moral instruction, possess a low degree of moral feeling, and therefore are not very conscientious in the preservation of domestic peace. Various families and individuals of different feelings are crowded together, so as to produce fierce contention. This disturbs the peace of the master's own family. Again: as slaves consider themselves working for others, they seldom do their work properly. This provokes the masters and overseers to acts of severity and even cruelty. The slaves, too, when they can, very often indulge in falsehood, treachery, dishonesty, lewdness; and their conversation, in the hearing of the master's children, is of the most vitiating description, calculated to pollute the minds of young persons, whether male or female. The vices of the slaves, as well as their corrupting conversation, and low ideas, are calculated to interfere with the peace of the families, as well as to affect them in other respects injuriously. And the frequent floggings, or various modes of punishment, form no very pleasant family incidents in the bosoms of families, or in reach of them in the negro quarters and kitchens.

The practice of slavery according to law tends to destroy natural affection, and even to brutalize the feelings of human nature. As all children born of female slaves are themselves slaves, it is no uncommon thing for fathers to sell their own children, to be slaves for perpetual generations, and therefore subject to the whole system of misery which belongs to a state of slavery. For a man to sell the children of another is, in some respects, worse than to sell his own; yet there are circumstances of horror peculiar to each of them. To sell the children of another appears more fiendish, because in that case the seller has no moral right of property in the child; but in the other case the father has a certain right of property in his own child, till it arrives at the age of twenty-one. In the case of a man selling his own children, he acts the most brutish; but the man who sells the child of another, acts the most fiendish.

That parents keep in slavery their own children, and sell them, the proofs are strong, and the instances innumerable. It is pretty well ascertained that the descendants of at least one of the Presidents of the United States are now slaves. We will content ourselves now by adducing the testimony of Miss A. E. Grimke, of South Carolina, in her address to the Christian women of the south. She asks: "Were the female slaves of the south sold by their fathers? How shall I answer this question? Thousands and tens of thousands never were. *Their* fathers *never* have received the poor compensation of silver or gold for the tears and toils, the suffering and anguish, and hopeless bondage of *their* daughters. They labor day by day, and year by year, side by side, in the same field, if haply their daughters are permitted to remain on the same plantation with them, instead of being—as they often are—separated from their parents and sold into distant states, never again to meet on earth. But *do the fathers of the south ever sell their daughters?* My heart bleeds, and my hand trembles, as I write the awful affirmative, YES! The fathers of this Christian land often sell their daughters, *not* as Jewish parents did, to be the wives and daughters-in-law of the men who buy them, but to be the abject slaves of petty tyrants and irresponsible masters. Is it not so, my friends? I leave it to your own candor to corroborate my assertion.

"In 1834 a man who had resided three years in New York, and bore a good character, was taken out of his bed at midnight, and, with his wife and son, carried back into slavery by his *own cousin.*

"In the same year a white man, of Newbern, North Carolina, carried his four *slave children* to New Orleans, by way of New York, having sold his *wife, their mother,* to a New Orleans trader, three years before.

"In the same year a man by the name of Phillips was taken up in New York, by a 'speculator,' *to whom he had been sold by his father,* and carried to Virginia as a slave. Many *honorable* names might be mentioned in connection with such facts." (Antislavery Record, i, 29.)

A distinguished Methodist clergyman, a native of the south, who exercised his pastoral functions long in Kentucky and Tennessee—but for the twenty-eight years last past of Illinois—on a visit a few years ago to Burlington, Iowa, fell into conversation with a very intelligent and pious lady, formerly from one of the most wealthy districts of Kentucky. The lady lamented the disadvantages of her new home for want of domestic aid in doing her work. The preacher remarked to her that times had very much changed in Kentucky since they left there—now over some twenty years ago—that in consequence of the forbidden connections of white husbands with the slaves, the lives of the slaveholders' wives were embittered; and confusion reigned in the families, owing to the unnatural alliances, eventuating in white brothers and sisters mingling with colored brothers and sisters, whose future lot was that of slavery. The lady could hardly credit the narrative. The preacher requested her, that, as she was soon to visit her friends in Kentucky, she might inquire of her former sisters in the Church, and ladies of her acquaintance, and learn for herself the truth of his statements, which he had learned on a recent visit to Kentucky. The lady paid her visit, instituted her inquiries, and learned to her sorrow the truth of what she had been informed. The result was, that she joyously thanked God for her deliverance from the domestic evils of slavery, and very contentedly bore the inconveniences of her situation in a new free state, released, as she was, from the domestic broils and disturbances of slavery.

Miss Martineau, in her Views of Slavery and Emancipation, p. 46, gives the following description, true, without doubt, of the cares of a slaveholder's wife of a certain class:

"But the wives of slaveholders are, as they and their husbands declare, as much slaves as their negroes. If they will not have every thing to go to rack and ruin around them, they must superintend every household operation, from the cellar to the garret; for there is nothing that slaves can do well. While the slaves are perpetually at one's heels, lolling against the bedposts before one rises in the morning, standing behind the chairs, leaning on the sofa, officiously undertaking and invariably spoiling every thing that one had rather do for one's self, the smallest possible amount of real service is performed. The lady of the house carries her huge bunch of keys—for every consumable thing must be locked up—and has to give out, on incessant requests, whatever is wanted for the household. She is forever superintending and trying to keep things straight, without the slightest hope of attaining any thing like leisure and comfort.

"What is there in retinue, in the reputation of ease and luxury, which can compensate her for toils and cares of this nature? How much happier must be the lot of a village milliner, or of the artisan's wife, who sweeps her own floor and cooks her husband's dinner, than that of the planter's lady, with twenty slaves to wait upon her—her sons migrating, because work is out of the question, and they have not the means to buy estates—and her daughters, with no better prospect of marrying, as she has done, to toil as she does!

"Some few of these ladies are among the strongest-minded and most remarkable women I have ever known. There are great drawbacks, as will be seen hereafter; but their mental vigor is occasionally proportioned to their responsibility. Women who have to rule over a barbarous society—small though it be—to make and enforce laws, provide for all the physical wants, and regulate the entire habits of a number of persons who can in no respect take care of themselves—it must be strong and strongly disciplined, if they in any degree discharge this duty. Those who shrink from it become, perhaps, the weakest women I have any where seen—selfishly timid, humbly dependent, languid in body, and with minds of no reach at all. These two extremes are found in the slave states, in the most striking opposition. It is worthy of note, that I never found these women strong enough voluntarily to brave the woes of life, in the presence of slavery, nor any woman weak enough to estimate the vices of the system, each knowing, prior to experience, what those woes and vices are." (Miss Martineau's Views of Slavery, p. 46.)

"A kind slave-master, in one of the Carolinas, had a large family, of various colors—some enslaved, some free. One of the slaves was his favorite daughter. She grew up beautiful, elegant, and much accomplished. Dying, he willed his heir, her brother, to provide for her handsomely, and make her free. But her brother was a slave-master, and she was a slave. He kept and debauched her. It would be unlawful even to speak of such things, were it not taking the part of tyrants to conceal them. At the end of four or five years he got tired of her; and that notorious slave-dealer, Woolfolk, coming down to collect a drove, he sold his sister to him. 'There is her cottage,' said he to Woolfolk; 'she is a violent woman. I don't like to go near her; go and carry her off by yourself.' Woolfolk strode into the cottage, told her the fact, and ordered her to prepare. She was dreadfully agitated. He urged her to hasten. She rose and said, 'White man, I don't believe you. I don't believe that my brother would thus sell me and his children. I will not believe, unless he come himself.' Woolfolk coolly went and required her brother's presence. The seducer, the tyrant came, and, standing at the door, confirmed the slave-dealer's report. 'And is it true? and have you indeed sold me?' she exclaimed. 'Is it really possible? Look at this child! Don't you see in every feature the lineaments of its father? Don't you know that your blood flows in its veins? Have you—have you sold me?' The terrible fact was repeated by her master. 'These children,' she said, with a voice only half articulate, 'never shall be slaves.' 'Never mind about *that*,' said Woolfolk; 'go and get ready. I shall only wait a few minutes longer.' She retired with her children. The two white men continued alone. They waited. She returned not. They grew tired of waiting, and followed her to her chamber. There they found their victims beyond the reach of human wickedness, bedded in their blood." (See Antislavery Record, vol. i, p. 159.)

"I have been told of a young physician, who went into the far southern states to settle, and there became in love with a very handsome and modest girl, who lived at service. He married her; and about a year after that event a gentleman called at the house, and announced himself as Mr. J——y, of Mobile. He said to Dr. W., 'Sir, I have a trifling affair of business to settle with you. You have married a slave of mine.' The young physician resented this language, for he had not entertained the slightest suspicion that the girl had any other than white ancestors since the Flood. But Mr. J. furnished proofs of his claim; and Dr. W. knew very well, that the laws of the country would uphold him in it. After considerable discussion the best bargain he could make was, either to pay eight hundred dollars, or have his wife put up at auction. He consented to the first alternative, and his unwelcome visitor departed. When he had gone, Dr. W. told his wife what had happened. The poor woman burst into tears, and said, that, as Mr. J. *was her own father*, she had hoped, that when he heard she had found an honorable protector, he would have left her in peace." (Antislavery Catechism, by Mrs. Child, pp. 16, 17.)

13. There is a recklessness manifest in the slaveholding spirit among the higher classes of society. Indeed, it frequently runs into downright ruffianism. It tramples on the decencies and proprieties of life, unchecked by considerations of station, character, law, national honor, and the like, to say nothing of the principles of religion or the dictates of conscience. In the national Legislature this spirit has shown itself so frequently and so strikingly, as to throw off all considerations for character, the honor of the country, or even the common decencies of civilized life. In state legislatures the same outbreaks have been equally disgraceful. The practice of dueling, with all its vicious and barbarous accompaniments and consequences, is a favorite resort, especially among slaveholders. The following is a specimen of ruffian and barbarous conduct, such as the most savage acts of heathenism and human depravity in any age can scarcely equal. The following regulations of a duel, between two southern lawyers, is published in the North Carolina Standard, of August 30, 1837:

"The following conditions were proposed by Alexander K. M'Clung, of Raymond, in the state of Mississippi, to H. C. Stewart, as the laws to govern a duel they were to fight near Vicksburg:

"Article 1. The parties shall meet opposite Vicksburg, in the state of Louisiana, on Thursday, the 29th inst., precisely at four o'clock, P. M. Agreed to.

"2. The weapons to be used by each shall weigh one pound, two and a half ounces, measuring sixteen inches and a half in length, including the handle, and one inch and three-eighths in breadth. Agreed to.

"3. Both knives shall be sharp on one edge, and on the back shall be sharp only one inch at the point. Agreed to.

"4. Each party shall stand at the distance of eight feet from the other, till the word is given. Agreed to.

"5. The second of each party shall throw up, with a silver dollar, on the ground, for the word, and two best out of three shall win the word. Agreed to.

"6. After the word is given either party may take what advantage he can with his knife; but on throwing his knife at the other shall be shot down by the second of his opponent. Agreed to.

"7. Each party shall be stripped entirely naked, except one pair of linen pantaloons, one pair of socks, and boots or pumps as the party please. Acceded to.

"8. The wrist of the left arm of each party shall be tied tight to his left thigh, and a strong cord shall be fastened around his left arm at the elbow, and then around his body. Rejected.

"9. After the word is given each party shall be allowed to advance or recede, as he pleases, over the space of twenty acres of ground, till death ensues to one of the parties. Agreed to—the parties to be placed in the center of the space.

"10. The word shall be given by the winner of the same, in the following manner, namely: 'Gentlemen, are you ready?' Each party shall then answer, 'I am.' The second giving the word shall then distinctly command, 'Strike!' Agreed to.

"If either party shall violate these rules, upon being notified by the second of either party, he may be liable to be shot down instantly. As established usage points out the duty of both parties, therefore notification is considered unnecessary." (See American Slavery, p. 185.)

Cock-fighting, too, with all its demoralizing connections, is also a favorite sport of slaveholders, as well as of others of a like spirit; and horse-racing is a passion among the dignitaries of the south, which is followed with great ardor.

It is true, there are some in the north who follow the same barbarous vices; but the number is small, and they are greatly aided or encouraged by the countenance and visitation of the southern sons of chivalry.

Not that slaveholders are naturally worse than other men, nor are they any better; but arbitrary power has wrought in them its proper work, and poisoned their better nature. The idleness, contempt of labor, sensuality, and cruelty engendered by the habit of making men and women work without pay, and punishing them if they refuse, prepares the human heart for the demoralizing and barbarous customs of dueling, horse-racing, and cock-fighting.

14. The brutal outrages of masters to each other can only be accounted for, that slaveholding leads those who are engaged in it to such overt acts. Slaveholders, exercising from childhood irresponsible powers over human beings, become, in a great measure, unfitted for self-control, in their intercourse with each other. Tempers unaccustomed to restraint, in reference to slaves, will not be well controlled toward equals. The state of society in slave states producing duels, open murders, so that the murderers are lauded as honorable men, is nearly allied in spirit with the treatment toward slaves. When slaveholders are in the habit of caning, stabbing, and shooting each other, to an extent not found in the free states, we must criminate the slave system as the cause. It is allowed, that cases of great atrocity occur in the free states; but they are neither so numerous nor so flagrant as those which occur among slaveholders Besides, the laws in the free states are, as a general thing, faithfully executed against such crimes; whereas, the contrary is the case in the slave states. Public opinion, too, in the free states, raises its voice against such crimes and in support of the laws which punish them; whereas, public opinion, in the slave states, is either feeble or powerless, so that the guilty go unpunished. Innumerable

proofs could be adduced, from the public prints of the country, proving, without gainsaying, that the foregoing view of this matter is no more than the truth. Several writers have already given ample specimens of these enormities, and yet the public newspapers are themselves the bearers of testimonies on these points which no one can gainsay, who is acquainted with their contents. (See American Slavery As It Is, pp. 187–210, and Lewis Tappan's Address to Non-Slaveholders, pp. 12–16, for much matter on this topic; and the southern papers, *passim.*)

15. The bad effects of slavery are manifest on all who administer the system. It has a reaction which suffers neither the slave-owner nor his white dependents to escape with impunity. Such is the constitution of things, that we can not inflict an injury without suffering from it ourselves. In doing good we receive good; but he who does wrong to his fellow-creatures does also a great wrong to his own soul. The oppressor is, in reality, in a worse condition than the oppressed. If we consider the case of those who administer this system, the scenes to which they have been familiarized from their infancy, the habits which they have formed, the prejudices which they have acquired, and the inevitable tendency of the unlimited power to corrupt the human heart, the slaveholders are as much the object of pity, in a moral sense, as the slaves themselves. Perhaps it is in its depraving influence on the moral sense of both slave and master that slavery is most deplorable. Brutal cruelty may be a rare and transient mischief; but the degradation of soul is universal.

Who, indeed, with a knowledge of the human heart, could consider the peculiar character of modern slavery, independently of the facts in its practical workings, but must come to the conclusion, that its influence on the moral character is most pernicious and demoralizing? To have an absolute possession of human beings—to work them, punish them, dispose of them as the owner pleases—to have them trembling at his frown, crouching beneath his authority, subservient to his wishes—is more than human nature can endure, without serious injury. It must minister to some of the worst passions of human nature, as selfishness, pride, haughtiness, revenge, and a spirit of domination which will not brook restraint. Neither Howard, Wilberforce, Wesley, nor any saint on earth can be trusted, under such circumstances, without receiving damage—much less the great crowd of slaveholders, many of whom are greatly deficient in moral principles, education, and the decencies of cultivated society.

And in relation to the facts, or acts of cruelty or oppression, they are not insulated and detached facts, affecting only the individuals who were engaged in the cruelties they involved. They would not be at all important in this view; for mere acts of atrocity, affecting only the characters of the perpetrators, might be found in any other community. But they are facts such as to be most intimately connected with the general character and temper which slavery never fails to create. They are the most horrible proofs, not of the guilt of this or that individual, but of the moral effect of slavery—of the exercise of despotic power in corrupting and degrading the mind of the owner, and thus insuring the misery, degradation, and oppression of the slave. Slavery first produces horrid passions in the mind of the master, and, hence, these passions inflict the greatest cruelties on the slave. Its road, indeed, leads to physical misery, but it is through moral guilt, and atrocity, and barbarity of the worst kind, that it travels thither.

"While on the Alabama circuit I spent the Sabbath with an old circuit preacher, who was also a doctor, living near 'the Horse-shoe,' celebrated as General Jackson's battle-ground. On Monday morning early he was reading Pope's Messiah to me, when his wife called him out. I glanced my eye out of the window, and saw a slave-man standing by, and they consulting over him. Presently the doctor took a raw-hide from under his coat, and began to cut up the half-naked back of the slave. I saw six or seven inches of the skin turn up perfectly white at every stroke, till the whole back was red with gore. The lacerated man cried out some at first; but at every blow the doctor cried, 'Won't ye hush? won't ye hush?' till the slave finally stood still and groaned. As soon as he had done, the doctor came in, panting, almost out of breath, and, addressing me, said, 'Won't you go to prayer with us, sir?' I fell on my knees and prayed, but what I said I knew not. When I came out, the poor creature had crept up and knelt by the door, during prayer; and his back was a gore of blood quite to his heels." (Rev. J. Boucher.)

16. The effects of slavery on the female character present, in a striking manner, its lamentable tendency to harden the heart and to suppress the benevolent feelings. The charities of our nature are enthroned in the heart of woman. A kind and tender-hearted compassion is identified with her character. Such is woman, in every clime and of every color. Mr. Park, the African traveler, was frequently indebted to the humane sympathies of negro females for food, shelter, and every hospitality. But nothing can withstand the hardening influences of slavery. We do not wonder that men lose all feeling, and become, by degrees, accustomed to the cruelties of slavery; though, when at first they beheld the miseries of the enslaved, they were horrified. But we are shocked, when females are rendered so totally indifferent, through habit, to the sufferings of their slaves, as not only to be reconciled to them, but to take an active part in their infliction. Mr. Stewart—Past and Present State of Jamaica, pp. 171, 172—remarks, in regard to slavery in Jamaica, and the remark will apply with equal truth to the United States, that "it unfortunately

happens that the females, as well as the males, are too apt to contract domineering and harsh ideas with respect to their slaves—ideas ill-suited to the natural softness and humanity of the female heart." And alluding to the punishment of slaves in the presence of children, he adds: "Such inflictions may in time be viewed with a sort of savage satisfaction. In the males it may produce brutality of mind, and in the females, to say the least of it, an insensibility of human misery, and a cold contemplation of its distresses. . . . Such is the power of habit over the heart, that the woman accustomed to the exercise of severity soon loses all the natural softness of her sex."

The following fact, stated upon the unquestionable evidence of Captain W. F. Owen, of the British navy, will be an appropriate illustration of this subject:

"When his Majesty's ships, the Leven and Barraconta, employed in surveying the coasts of Africa, were at Mozambique, in 1823, the officers were introduced to his family; and it was an opinion agreed in by all, that Donna Sophia d'Almeydra was the most superior woman they had seen, from the time they had left England. Captain Owen, the leader of this expedition, expressing to Senor d'Almeydra his detestation of slavery, the Senor replied, 'You will not be long here before you change your sentiments. Look at my Sophia there. Before she would marry me she made me promise that I should give up the slave-trade. When we first settled at Mozambique, she was continually interceding for the slaves; and she constantly wept when I punished them; and now she is among the slaves from morning to night. She regulates the whole of my slave establishment. She inquires into every offense committed by them, pronounces sentence upon the offender, and stands by and sees him punished." (London Antislavery Reporter, vol. ii, No. 8, for January, 1828, pp. 171, 172.)

A brutal depravity of character is, indeed, inseparable

from slavery; and this depravity is frequently urged as an apology for the cruelty of the masters. But the evils in both cases are principally to be ascribed to the *system;* and they form an irresistible argument for its destruction. Men, in a state of slavery, in general, are effectually acted upon by *fear* only; and masters can not, as a general thing, manage slaves without being changed into tyrants. When, at a distance, we look at the cruelties of slavery, we are shocked at the brutality of the oppressor; but we may forget how large a share of that brutality is to be ascribed to the system. Many of the individuals now engaged in the practice of slavery were, before they entered it, as humane and kind-hearted as those who held their conduct in abhorrence. Nero wept, when first called upon to put his hand to the warrant of death.

17. We will here give some testimonies to the evil effects of the system of slavery on the moral character of those who administer it. The number of these is legion. We must content ourselves with a few.

Mr. Fearon, in his Sketches of America, pp. 378, 379, declares, that "the existence of slavery in the United States has a most visible effect on the national character. It necessarily brutalizes the minds of the southern and western inhabitants. It lowers, indeed, the tone of humane and correct feeling throughout the Union, and imperceptibly contributes to the existence of that great difference which there exists between theory and practice."

The testimony of Jefferson, on this subject, has already been adduced.

Mr. Stewart—Past and Present State of Jamaica, p. 170—says: "Wherever slavery exists, there must be many things attending it unfavorable to the improvement of the minds and manners of the people; arbitrary habits are acquired; irritation and violent passions are engendered, partly, indeed, by the perverseness of the slaves; and the feelings are gradually blunted by the constant exercise of a too unrestrained power, and the scenes to which it is continually giving birth. Human nature is shaped and governed by the force of early habits and of example. The very children, in some families, are so used to see or hear the negro servants whipped for the offenses they commit, that it becomes a sort of amusement to them."

Bishop Smith, of Kentucky, who is intimately acquainted with the state, and a competent and impartial witness, in his testimony concerning homicides, speaks thus of the influence of slavery as an exciting cause of homicides and other sins:

"Are not some of the direct influences of a system, [slavery,] the existence of which among us can never be sufficiently deplored, discoverable in these affrays? Are not our young men more heady, violent, and imperious, in consequence of their early habits of command? And are not our taverns and other public places of resort much more crowded with an inflammable material, than if young men were brought up in the staid and frugal habits of those who are constrained to earn their bread by the sweat of their brow? . . . Is not intemperance more social, more inflammatory, more pugnacious, where a fancied superiority of gentlemanly character is felt, in consequence of exemption from severe manual labor? Is there ever stabbing where there is not idleness and strong drink? . . . . Has not a public sentiment which we hear characterized as singularly high-minded and honorable, and sensitively alive to every affront, whether real or imaginary, but which strangers denominate rough and ferocious, much to do in provoking these assaults, and then in applauding instead of punishing the offender?" (See American Slavery, pp. 204–206.)

CHAPTER IV.

EFFECT OF SLAVERY ON THE NON-SLAVEHOLDERS OF SLAVE STATES.

1. THE non-slaveholders, in the slave states, partake greatly of the evil effects of slavery, in a great variety of views. Different from the slaveholders in rank, wealth, and associations, they can not find equality among the owners of slaves. Unaccustomed to labor, and unacquainted with the mechanical arts to a great degree, they are poorly provided for. By their position in society they are virtually shut out from political offices of profit, honor, and trust. Their deficiency in education, too, is a serious barrier against them. We will survey the principal matters in which their great disadvantages will appear.

2. Slavery makes labor disreputable in the slave states. The result of this is to impoverish the white non-slaveholders, by deterring them from work. We will see this very clearly, by quoting the sentiments of slaveholders on this subject:

"Our slave population is decidedly preferable, as an orderly and laboring class, to a northern laboring class, that have just learning enough to make them wondrous wise, and make them the most dangerous class to well-regulated liberty under the sun." (Richmond, Virginia, Enquirer.)

"We believe the servitude which prevails in the south far preferable to that of the *north* or in Europe. Slavery will exist in all communities. There is a class which may be nominally free, but they will be virtually *slaves*." (Mississippian, July 6, 1838.)

"Those who depend on their daily labor for their daily subsistence can never enter into political affairs; they never do, never will, never can." (B. W. Leigh in Virginia Convention, 1829.)

"All society settles down into a classification of capitalists and laborers. The former will *own* the latter, either collectively through the government, or individually in a state of domestic servitude, as exists in the southern states of this confederacy. If LABORERS ever obtain the political power of a country, it is, in fact, in a state of REVOLUTION. The capitalists north of Mason and Dixon's line, have precisely the same interest in the labor of the country that the capitalists of England have in their labor. Hence it is, that they must have a strong federal government [!] *to control* the labor of the nation. But it is precisely the reverse with us. We have already not only a right to the proceeds of our laborers, but we OWN a *class of laborers* themselves. But let me say to gentlemen who represent the great class of capitalists in the north, beware that you do not drive us into a separate system; for if you do, as certain as the decrees of Heaven, you will be compelled to *appeal to the sword to maintain yourselves at home.* It may not come in your day; but your children's children will be covered with the blood of domestic factions, and *a plundering mob contending for power and conquest.*" (Mr. Pickens, of South Carolina, in Congress, 21st January, 1836.)

"In the very nature of things there must be classes of persons to discharge all the different offices of society, from the highest to the lowest. Some of these offices are regarded as *degraded,* although they must and will be performed. Hence those manifest forms of dependent servitude which produce a sense of superiority in the masters or employers, and of inferiority on the part of the servants. Where these offices are performed by *members of the political community,* a DANGEROUS ELEMENT is obviously introduced into the body politic. Hence the alarming tendency to violate the rights of property by agrarian legislation, which is beginning to be manifest in the older states, where UNIVERSAL SUFFRAGE *prevails without* DOMESTIC SLAVERY.

"In a word, the institution of domestic slavery supersedes the *necessity* of AN ORDER OF NOBILITY AND ALL THE OTHER APPENDAGES OF A HEREDITARY SYSTEM OF GOVERNMENT." (Gov. M'Duffie's Message to the South Carolina Legislature, 1836.)

"We regard SLAVERY *as the most safe and stable basis for free institutions in the world.* It is impossible with us, that the conflict can take place between labor and capital, which makes it so difficult to establish and maintain free institutions in all wealthy and highly-civilized nations where such institutions do not exist. Every plantation is a little community with the master at its head, who concentrates in himself the united interests of capital and labor, *of which he is the common representative.*" (Mr Calhoun, of South Carolina, in the United States Senate, Jan. 10, 1840.)

"We of the south have cause now, and shall soon have greater, to congratulate ourselves on the existence of a population among us which excludes the POPULACE which in effect rules some of our northern neighbors, and is rapidly gaining strength wherever slavery does not exist—a populace made up of the dregs of Europe, and the most worthless portion of the native population." (Richmond Whig, 1837.)

"Would you do a benefit to the horse or the ox by giving him a cultivated understanding—a fine feeling? So far as the MERE LABORER has the pride, the knowledge, or the aspiration of a freeman, he is unfitted for his situation. If there are sordid, servile, *laborious* offices to be performed, is it not better that there should be sordid, servile, laborious beings to perform them?

"Odium has been cast upon our legislation on account of its forbidding the elements of education being communicated to slaves. But, in truth, what injury is done them by this? *He who works during the day with his hands,* does not read in the intervals of leisure for his amusement, or the improvement of his mind, or the exception is so very rare as scarcely to need the being provided for." (Chancellor Harper, of South Carolina. Southern Literary Messenger.)

"Is there any thing in the principles and opinions of the other party—the great *democratic rabble,* as it has been justly called—which should induce us to identify ourselves with that? Here you may find every possible grade and hue of opinion which has ever existed in the country. Here you may find loafer, and loco-foco, and agrarian, and all the rabble of the city of New York, the most corrupt and depraved of rabbles, and which controls, in a great degree, the city itself, and through that, as being the commercial metropolis, exercises much influence over the state at large.

"What are the essential principles of democracy as distinguished from republicanism? The first consists in the dogma, so portentous to us, of the natural equality and inalienable right to liberty of every human being. Our allies, [!] no doubt, are willing, at *present,* to modify the doctrine in *our favor.* But the spirit of democracy at large makes no such exceptions, nor will these—our allies, the northern democrats—continue to make it longer than necessity or *interests* may require. The second consists in the doctrine of the divine right of majorities; a doctrine not less false, and slavish, and absurd, than the ancient doctrine of the divine right of kings." (Chancellor Harper's Oration, in 1840.)

"Gentlemen wanted to drive out the black population that they may obtain WHITE NEGROES in their place. WHITE NEGROES have this advantage over black negroes—they can be converted into voters; and the men who live upon the sweat of their brow, and pay them but a dependent and scanty subsistence, can, if able to keep ten thousand of them in employment, come up to the polls and change the destiny of the country.

"How improved will be our condition when we have such white negroes as perform the servile labors of Europe, of Old England, and he would add now of *New England*, when our body servants, and our cart-drivers, and our street-sweepers, are *white negroes* instead of black? Where will be the independence, the proud spirit, and the chivalry of Kentuckians then?" (R. Wickliffe, of Kentucky, in Louisville Advertiser.)

3. Slave labor tends to drive the non-slaveholding whites from the slave countries, or to degrade them toward the condition of slaves. The following is from the pen of a Virginian:

"Being born in 1801, in the valley of Virginia, and having resided here to this day, as may be expected, I have seen some of the workings of slavery. The valley has good land in it; some of which lies along the streams of water, while other portions, of heavy limestone soil generally, compose the middle part of the valley. In addition to these lands there are others of a thin, gravelly nature, generally ranging nearest the mountains. The entire valley is and has been settled for a number of years already, but at what date the slaves were brought in I have no knowledge. They were here at my earliest recollection, when they were but few, but their number has been constantly and steadily increasing to this time. Then the owners of them were also few, and each owned, perhaps, on an average, two, three, four, or six slaves. Alongside of the slaveholders were living eight or ten times their number who did not own any slaves, generally holding small farms of one hundred, one hundred and fifty, or two hundred acres. But through some cause, which one can better imagine than tell, the most of these persons, living contiguous to their black neighbors, sold their lands to the slaveholders, and have gone to the west to find homes more congenial to their wishes and interests. Thus it has come about that, in some places, four, five, or six *free soil farms were smelted into one slave farm;* and where the smelting could not be effected, a slave-owner has made himself proprietor of so many detached farms. In this way, slavery in general has been getting the ascendency in the possession of the lands, while the white man, who would not involve himself in negro servitude, has, as already stated, gone to some western state; while, perhaps, two-thirds of the residue of that class yet here are the occupants of the poorer lands which have been mentioned, when, at the same time, in three or more counties of the valley, seven-tenths of the voters are non-slaveholders. But the time is coming when these, too, must leave our valley, as the farms they own are generally small, their families large, and, of course, without sufficient employment. Their slave neighbors, who own the larger and most productive tracts of land, will not give them employment, having slaves to do their work; and, therefore, being thus situated, necessity—not choice, as we all love home—will force them to seek a country of strangers for future homes. Thus slavery, like a huge serpent, is creeping on in our valley, and will finally blight the whole of it. It has increased, perhaps, fifty or one hundred fold during my time, and has done its work of monopoly in more than one way.

"There was a time when our *young men here could get employment* on farms at pleasure, and receive good prices. I recollect, when but a boy, that my brother, then a young man, got wages from fifteen to twenty dollars per month. The last two years of his service in that way he got twenty dollars per month, and then married the old farmer's daughter, which at once made him heir to the stock; but, had the old man been a slaveholder, he would hardly have been willing for *Sam* to marry his daughter, for the good reason that his qualities would never have developed themselves to the old gentleman. But a series of labor on the farm brought them to light, and the result was not a bad one. But where is the man in our valley now that can get half that sum as wages for the same service? Ah! those days and those wages are gone by, and, I fear, will never return for our young men. And why? Slavery is doing the labor on the rich lands of the valley, and the sturdy young free white man must now learn a trade, contrary to his wishes, or leave the country and his friends, and go where the strength of his body and bent of his mind may find employment more congenial to his health, and which may suit him best. Blessed, thrice blessed, be the memory of those wise and good men, who, in the formation of this vast republic, secured some portions of it from the curse of slavery, where the young and enterprising men of Virginia may find an asylum. They love Virginia, its mountains and dales, and sincerely regret to leave her; but slavery drives them, and they must go. Peace be to the ashes of their sires, whom they leave behind them, sleeping beneath the soil now trampled by the slave, while the children, the offspring of their affection, are seeking a refuge in other countries, where slavery can not oppress them.

"The Governor of our state, [Virginia,] in his recent message has missed it vastly, when he says: 'The moral necessity for the emigration of no inconsiderable portion of our laboring white population is occasioned by the free blacks of the state.' Ah, Billy, this will not do. It certainly is a *very* inconsiderable number of our good, honest white men who leave this portion of our country through the influence of free black labor, and its low wages. We have as little relish for free blacks among us, as your honorable self, but we pray you, charge not this moral evil to the *very least* of its causes. *Slavery,* slavery *does this work.* Slaves owned here, and the thousand and one hired here from eastern Virginia annually, at a price lower than the white man can work for—this has caused, and always will cause, the emigration from this section; and if from here the emigration is caused in this way, how much more terrible must be the effect on that portion of the state where the excess of slaves is such that labor can not be produced sufficient to keep them employed; so much so, that swarms of them are hired out in other sections annually! How many of the farms in the valley now work from ten, twenty, sixty, to a hundred or more slaves! These take just that amount of labor from the free but poor white men, who must depend upon that kind of labor to make their living. The result is obvious. The land is held by but a small portion of white citizens, yet working many hands, [slaves;] consequently, the profit arising from products of the earth is, in this way, thrown into the hands of the few whites, and they and their families made very rich. The abominable system of black slavery does this; for, were it not for this, these rich landholders would be bound to sell some of their lands, or let tenants or renters farm it, and thus divide the spoils. Now, then, let this thing grow and spread over our entire nation, and the poor white people of this country would be in a worse condition than the paupers of Europe.

"We say, again, blessed be the memories of those worthies who secured to us better things, by fixing a limit to the slave power in the country they then possessed; and we fondly hope that our present rulers will effect like favors for future generations, in that territory which has lately been added to our large domain. This certainly is of the most weighty importance, as the evils of slavery are inevitable, the slaveholder himself will, in most instances, confess; yet, like the drunkard, indulge in it to the very brink of destruction. He lives in ease and comfort, and sometimes in extravagance; makes money by slave labor and slave traffic; and in the latter way of making money, he would like to have the whole world to be his market, and thus finally depopulate the earth of her white inhabitants, if he could but be the last one to ride out on the back of a slave; so completely is he infatuated with it, and so unmanned within himself as to move about in the general wreck of its pernicious effects, without attempting to stay its progress in the least. Who, then, must save [if saved at all] from the ruin of slavery, New Mexico and California? The west and the north must do it. This lies particularly heavy and important as a duty on western members in Congress, to reciprocate to others what they now enjoy through favors bestowed on them by good men in former days, of a like nature. What would be the condition of the western states now, had not Mr. Jefferson and other worthies of the south and north stayed slavery at the Ohio river? Let them think of this, and go and do likewise.

"Southern men who would like to see bounds set to slave territory, can do nothing to effect it. They scarcely dare open their lips to say a word favorable to it, as the abuse would be bitter; yet there are none who know and feel the evil effects of slavery better than they do. They also fear, that to abolish slavery in the south, and have the blacks as free as white men are, mingled and mixed in one community, would be worse than slavery itself. But many believe here, that if slavery were not allowed to spread over more territory than it now has, God, in his wise providence, would, perhaps, in his own appointed time, make a way possible for the final emancipation of the blacks. It is true, in many instances, the slave is cruelly treated, and shamefully bound down to ignorance; nor is his condition at all likely to be made better while in servitude, only where his master lives properly under the influence of the Gospel of Christ; then better things are sometimes seen. The slaves generally in the valley are well fed and clothed; and, so far, their condition is not bad. But the great evil of them is felt by the poorer class of white people, in the way already stated, and in petty thefts, of which most of the blacks are guilty. Put slavery, then, in the best form you can, and it is an abominable thing; and the people of the United States can never be considered a happy and great people, in the true sense of the word, while *these things* remain among them. Turn it which way you will, and it remains black; and the white people that dabble with it, will not fail to find themselves smutted by it. How, then, shall this stain be obliterated from our otherwise happy nation, and who shall he be that may accomplish this thing?" (J. H. Steffy, Dec. 22, 1848, in the National Era, January 11, 1849.)

4. The principal political offices are filled by slaveholders. Of this we have already given sufficient proof elsewhere. We now barely add the conclusion of Mr. Steffy's letter quoted above:

"Another idea, founded on fact, may be noticed here. In several counties, where seven or eight-tenths of the voters are without slaves, there are *very few instances where civil offices are held by any of them;* perhaps there may be a small number of magistrates who do not hold slaves. Several reasons may be assigned for this. Slavery has got such undoubted preponderance in these things, that both classes seem to think that the slaveholder alone should hold these stations. He has such a habit of domineering and ruling, that he seeks every opportunity to work himself into power, which he generally accomplishes by making those his friends already in power, and these then unitedly, by craft, working on the credulity of the unsuspecting laboring white man—where he has any thing to say to it—his designs become accomplished; while, on the other hand, the laborer seldom seeks an office, believing it useless, from the persuasion that he can not obtain it, in which his friends concur, from the notion they have of slave preponderance. Thus *civil offices* have become somewhat hereditary with slaveholders, and I verily believe ever will be so, where slaveholders and non-slaveholders live together in one community. The man of *slaves* will bear rule. In *his social intercourse*, he there, too, is one-sided. The laboring white man has no pleasures in his house and family for him. In short, the two classes can not properly live in the same community; they should and must be separate. But if the laws of our land do not effect this separation, by setting limits for slavery, then, without a shadow of doubt, it will spread to the remotest parts of our land; and then every white man must either become a slaveholder or a vassal to slaveholders; and, finally, the black and white, in a smelted [mixed in blood] form, occupy this vast and rich territory. More than one slaveholder actually believes this. May God, in his infinite mercy, avert it! Slavery is an evil in itself, and every one must see its evil and wicked consequences. How, then, can a true patriot give his aid to extend it one mile further on our continent; but how much less the believer in Christ? J. H. STEFFY.

"*December* 22, 1848."

5. Slavery is extremely injurious to the general interests of white non-slaveholders. We quote on this the well-sustained argument of S. S. Nicholson, of Kentucky, who is well acquainted with this subject:

"It is well known, that a majority of the slaveholders are opposed to the importation of more slaves. How, then, do the members of the last Legislature expect to be sustained in this new policy? Is it by reason of their supposed influence over the poorer class of men, who are not slave-owners, most of whom have no prospect of becoming so, none of whom have any personal interest in maintaining slavery, and who constitute four-fifths of the voters of the state? There must be some plausibility in the argument which goes to show that slavery is beneficial to the owners of rich lands, who are also the most exclusive owners of slaves, or so many respectable and intelligent men would not avow that opinion. But, what is the course of reasoning by which it is expected to prove to the great laboring class, who own no slaves, but do their own work in tilling the thinner and less productive lands, that their *interests* are promoted, that they are benefited by the system? Kentucky has been trying the experiment for between sixty and seventy years, and thus far the direct benefits of slavery—if there be such—have never yet reached the poor lands. We need no further experimenting, to prove that those benefits never will reach them. All know that negro slavery never did and never can thrive on poor land, while there is a slave market in richer lands. The inhabitants of our thinner lands must by this time be sufficiently convinced that, whatever may be the direct benefits of negro slavery to others, they are never to reap any of them. What, then, are the collateral benefits of slavery to that class of our population who constitute so large a majority of the whole? This development the pro-slavery men have never yet made. No one has yet attempted to prove that the system was beneficial to that class of our population. There are, perhaps, more rich men in Kentucky, in proportion to white population, than there are in Ohio. One of the evils of the system is to accumulate too much wealth in few hands, and the rich part of our population may be conceded to be in a sufficiently-prosperous condition. But the rich are a very lean minority of the population of any country. They are so few in number, that with no propriety can the fundamental institutions of society be adjusted with a peculiar view, much less with an exclusive eye to their interests. The great interest to be attended to, not to the exclusion of others, however, but that which is most entitled to respectful consideration, is the interest of the laboring masses—of those who constitute four-fifths if not five-sixths of our white population. Let it be shown how slavery benefits them; what interest they have in the perpetuation of slavery and the increase of slaves in our state. It is precisely in its evil operations on them, by its destructive influence on their best interests, that the system produces most of its pernicious effects on the well-being of the whole state.

"They are mostly small farmers, remote from market. The mechanic arts and manufactures are but little pursued among them. They have not been reared to such pursuits, and do not voluntarily fall into them. The institution of slavery keeps mechanics and manufacturers from coming to the state and settling among them. That is what they want. Agricultural labor is overstocked. They want an industrious, consuming population near them, which they can have the benefit of feeding, and which can teach them the mechanic arts. The labor of one producer can feed himself and five or six others. All producers and no consumers can never constitute a prosperous community. They especially need the facilities for educating their children and teaching their sons good trades. They can not give all their sons farms; but they know that if they can make them good mechanics, they will make them independent. How does the large slaveholder of an adjacent county aid or assist that class of our community? He raises his own provisions, and is a competitor in the market with his surplus. He grows his own wool and flax, weaves and makes up his own coarser clothing, imports his furniture and finer clothing, ready-made, from a free state, and encourages no mechanic but the blacksmith and the house builder, and that because he can not import a ready-made house, and because he can not send to a free state to have his wagon mended or his horse shod. Nor is this state of things at all likely to improve, but it is every day getting worse. It is an undoubted fact, that forty years ago there were more hats, shoes, boots, saddles, and various articles of furniture, manufactured in Kentucky than there are at this day.

"The great mass of every community is, always has been, and always will be, poor. In other words, the great majority must always be made up of those who are not and never can be slaveholders. Hence the necessity of constantly keeping in view the interests of this greater mass, in every discussion of negro slavery. Let it be shown how or in what way it is that they are benefited by the system. Directly it can not be, for it does not reach them. So long as the southern states afford better markets for slaves than even the rich lands of Kentucky, it is in vain to expect that slaves will be generally owned by the small proprietors of our thin lands. If there be collateral benefits to the class, let them be shown. You may rely upon the sympathies and the supposed sense of justice of this great majority, to suffer and endure the system as it is. But, when you venture upon a new course of measures to spread and perpetuate it, then, surely, you rely too much on the gullibility of the masses, if you do not show how they are to be benefited. You must satisfy them by pointing to the comparative superior prosperity of the slave states over the free. In what particulars will you find this superiority? In commerce, in manufactures, in mechanic arts, in individual or public enterprise, in roads and canals, in arts, in learning, in common schools for the poor, or in the general diffusion of the common elements of education, or will it be in the proper appreciation of the working man, and of all industrial pursuits? None of these—no, not one of them—furnishes the means of an illustration in favor of the slave system, but each and all of them tell a tale the other way, which must carry uncontrollable conviction to every poor man's mind, that the system of slavery is not good for him." (S. S. Nicholson, in Louisville Journal of March 7, 1849, and quoted in National Era, March 19, 1849.)

6. The education of the free white people in the slave states, too, is most injuriously affected by slavery. On this

we will barely adduce the testimony of Mr. Nicholson quoted above. What he says in the conclusion of his letter, respecting Kentucky, will apply equally well to other slave states:

"Kentucky has recently declared, with unprecedented unanimity at the polls, that she will be taxed for the support of a system of *common schools.* Her Legislature will pass law after law in obedience to this mandate. But still she will have no common schools. The poor man will still be without the facility of giving the elements of a plain education to his children. We have not the teachers for the schools, but, above all, we have not the men to put the schools in operation and supervise them when started. Louisville has the honor of being the first city in the west to start a system of common schools. This was done under the influence and guidance of New England men—it has been kept up for twenty years under their superintendence; it is so extended that it is annually imparting its benefits to some four thousand children. Not a hundred votes could be obtained in the city for its abolition. Yet, it is the firm conviction of one who has been intimately acquainted with it for ten years, that, if the northern men among us were to withdraw from it their gratuitous supervision and care, it would, in a very few years, die out of inanition and neglect. It is one of those small kind of public concerns which our Virginia stock have not been trained to in early life, and, therefore, deem beneath their attention. This is but one of the many illustrations of the erroneous structure of society, where negro slavery is part of the structure. The rich are not brought into sufficiently-near contact with poor men to feel their dependence on them, or elicit sufficiently-active sympathy for them. The general policy of all the slave states is, to let every man do for himself and to take care of himself; there are no general provisions in aid of the masses—nothing to call forth and combine their small means for even their own general benefit. Nearly all local and public trusts are conducted in the most slothful and slovenly manner. Roads, bridges, and public edifices, all speak in most intelligible and unmistakable language. The most casual observer and inattentive traveler can not cross the line from a slave state into a free state, without at once being struck with the contrast in all the elements of visible prosperity. It is the contrast between sloth and premature decay, and all the active bustle of thriving industry and rapid improvement in all the elements of a state's well-being and prosperity. Ask the cause of the contrast, and there is one uniform, invariable answer, from all men of intelligence, 'that it is to be found in the system of negro slavery.' "

7. The following picture of the ignorance, degradation, and poverty of non-slaveholders, is from the pen of Mr. Vaughan, a native of South Carolina, a devoted friend to liberty and to man. What he says respecting the *Sand-hillers* of the Carolinas, will apply to non-slaveholders generally in all slave countries:

"*The Sufferers; or, Sand-hillers.*—We find in the Winyan Intelligencer, published at Georgetown, South Carolina, the following notice:

"'The poor laborers on Black river, and in that neighborhood, are in a state of starvation, many of them being without corn or meal, and none of them having meat. The occasion calls for the aid of the charitable, and efforts will be made to obtain relief for them.'

"Who are these 'poor laborers?'

"There is a class of poor whites in the Carolinas, and most of the southern states, peculiar in character, and unknown generally to the country. They are called *Sand-hillers.* They are so called because they cluster together in the poorest regions, and there live by hunting, fishing, raising a little stock, making tar and charcoal, and attending to poultry. They are very ignorant. Not one out of fifty can read or write, and, what is worse, they change not as time winnows down the old and supplies their places with the young. As is the sire, so is the son.

"And these Sand-hillers are as peculiar in dress and looks as they are in character. You know them whenever you see them. They are *marked* in any crowd. Dressed always in the plainest homespun, home-made and widely cut, often without shoes, but when using them wearing the coarsest kind, with slouched hats of cheapest texture, having no blood in their cheeks, their eyes black, and their hair lank, they are as distinct a race as the Indian. In some respects they are not unlike them. They love to roam the woods, and be free there; to get together for frolic or fun; to fish and hunt; to chase wild cattle; but here the similarity ends; for they are wanting in personal daring, and in that energy of character which makes a man. We do not know one of them who ever gained station in society, or became distinguished by his deeds. And it is this class to whom the Georgetown Intelligencer alludes, we conclude, when it speaks of the 'poor laborers' on Black river, and neighborhood.

"How came they in their present condition?

"Their history is quickly told. It is a sad one, and we never think of it without sorrow.

"In the early settlements of the Carolinas, every body pressed upon the water courses. Poor, as well as rich, made lodgment upon, or near their banks. There were, at first, very few negroes; consequently the latter needed the labor of the former to house their crops, and clear their lands. All got along well, then. But the slave traffic, with its accursed ills, began soon after, and, by and by, planters had their places stocked with slaves. As these slaves increased, the poor began to feel their degradation. A bitter hatred grew up between these classes. It led often to violence. The large planters, in consequence, began to buy up the poor men's land, and the poor men, in turn, became anxious to sell. And they did so. But where were they to go? South of Carolina was a wilderness; the good lands on the water courses, in the state, were in possession of rich planters. They had no alternative left, as they thought, but to herd together on the sand-hills, and there they and theirs still live.

"Their choice of place is significant enough of their feeling, and of the *cause* of their removal. They made their location in neighborhoods where neither large nor small planters could molest them. They got where they could live without being disturbed, or worried, by the continued sight of slaves. Now and then you will find a few of the more debased sort gathered close by towns; but generally they are some ten, or fifteen, or twenty miles back. What the land would yield which they call their own—for often they 'squat,' as the phrase is, on the state's or others' property—it is difficult to say. But the best of it, on the average, would not return ten bushels of corn to the acre; the most of it, not five. They grow sweet-potatoes, melons, a little cotton for home use, and now and then a bag or half a bag for market. But things are where they are, and as they are, because slavery, with its biting social ills, beats them away, from the richer soil, and keeps them hopelessly down and debased on the barren hills.

"What are their peculiarities of mind?

"The fact, that they left the neighborhood of large plantations, and sought a sort of wild-wood liberty, shows that they have some notions of personal freedom They have. But they are very crude. It was their condition which induced us to think first on the subject of slavery, and we endeavored, in conjunction with the lamented GRIMKE, to hit upon some plan by which we could improve this. We sought them out in their hovel-homes. We endeavored to

win their regard, and secure their confidence. We succeeded in this, but we failed, wholly, in every effort to induce them to change their mode of life. The ruling idea uppermost in their minds seemed to be, *hatred of labor*, under the conviction, that it degraded them, because it put them on an equality with the slaves. An anecdote will illustrate this feeling.

"One of their number had a fine, intelligent boy. He was one that would have attracted notice in any boyhood gathering. We proposed to the father that he should be educated. 'Let him go with us to town,' said we, 'and we will send him to school, and see what can be done with him.' 'And what then?' asked he, eyeing us, as if suspicious that something wrong was to follow. 'Why,' we continued, 'when he has been educated, we can send him to the carriage maker's, Mr. C., and let him learn a trade!' 'Never,' he quickly, almost fiercely, rejoined, with a harsh oath. 'My son shall never work by the side of your negroes, and Mr. ——'s negroes'—calling certain planters' names whose slaves were being taught the trade—'and be ordered about by Mr. C. as he ordered them about.' He was fixed. No argument, entreaty, appeal to interest, could move him. The idea uppermost in his mind was the idea of his class—that labor was degrading—and he would rather his son should be free in the forest, if ignorant, than debased in the city, though educated, by a menial task.

"What hope is there for them?

"We see none. Nothing, certainly, but the removal of slavery can induce them to change their present condition. They will not labor in the field while they think it degrading; nor become artisans or mechanics while slaves are such. And as for educating them, scattered as they are, the effort seems almost hopeless! Up and down the river where these 'poor laborers,' that the South Carolina paper talks of, live, and all around Georgetown, there are large rice and cotton

estates. Many of the owners of them are very wealthy; a majority rich. Yet there is no sort of connection, or sympathy, between these planters and the Sand-hillers! They are as far apart as two races well can be. We speak now of social separation; for we are sure the moment they heard the 'poor laborers' were starving, these planters did what was necessary, and more, to relieve their wants. But, we fear, coming time will find them as they are now—alone, ignorant, degraded, the victims of a blighting curse!

"The condition of these Sand-hillers illustrates the effect of slavery in its extreme, or when pushed to its farthest limit. Take one town, near the center of South Carolina, and make a line for ten miles south of it along the river on one side, looking three miles back, and we question whether you will find over ten planters! They have each from one hundred to two, three, four, or five hundred slaves! Many of these slaves, too, are mechanics! Necessarily, therefore, the towns wane, the poorer classes emigrate, as well as the young and enterprising; and the ignorant, or Sand-hill class, escape to the barrens for freedom! according to their notion of it.

"So much for the 'poor laborers' of Black river and its neighborhood! for the unfortunate Sand-hillers of the Carolinas!" (J. C. Vaughan, in the Louisville Examiner of July 24, 1847.)

CHAPTER V.

OPPOSITION OF SLAVERY TO CHRISTIANITY.

1. The effects of slavery on the state are no less striking and injurious, than they are on the masters and their families—on the slaves and the white population generally. It furnishes an antagonism to Christianity, in a Christian country, of the most injurious character, preventing its progress, or totally forbidding pure Christianity, or greatly vitiating it, and lowering its standard in morals, when it does not entirely prevent its propagation. The slave code runs into actual or virtual persecution, violating the rights of conscience, and virtually banishing its conscientious citizens into other states, by the impediments or disabilities thrown in the way of emancipation.

And what is morally wrong in itself never can be politically right. This maxim—an axiom in true politics—is fully exemplified in the history of all countries where slavery has existed; and the developments in the United States now clearly show, that this great country can not be excepted from the general course of things, in which moral causes will lead to their natural consequences. The elementary operations of slavery in this country are operating adversely to general education and national morals—the monopolies of offices by slaveholders—the martial spirit produced by it—the impoverishment of the country by an indolent and improvident agriculture, and want of energy and enterprise in commerce and manufactures—the disaffection and discord produced by the system—the disregard for constitutional obligation, and the difficulty of conducting government harmoniously—the state weakened—want of allegiance to law, in the encouragement given to mobs and lynching—interference with the very elements of political liberty, in the freedom of speech, freedom of the press, trial by jury, and the right of petition, etc.—these political evils, growing out of slavery, and all proceeding from *moral wrong, injustice,* and evil habits and principles, are working most mischievously in the United States, so that the sinful and moral taint in the system is as easily distinguished as a tree is known by its fruits.

Slavery, we maintain, both in its principles and its practice, is in antagonism to Christianity, and is also producing effects adverse to the well-being and continuance of the body politic. Each of these will demand our attention; and, in the first place, we will survey the effects of slavery on the Church.

2. Slavery is antagonistic to Christianity.

Whatever stand the Church may take in reference to slavery, whether she condemns or sanctions it, its existence in her field of labor will cripple her energies and impede her progress. If the Church condemn slavery, this will excite the jealousy and hostility of slaveholders. If the Church approve of slavery, or utter no testimony against it, the world will conclude that religion is itself a corrupt thing, because it approves or winks at injustice or wrong.

There is a direct and irreconcilable antagonism between the principles of the slave system, as established by law, and the principles of the Christian religion.

The seizure of human beings as slaves, at their birth, by law, is violence and robbery, and is fundamentally wrong, according to the Christian religion. Robbing the slave of his property, in depriving him of the fruit of his skill, is a continuance or an addition to the original theft; and his deprivation of liberty, growing out of these, is only a link in the chain of robbery. Reducing man to property, or making him a chattel, and then depriving him of his liberty, his property, and other rights, stand in the most antagonistic attitude to the principles of Christianity; and whether this is done by stealing the child from Africa, buying the stolen man, or seizing the child of a slave-mother, the effect is the same on the slave. He is deprived of himself, his liberty, and his property; and the *mode* of doing it has no more to do with the nature of the wrong, than the different modes of murder and theft have to do with the nature of wrong done in theft or murder.

Christianity is *light*, and instructs man intellectually, morally, and religiously; slavery hinders, neglects, or forbids the intellectual, moral, and religious instruction of the slaves

Christianity gives all men credit for declaring the truth or bearing witness thereto; but slavery rejects the testimony of slaves, even when they tell the truth, as when they utter untruth, and by this means subjecting them to cruel treatment, degradation, and even death.

Slavery, in its code, knows nothing of marriage; but Christianity enjoins and commands it.

Slavery exposes, without protection or redress, females to indecent and licentious treatment; but Christianity condemns this with its heaviest anathemas.

Christianity places children and parents in close connection; but slavery separates them, although God himself has joined them together.

Slavery inflicts severe and cruel punishments on its victims for no crimes, or for trivial faults, and extends this to the most shameful exposure of the bodies of females; and all this at the caprice of the master, without judge, jury, examination, or trial. Christianity condemns all such cruel acts, and enjoins a different course.

Slavery either forbids or impedes the acquisition of freedom, and renders it insecure when enjoyed. Christianity teaches, "If thou canst be free, use it rather." And the Gospel jubilee declares this to be one of the great works of Christianity. (Luke iv, 18, and Isa. i. See Duncan, pp. 94–97.)

Christianity *civilizes* man, because all its tendencies are toward the highest possible forms of social order and improvement; but slavery is essentially *barbarous.*

Christianity *humanizes,* for it develops the faculties and regulates the affections in every individual who receives it; but slavery brutalizes man.

The spirit of Christianity is love and good-will; the spirit of slavery is violence and fear.

Christianity makes all men *equal,* by the common privileges of creation, redemption, provision, and future prospects; but slavery reduces one portion of the human family to brutal degradation, and raises another portion to arrogant assumption of the rights of God and man.

In brief, it were easy to increase this list of antagonistic principles between Christianity and slavery. The points of antagonism have been already discussed. We will now proceed to point out the antagonistic workings of Christianity and slavery in the same body politic.

3. There are duties or practices enjoined by Christianity which are forbidden or counteracted by the system of slavery.

It is impossible to declare the whole counsel of God, without coming in opposition to some branch of the system of slavery, such, especially, as that great branch of duties which teaches us our duty toward man, and renders to all their due. But the laws of most of the slave states render it criminal for a preacher to preach against slavery. Hence, preachers of the Gospel are prevented from preaching the whole counsel of God; and, indeed, they can not preach it, in whole or in part, to the slaves, without the good leave of the masters; so that here again the commission of Christ, which teaches ministers to preach the Gospel to every creature, is met with the hinderance of the master's will.

Many preachers have been fined for preaching against slavery; others have been maltreated in various ways; and all have been hindered in enforcing the morals of the Gospel.

Take the institution of *marriage*. In reference to this, adultery and fornication, and all concubinage, or illicit commerce between the sexes, is expressly forbidden in the Christian religion; and the obligation of marriage is enjoined on all, without exception, who live together as husband and wife. But the slave laws know nothing of marriage as an ordinance of God. Any connection among slaves answering to marriage is broken up by the will of the master; and the slave laws repudiate marriage. They acknowledge a *mother*, but no father. The abominable sentiment of the heathen and Roman slave law is adopted by Christian America—"*partus sequitur ventrem*"—the child follows the condition of the mother.

As a specimen of this, while we are writing, the Southern Christian Advocate, of February 2, 1849, contains the following resolutions of the Georgia conference, on the "MARRIAGE OF COLORED MEMBERS," attested thus: E. H. Myers, Secretary, Macon, January 25, 1849:

"*Resolved*, 1. That this conference instruct the preachers in charge of circuits, stations, and missions within its bounds, to require the colored members under their charge, who may hereafter take husband or wife, to be married in due form by an ordained minister, or authorized officer of the law, provided the owners do not object.

"2. That no leader, exhorter, or unordained preacher, much less a private member, has any authority to perform the marriage ceremony, and that, therefore, in the judgment of this conference, no unordained person, not an officer of the law, should perform that ceremony.

"3. That our preachers in charge pay special attention to this subject in the future, and that where our members have heretofore agreed to be man and wife, or may hereafter be married, they shall not be allowed voluntarily to separate except for Scriptural cause."

In Georgia, it appears, from the foregoing, that the marriage of colored persons is held by the state laws and customs in no very high repute. Colored persons, even members of Churches, "take husband and wife," and "agree to be man and wife." Again: the "owners may object;" that is, they may object to the institution of almighty God, sanctioned and enjoined by Jesus Christ, and refuse that persons should be married whom the laws of God require to be married. Here the Church and the state are at direct issue. The Church is attempting to adhere to Christ's institution, and the state is setting it at naught, and establishing adultery, fornication, and concubinage in the place of the holy matrimony of God's own appointment. The twenty-first article of religion, of the same Church, declares that "Christians and ministers may marry at their own discretion, as they shall judge the same to serve best to godliness." But the state—by the power allowed to slaveholders—here interposes, and places this at the arbitrary disposition of an interested, and frequently a licentious master, thus annulling marriage, and establishing in its place concubinage or unbounded licentiousness, such as heathenism never exceeded in its worst forms of moral pollution.

4. The system of slavery and Christianity are opposed in the exercise of Church discipline. We will adduce a few cases, in which the irreconcilable antagonism of slavery and the Scriptural exercise of discipline will appear.

The government of the Church takes cognizance of fraud, theft, robbery, and the like. The crime of defrauding the laborer of his stipulated wages, can be no greater than taking the labor of a slave without wages. Indeed, the sin is less. The first is an act of theft or fraud; the last is an act of double robbery; for slavery robs the slave of his liberty, and then of his labor, which is his property. If the government of the Church takes cognizance of fraud and theft in ordinary cases, it must also of acts of robbery. Therefore, the just government of the Church is opposed to the government of slaves; and a slaveholder, who is such of choice, or continues such by choice, can have no more right to Church membership than swindlers, thieves, or robbers.

When slaveholders and slaves are both members of the Church, if the slave accuses his master to the Church for a crime, in support of which he can bring no testimony but that of slaves, the Church, by the laws of Christ, are bound to give credit to true testimony, from whatever source it may come. But the laws of the state will not allow the testimony of slaves to be taken. Here again the state is opposed to Christianity, because Christianity obeys the laws of God.

Again: the laws of the state allow the master to *beat* the slave, *brand*, or *crop* him. But the laws of the Church forbid one brother to *strike* or *beat* another, much less to brand him, crop off his ears, or the like. The law of Scripture in the case, (Matt. xviii, 15,) gives the master no authority to *beat* or *whip* his offending brother; but directs him to take different measures. Thus, the government of the Church is at variance with the government of slaves. If the Church forbids the masters to whip and abuse the slaves in the same Church with them, it will amount to an emancipation of the slaves; for no one can be a slaveholder, without possessing authority to compel the slaves to submit to his will, and, therefore, to whip, beat, or otherwise correct them if need be.

Again: suppose a slave, in the same Church with his master, deserts his service, but is again brought back, and placed under the government of the master, and also that of the Church. Now, how could the Church court condemn the slave for the crime of offending God and his brethren, when he only attempted that which every member of the court would justify in himself, had he been in the same condition with the slave?

No ecclesiastical court can restore an offending brother to the communion of the Church again, but upon confession of sin, and an engagement, through divine grace, to avoid a repetition of the same offense. But it is impossible to bring a slave to such a confession for deserting his master's service, without lying both to God and man.

5. Accordingly, we find leading slaveholders in the south openly declare against the Church, unless it shapes its doctrines and discipline to suit their views, and to accommodate Church discipline to the laws and practice of slavery.

Mr. Calhoun declared in the senate, January 10, 1838, that "many in the south once believed that slavery was a moral and political evil: that folly and delusion are gone. We see it now in its true light, and regard it as the most safe and stable basis for free institutions in the world." Governor Hammon, February 1, 1836, declared: "I do firmly believe that domestic slavery, regulated as ours is, produces the highest-toned, the purest, the best organization of society, that has ever existed on the face of the earth."

Mr. Seabrook, in no obscure terms, considers Christianity in any efficient form, as at variance with slavery. He says: "Whoever believes slavery to be immoral or illegal, and, under that belief, frames a code of laws for the government of his people, is practically an ENEMY TO THE STATE." Alluding to the decisions of the synod of South Carolina and Georgia, he says: "The sentences quoted contain the foundation argument on which the emancipationist proposes to erect the structure of his scheme."

A large number of southern Christians have lately conceded to Mr. Seabrook, and the other politicians, all they could desire by way of submission. Presbyterian synods and presbyteries have allowed, "that holding slaves, so far from being a sin in the sight of God, is no where condemned in his holy word; . . . that slavery is a civil institution with which the General Assembly has nothing to do." Baptist associations have issued similar decrees; and several Methodist conferences as well as individuals in the south have declared, that slavery is no moral evil, but a civil and domestic institution.

The Rev. Leroy M. Lee, D. D., editor of the Richmond Advocate, of June 14, 1849, brings out this antagonism between the Church and the slave laws of Virginia. The state properly allows no negro to preach or exercise pastoral oversight. The Methodist Episcopal Church has all along endeavored to follow the command of the Savior in this matter, as far as the slave states would allow. Mr. Lee condemns the Church. He says: "The laws of Virginia do not allow slaves and free people of color either to teach or preach. The Baltimore conference preachers here in Virginia are in the habit of violating the laws of the state on this subject." Again, he says: "We have a class of ministers in Virginia who violate the civil laws of the commonwealth on one of the most delicate and dangerous subjects of legislation, and who, by conferring authority to teach upon slaves and free people of color, show their disregard of the law and their contempt for the reasons on which it rests for support. We think it high time the persons in question had conformed to the requirements of law, or ceased to exercise their functions within its control or under its jurisdiction. If they will do neither, let them protest against the law, and seek its abrogation. Then, whatever men may think of their opinions, they will at least give them credit for honesty and uprightness." The ministers referred to have long since protested against the law; but whether they have used their influence to have the law altered we can not tell. One thing is sure, that slavery is at war with the Gospel, when those called of God are not permitted to preach, or to teach, or exercise pastoral functions. We have quoted here the Richmond Advocate principally to show, historically and by way of testimony, that slavery was antagonistic to the exercise of the functions of a pure Gospel ministry.

In 1835 the pro-slavery politicians became alarmed for the safety of the domestic institution, and took it upon them to catechise the Churches. At one of these meetings in Clinton, Miss., among other resolutions the following was passed:

"That the clergy of the state of Mississippi be hereby recommended at once to take a stand upon the subject, and that their further silence in relation thereto, at this crisis, will, in our opinion, be subject to serious censure."

At Charleston, South Carolina, at a public meeting the clergy seem to be willing to do their part; for "the clergy of all denominations attended in a body, lending their sanction to the proceedings, and adding by their presence to the impressive character of the scene." It was then resolved by the meeting,

"That the thanks of this meeting are due to the reverend gentlemen of the clergy in this city, who have so promptly and so effectually responded to public sentiment, by suspending their schools in which the *free colored population were taught;* and that this meeting deem it a patriotic action, worthy of all praise, and proper to be imitated by other teachers of similar schools, throughout the states."

6. Slavery is criminal, because it violates the rights of conscience, and, therefore, is chargeable with persecution.

All Christians, especially ministers, are bound to teach the ignorant and make them acquainted with the truths of religion. But the laws of the slave states, by fines and penalties, prevent the free citizens from teaching the slaves to read the word of God. The reason is, that slavery can not be supported without restrictions on the means of knowledge; and this restriction interferes with the rights of conscience, for all good men are bound in conscience to instruct the ignorant, as well as to clothe the naked and feed the hungry.

If a slave feel in conscience bound to learn to read the word of God—and many feel themselves thus bound—the attempt would expose him to punishment of great severity.

If a slave possess gifts to preach, and the Church, as it is right she should, license and ordain him, he is prevented by the slave laws from going forth, according to Christ's commission, to preach the Gospel to his fellow-men, and if he persists he falls by the hand of the executioner. There are circumstances of horror in the persecutions of slavery unknown to the Popish persecutions, those of the inquisition not excepted. These professed to have the glory of God in view, and thought, in persecuting heretics, they were doing God service. But *gain* is the motive which weighs in the persecutions of the slave system. A chief reason for Popish persecution was the use of the Bible. It comes to the same thing whether the Bible is by force withheld from the people, or the people by force kept from the Bible. The Popish persecutors never restrained the Protestants from learning to read. But our slaveholders will not suffer the slaves to learn to read.

There is another case in which slavery most directly violates the rights of conscience: we mean, in its preventing, by prohibitory laws or impeding disabilities, conscientious masters from emancipating their slaves. The atrocious wrongs of slavery are such, and its moral evils so great, so palpable, and so repulsive to all men of enlightened consciences, that multitudes of slaveholders, since slavery commenced to this day, have felt themselves conscientiously bound to emancipate their slaves. But in the slave states the genuine slaveholders have succeeded to pass such laws as to prevent emancipation altogether, or so embarrass it as to render it impracticable or exceedingly difficult. In many states the laws prevent emancipation, except by legislative authority—a privilege very rarely granted; and, indeed, to ask such a privilege, in ordinary cases, would be to expose the petitioner to the imputation of being an abolitionist, and thus exposing him to scorn, if not to insult, or even death by Lynch law. In other states, where the laws allow of emancipation by the decision of the county courts, the emancipator must give security for maintenance and good behavior, which amount to more than most men can give; and thus, by these unreasonable and unjust impediments, emancipation is prevented. Thus the conscientious man, by these unjust laws, is prevented from following his sober convictions; and, hence, the rights of conscience are invaded. The consequence is, the system of slavery, in the slave states, has persecuted out of its territory multitudes of intelligent and conscientious men—the very best citizens in the state; for the intellectual and moral culture of those who are not conscientiously opposed to slavery must be low indeed, and much perverted. Certain it is, that the best and most enlightened men in the slave states, since slavery began, were opposed to slavery on the principles of right, and on high moral grounds. The true slaveholders took advantage of their position, and enacted law after law, so as to shut the door against emancipation. Multitudes of the conscientious and enlightened men left the slave states, and emigrated to the new free states. Maryland, Virginia, and Kentucky have persecuted this class of worthy men from their territories; and, to some extent, the other old slave states have done the same. The greater portion of the original settlers in middle and southern Ohio, Indiana, and Illinois were refugees from slavery. They left their country on account of the moral evils of slavery and its prospective influences on their families. They settled in these new states because they were free. Never was any country settled with better citizens than the refugee slaveholders, who have been the first and principal pioneer settlers of Ohio, Indiana, and Illinois. The states that expelled them have lost much; the states that have furnished them with homes are enriched and benefited every way by so noble a race of men; and their children have grown up to a maturity in intellectual and moral culture, that gives guarantee for the excellency of their future generations.

8. Nor is the south by any means compensated for banishing her conscientious antislavery citizens, by the reception of emigrants from the free states and from Europe, who settle in the south for the purpose of being slaveholders, or who after awhile glide into the class of slaveholders, although at first they had a strong repugnance to the system.

Those from free countries, who from choice settle in the slave states, must be ranked, in general, with the most debased of the human family. Either such never had right principles, or they have abandoned them. If they never had good moral principles, they can enter into practical slavery, exactly prepared to carry out the system; for just sentiments of moral conduct—of right and wrong—have no place in the slave system. Such persons are the very men to emigrate to the south, and there become overseers, clerks, and the like, and thus become initiated into the slave system. They are then ready to go to the slave market, inspect the gang, and bid off such as they want, with which to commence the business of slaveholding. Then the work can be prosecuted, by driving their gangs to the utmost, selling and separating husbands and wives, parents and children, without remorse, because they have no strong moral principles to produce conviction in their conscience; and those, who, with better teaching and in possession of better principles, can deliberately enter, practically, into slaveholding, must have abandoned their better teaching, and done violence to their conscience, and by this means have made shipwreck of faith and a good conscience. Such are now prepared, by their apostasy from the principles and the moral obligation of right, to do as most apostates do, to become threefold more the children of hell than others. Those, then, of no moral principles, or apostates from moral principles, form a large portion of those from free countries who enter practically into slavery.

There is, however, a class of persons from free countries who can not be ranked with the foregoing, whose general moral principles and sentiments are good. They have become citizens of slave states, with no such views as the unprincipled or the apostates from good morals. From the circumstances around them, they have been led to become slaveholders. They have never considered the vices which are inseparable from slavery. Ignorant of the force of long-established habits, and of the state of the human mind in slavery, they flatter themselves that every thing is to be gained by lenient means; but when they find their property purloined, or think that the labor obtained from their slaves is small in quantity, they are apt to give them up as incorrigible, and to lay it down as a settled maxim, that nothing will do with their slaves but the horse-whip. One of this class will then be heard confessing, that, on his arrival in the slave state, he formed an erroneous opinion of slavery and of slave treatment; that he imagined every thing might be done by kindness, and that he was too severe upon the discipline of slave states; but he now sees that these people are fit for nothing but for being slaves, and that nothing will do for them but the lash. There are only few raised in free states who are not, in the first instance, shocked at the sight of the evils of slavery. There is, however, something so insidious in its nature, and so congenial also to certain dispositions of mind, that this repugnance is, in general, speedily overcome. And as a last proof of the demoralizing effects of slavery, the new slaveholder is so much intoxicated with the love of this baneful system, so enraged against every one that condemns it, and so loud in his execration of emancipation, that he is foremost with those who proclaim death to the abolitionists and emancipationists.

CHAPTER VI.

EFFECTS OF SLAVERY ON THE STATE.

In the foregoing chapter we undertook to show the antagonism between Christianity and the system of slavery, and the injurious effects of this on the state, in consequence of the impediments thrown in the way of Christianity, which alone can reform the hearts and lives of men; and, by this means, the state is preserved from corruption, by the extension of good morals and good order. We will now proceed to present the evil effects of slavery on the best interests of the state, in a great variety of particulars.

1. We begin with the impediments which slavery throws in the way of *general education* in the state. This will divide itself naturally into three parts—the education of the slaves and colored people, the education of the white non-slaveholders, and the education of the slaveholders.

Education elevates the inferior classes of society, teaches them their rights, and points out the means of securing them. Of course this tends to diminish the influence of wealth, birth, and rank. It is a fundamental element in slavery, that the arts of reading and writing—the very elements of literary education—are acquirements which can not be allowed to the slave without diminishing his value as a laborer, facilitating his escape from bondage, and jeoparding the life of his master. Hence, *custom* or the *laws* of slave states deprive the slaves of all education. The exclusion of so large a portion of the inhabitants from the very elements of education, is an immense loss to any country, intellectually and morally considered, and throws an amount of ignorance into the community which must be felt in every grade in society, bond and free, white and colored. The seclusion of the same proportion of the community in the free states, from the common school cause, would

utterly ruin that system, which is the foundation and the elementary part of the whole educational interests of the country.

The education of the free white population in slave states is surrounded with great obstacles. The property, in the agricultural districts, is mostly in the hands of the slaveholders. Large masses of the free white population are poor. Thus, a common school system of education, in slave states, is impracticable, by secluding totally the colored population, by the pride of the slaveholders, who give little countenance to common schools, and by the inability of the non-slaveholders to support them.

A comparative view of the matter will appear from the the following table, the result of the census of 1840, by which the proportion of those who can not read and write to those who can, is pointed out:

Connecticut	1	to every	568	Louisiana	1	to every	38½
Vermont	1	"	473	Maryland	1	"	27
N. Hampshire	1	"	310	Mississippi	1	"	20
Massachusetts	1	"	166	Delaware	1	"	18
Maine	1	"	108	S. Carolina	1	"	17
Michigan	1	"	97	Missouri	1	"	16
Rhode Island	1	"	67	Alabama	1	"	15
New Jersey	1	"	58	Kentucky	1	"	13½
New York	1	"	56	Georgia	1	"	13
Pennsylvania	1	"	50	Virginia	1	"	12½
Ohio	1	"	43	Arkansas	1	"	11½
Indiana	1	"	18	Tennessee	1	"	11
Illinois	1	"	17	N. Carolina	1	"	7

Even according to the census, Indiana and Illinois are the only free states which, in point of education, are surpassed by any of the slave states. The principal cause of this is from their recent settlement, the influx of foreigners, and the emigration from the slave states. We are certain, however, that many of the foreigners who can read and write in their own language, yet, because they can not read and write in English, were returned as unable to read or

write at all. The same will apply to the northern states generally, where the foreign emigration is great. The gross ignorance prevailing in the old states of South Carolina, North Carolina, and Virginia, is a striking commentary on slavery and slaveholders.

Furthermore, the census gives a return of "scholars at public charge." Of these, there are in the free states 432,173, and in the slave states 35,580. Ohio has 51,812 such scholars, which are more than are to be found in the thirteen slave states. Kentucky has only 429 such scholars. Virginia, the largest state, has 9,791 scholars at public charge; while Rhode Island, the smallest state, has 10,912 such scholars. In the whole United States only 8.54 per cent. of the white adult population are unable to read and write; in the free states only 4.55 per cent. are so, while in the slave states the per cent. is 17.64, being more than *twice* as great a proportion in the slave states as in all the states together, and more than *four* times as great as in the free states; or, in other words, more than *one-seventeenth* of the white population in the slave states are unable to read or write; while not the *one hundred and fiftieth part* of the same class in the free states are in the same condition. There are more than *twelve times* as many scholars at public charge in the free states as in the slave states.

We have, also, some statements of public southern functionaries, which declare very startling facts in this matter.

In 1837 Governor Clarke, of Kentucky, in his message to the Legislature, says: "By the computation of those most familiar with the subject, one-third of the adult population of the state are unable to write their names."

Governor Campbell reported to the Virginia Legislature, that from the returns of twenty-eight clerks of counties, it appeared that of four thousand, six hundred and fourteen applications for marriage licenses in 1837, no less than one thousand and forty-seven were made by men unable to write. And probably the proportion of the females who could not write was greater than the males. Mr. Birney thinks that in Alabama, in the course of his practice as a lawyer, he found one white man out of every seven who could not write his name. In one instance he knew of a *true bill* found by a grand jury against a schoolmaster for the crime of teaching colored children; and the bill was signed by the foreman with a *mark*, because he could not write his name. This, however, must have been a rare occurrence.

As the slaves and colored people of the south are excluded from common education, and the whites are so sparsely settled, common schools have but limited existence in the south. Hence, the poor white people have little or no education, because the slaves have none. The rich planters imperfectly supply the want by the aid of private tutors, and by sending their children to the north for education. But, in consequence of their indolent habits and sportive methods of life, intellectual culture is low even among them.

The slaveholders and their children, taken as a whole, are far from being well educated. A majority of them are ignorant men—thousands of them notoriously so—mere *boors*—unable to write their names or read the alphabet. Because labor is performed by the slaves, it becomes disgraceful to work. The children of slaveholders brought up in luxury and idleness, will rarely undergo the labor necessary to a liberal education. They have a stronger propensity for pleasure and amusement, and even vices, than for the acquirement of knowledge. They have, also, too high an opinion of their own dignity to submit to the government of well-regulated seminaries. Thus, an inclination to idleness, a love of pleasure, vicious habits, and intractable dispositions prevent them from making advances in learning. And though some noble minds will rise above these difficulties, the multitude will be seriously impeded by them. A *few* slaveholders in each of the slave states have been men of *ripe* scholarship, to whom the national literature is justly indebted. A larger number may be called *well* educated, and these reside principally in cities and large towns. But the crowd of slaveholders are steeped in ignorance. As speakers some of them excel, as this is the way to distinction in some of the departments in life. Yet, among them there are but few close students, and fewer still of profound authors in any department of literature and science.

In the south the colored population are excluded from all education of every kind. The non-slaveholding whites are greatly deficient, and the slaveholders in general not much better, with the exception of a few, who but limitedly affect the masses. Very few southerners, male or female, become instructors of youth, even when qualified. Very few of the non-slaveholders are qualified to teach schools. Hence, the south depends principally on the non-slaveholding states even for their teachers. Colleges do not flourish in the south, and common schools are sparse indeed. The blight of slavery occasions all this. It has recourse to darkness as its stronghold; and darkness, by the retribution of Heaven, becomes the deadliest plague of those who wrong and oppress their fellow-men.

2. The spirit and demands of slavery claim monopolies in government affairs inconsistent with equal rights and injurious to the non-slaveholding portions of the republic.

The Presidency.—Of the ELEVEN Presidents since 1789, the slave states have had seven, who will have served, at the end of the present term, forty-eight years. The free states have had four Presidents, who have served sixteen years, counting Gen. Harrison's term of four years. No northern President has ever served more than one term. By holding the Presidency, slavery controls the cabinet, the diplomacy, the army and the navy of the country. The power that controls the Presidency controls, to a very great extent, the whole nation.

The Vice-Presidency.—The President exercises much of his power by and with the aid of the senate. The Vice-President is, *ex officio*, president of the senate. As such, he has the casting vote in all questions before that body. For the most part, the Vice-Presidents have been slave-holders. From the adoption of the Constitution up to June, 1842, there were seventy-six elections in the senate of president *pro tem.* of these the slave states had sixty, and the free states sixteen.

The Senate.—In the senate the slave states have precisely as many votes as the free states; and as the senate has had a veto on every question, no law has been passed, nor a treaty ratified, but by their votes. They can not, therefore, impute their depressed condition to unjust and partial legislation.

Department of State.—The office of Secretary of State is the most important, perhaps, in the cabinet, as he conducts the foreign correspondence, negotiates treaties, etc. Of the fifteen who had filled this office up to 1845, the slave states have had ten; the free states, five.

The War Department.—The free states have generally furnished the seamen and the soldiers; but the officers are mostly from the south.

The Post-Office.—Many of the post-offices in the south do not pay their way. Thus, in 1842 the deficit in the slave states was $571,000, while the excess over the expenditures in the free states was $600,000; so that in this year the north paid its own postage, and $571,000 for the south. Besides, the whole number of miles of mail transportation, for 1842, was 34,835,991, at an expense of $3,087,796. The mail was carried 20,331,461 miles in the free states, at a cost of $1,508,413; and 14,504,530 miles, at a cost of

$1,579,383, in the slave states. That is, it cost $70,970 more to carry the mail in the slave states than in the free, while it ran 5,826,931 miles less.

Civil, Consular, and Diplomatic Agencies.—Of the seven full ministers, six are from the slave states. Of the thirteen charges, nine are from the slave states; and the four charges given to the north are among the most insignificant governments.

In the election of members of the house, as well as in the election of President, the people of the slave states have a disproportionate influence over the policy of the administration. In consequence of the operation of the rule of *federal numbers,* whereby five slaves are counted as three white men, extraordinary results are exhibited at every Presidential election. In the election of 1840, the electors chosen were two hundred and ninety-four—of whom one hundred and sixty-eight were from the free, and one hundred and twenty-six from the slave states. The popular vote in the free states was 1,726,737, or one elector for 10,278 votes. The popular vote in the slave states was 682,583, or one elector to 5,935 votes.

The electors from South Carolina, chosen by the Legislature, are not embraced in this calculation. These facts show that the slaveholding states have an unfair share in the representation in Congress, as well as in the election of President.

The slaveholders under the first appointment of representatives, which lasted from 1789 to 1793, secured seven Congressmen more than they would have been entitled to under an equal representation, based upon white population alone; under the second, or from 1803 to 1813, they had sixteen; under the third, which went to 1823, they gained twenty-two Congressmen; under the fourth, which went to 1833, they had twenty-four Congressmen; under the fifth, which went to 1843, they had twenty-five Congressmen more than they would have had under an equal representation, based on white population. We have no means of accurately calculating, just now, the present state of this point; but we may safely put the number down at twenty-five.

Nor are they at all behind in the distribution of the *patronage* of government. Appointments under the federal compact are made by the President, with the consent of the senate. The rule of federal numbers, confined by the Constitution to the appointment of representatives, has been extended, by the influence of slaveholders, to other and very different subjects, such as the distribution among the states of the surplus revenue, and the proceeds of the public lands. Out of the Presidents who have filled the Presidential chair, only four have been from the free states. One of these served only for a month, and his place was supplied by a slaveholder. Another of these is said to have been a northern man with southern principles, yet the south deemed him unsafe for re-election, and, by their influence, put another in his place. Most of the secretaries of state have been slaveholders. The chair of the house of representatives has been mostly filled, and its committees appointed, by slaveholders. A majority of the judges of the Supreme Court have always been from the slave states. In 1842 the United States were represented at foreign courts by nineteen ministers and charges d'affaires, of whom thirteen were from the slave states.

Accustomed to rule the slaves with despotic power, and to monopolize the fruits of their labors, slaveholders carry the same temper and principles with them into the management of public affairs. It is with them a business to control and monopolize, not to provide for themselves by their industry. Hence, the various political intrigues are resorted to, and all diligence used to accomplish their purposes, urged on by their accustomed principle of usurpation of the rights of others, and their practice of monopolizing to themselves the fruits of other men's toils, while at the same time to engage in labor and toil is the last thing to be thought of.

It seems, indeed, that a non-slaveholder has a poor chance for an office, unless he can obtain the aid of southern influence to secure it. As an example in point, Major Noah, in 1842, applied for a lucrative office in New York, and obtained some northern signatures for that purpose. Knowing well, however, the value of southern influence, he obtained the following recommendatory letter from two slaveholders, W. C. Preston and Willie P. Mangum, to T. Ewing, Secretary of the Treasury:

"*Dear Sir,*—Believing Major Noah to be eminently qualified for the office which he seeks, and a most meritorious man, we join in the request of the gentlemen inclosed. We do this, not only as friends of Major Noah, and citizens of a common country, but as *southern men,* feeling that his wise and *temperate* course, as the conductor of a press, for many years, on the subject of *southern institutions,* entitles him to our *grateful* interposition in his behalf."

Mr. Noah had recommended a bill to the New York Legislature for fining and imprisoning abolitionists. It is not marvelous that Mr. Preston, who was for *hanging* abolitionists when caught, should think Mr. Noah very temperate; for certainly to fine and imprison them is much more moderate than to hang them.

John Quincy Adams said: "Not three days since, Mr. Clayton, of Georgia, called that species of population—that is, slaves—the machinery of the south. Now, that machinery had twenty odd representatives in that hall—not elected by the machinery, but by those who owned it. And if he should go back to the history of this government from its foundation, it would be easy to prove that its decisions had been affected, in general, by less majorities than that.

Nay, he might go further, and insist that that very representation had ever been, in fact, *the ruling power of this government.*

"The history of the Union has afforded a continual proof that this representation of property, which they enjoy, as well in the election of President and Vice-President of the United States, as upon the floor of the house of representatives, has secured to the slaveholding states the entire control of the national policy, and, almost without exception, the possession of the highest executive office of the Union. Always united in the purpose of regulating the affairs of the whole Union by the standard of the slaveholding interest, their disproportionate numbers in the electoral colleges have enabled them, in ten out of twelve quadrennial elections, to confer the Chief Magistracy upon one of their own citizens. Their suffrages at every election, without exception, have been almost exclusively confined to a candidate of their own caste." (Speech in Congress, February 4, 1833.)

John Quincy Adams said, elsewhere: "The spirit of slavery has acquired not only an overruling ascendency, but it has become at once intolerant, proscriptive, and sophistical. It has crept into the philosophical chairs of the schools. Its cloven hoof has ascended the pulpits of the Churches; professors of colleges teach it as a lesson of morals; ministers of the Gospel seek, and profess to find, sanctions for it in the word of God."

Wilberforce said of slavery, that it is "a system of the grossest injustice; of the most heathenish irreligion and immorality; of the most unprecedented degradation and unrelenting cruelty."

3. Slavery imparts to a people a martial character, hostile to the arts of peace, and to the security of human life.

Slaveholders generally carry deadly weapons about their persons. This is deemed necessary for defense against the violence or insolence of the slaves. The spirit thus cherished, by correcting the slaves, and the frequent sacrifice of their lives, and the equipments for deeds of blood, is seen in the violent tempers and fatal encounters so frequent at the south, in duels and assassinations.

What but this very spirit, and pleas for the rights of slaveholders, originated the Florida war? A cotton planter's claim of property to the wife of an Indian chieftain, seems to have been the occasion of this war. The following is a note appended to an account of the celebrated Oceola, by M. M. Cohen: "Oceola, or Powel, as he was called by the whites, had a wife to whom he was much attached, whose mother was a mulatto slave, who ran away, was adopted by the Indians, and married one of the chiefs. Though the father was free, yet as children, by law, in the south, take the condition of the mother, Oceola's wife was seized as a slave by a person claiming her under the right of her mother's former master. The high-spirited husband attempted to defend her, but was overpowered and put into irons by Thompson, who commanded the party. The event is incidentally related above. This transaction is said to have been the origin of the Florida war."

The cost of this Florida war, including $5,000 for bloodhounds to catch runaway slaves, amounted to $50,000,000, the greater part of which must be paid by the free states.

The annexation of Texas was also a scheme got on foot for the purpose of extending slavery.

The Mexican war was another movement conducted in the spirit of slavery, and accompanied with the customary temper and means with which slaveholders are familiar. The cost to the United States is placed by some at one hundred and twenty millions; and the whole territory acquired, at a fair purchase, could be obtained for about ten or twelve millions of dollars.

4. The principles on which the relation of master and

slave are based are inconsistent with the principles of a free government, and subversive of it.

It is essential to the enactment of good laws, that the lawgiver should have a general identity of interest with those for whom he legislates, and a habitual sympathy with their feelings. But there is little or no identity of interest, of feeling, when the mass of the people to be governed are slaves, and the legislators and those who elect them are proprietors. The condition of slavery is, that the remuneration of the laborer is measured not by the value of his services, but by the amount of his indispensable wants; his interest, therefore, is to do the smallest possible amount of work, and to consume, at his owner's expense, the greatest possible amount of food, clothing, and other necessaries. The interest of the owner, on the other hand, is precisely the reverse; it is, that the greatest possible amount of labor should be obtained at the least expenditure which is compatible with the preservation of the laborer. The interest of the slave consists in the acquisition of his freedom. It is the interest of the owner to withhold freedom. The slave has a strong motive for desiring the abolition of those laws or customs by which his own class in society is degraded. The owner has an equally-powerful motive to maintain the exclusive privileges of his class. The general diffusion of religious knowledge and education is the highest interest of the slave, because it would prepare him for the participation of his rights, and enable him to assert them. The owner has an interest in obstructing the advance of knowledge among this part of the population. There exists between the slaves and their proprietors, that palpable contrariety of interests, by which, as all experience shows, men are habitually guided in their use of power.

In a slave country there is wanting a general *sympathy* of feeling between the lawgiver and those subject to his laws. Hence, it is impossible to reconcile the full enjoyment of civil freedom with the maintenance of domestic slavery. The equal protection of every class of men living beneath its rule, is elementary in the establishment of a free government, and this is wanting or greatly deficient in a slave country.

The experience of the past shows, that the very elementary principles which go to establish a system of slavery, are in practical opposition to a free government.

5. Indeed, the principles of the slave system are at variance with the fundamental principles of right, comprised in the Constitution of the United States.

Slavery is opposed to the fundamental principles of republicanism, maintained in the Declaration of Independence. That noble instrument asserts: "All men are created equal, and are endowed by their Creator with certain inalienable rights; among these are life, liberty, and the pursuit of happiness." These principles are denied by the slaveholding states. The Constitutions of Maryland, North Carolina, South Carolina, and Tennessee, declare, "that no freeman ought to be taken or imprisoned, or deprived of his freehold, liberties, or privileges, or outlawed, or exiled, or in any manner destroyed, or deprived of life, liberty, or property, but by the judgment of his peers, or by the law of the land." This plainly implies that the slave may be taken, imprisoned, and destroyed, without either judgment or law.

The Constitution of Kentucky tells us "that all freemen, when they form a social compact, are equal." Kentucky does not admit that all men are "created equal," nor that even freemen are equal, till they become so by social compact. This state, therefore, denies a fundamental principle of the Declaration of Independence.

The slave states widely differ from the free states, which declare, in their constitutions, "that all men are born equally free and independent." Slaveholding states practically maintain the fundamental principles of absolute monarchy, which are, that all men are not equal, and that all men are not born equally free and independent. Every slaveholder is, virtually, an absolute monarch to his slaves, and they are bound to approach him with all the submissions which absolute monarchy can require.

Again: the Constitution of the United States, article iv, section 2, declares, that "the citizens of each state shall be entitled to all the privileges and immunities of citizens of the several states." Notwithstanding this express provision, there are in most, if not in all slave states, laws for seizing, imprisoning, and then selling as slaves for life, citizens of other states, entering within their borders, because they are black or colored. This is done under the shallow pretense that such are fugitives from bondage.

By a law of Louisiana, every free negro or mulatto arriving on board any vessel as a *mariner*, or *passenger*, shall be immediately imprisoned till the departure of the vessel, when he is compelled to depart in her. If such negro or mulatto returns to the state, he is to be imprisoned for *five* years.

If any free negro or mulatto enters the state of Mississippi for any cause, however urgent, any white person may cause him to be punished by the sheriff with thirty-nine lashes; and if he does not immediately leave the state, he is sold as a slave.

In Maryland, a free negro or mulatto, coming into the state, is fined $20, and if he returns he is fined $500, and on default of payment is sold as a slave.

In 1833 seventeen slaves effected their escape from Virginia in a boat, and finally reached New York, in which state a judicial investigation would be requisite to prove property. The Governor of Virginia made a requisition on the Governor of New York for them, as fugitive *felons*, and the pretended felony was *stealing the boat* in which they had escaped.

Slaveholders hold even their *own* laws and constitution in contempt, as well as those of the federal government, whenever they conflict with the security and permanency of slavery. One of the most inestimable rights of constitutional privileges is trial by jury, and this is trampled on at the mandate of slaveholders.

"It is expressly provided [article iv, section 2] by the Constitution of the United States, 'that the citizens of each state shall be entitled to all the privileges and immunities of citizens in the several states.' This is a very simple, plain, and imperative sentence. Free blacks and mulattoes are citizens in all the states, I believe, east of the Delaware, as well as in the states north-west of the river Ohio, and they can not be dispossessed of the right to locate themselves where they please.

"The Constitution of the United States equalizes the privileges of the citizens of the states, without respect to color, or the countries from whence they may be derived. This principle must be maintained. The free blacks and mulattoes in the United States are not to be considered. It is the disfranchisement of citizens who are citizens, and can not be disfranchised. Shall we open the door to what may become the foulest proscriptions?" (Niles' Register, 1820.)

6. The practical operations requisite to carry out with safety the system of slavery are at variance with allegiance to law.

Practical slavery, when the system is in danger by the inculcation of liberal principles, or the requirements of strict moral justice, is forced to have recourse to mobs and Lynch law. It would be a tedious recital to go through half the instances of Lynch-law decisions and mobocratic acts, to which the citizens of the south have had resort, within these last fifteen years, in order to enforce their unjust and cruel slave laws, as well as to extinguish every rising spark of liberty. White men have been summarily visited by capital punishment by the decisions of Judge Lynch. Colored persons have been murdered, whipped, tortured, and maltreated, in many places; and all this by the general approbation and public opinion of the slave community.

Add to this, the close sympathy and interests existing between the slaveholders of the south and their commercial friends in the north have succeeded to raise mobs, almost without number, in the free states, with a design, directly or indirectly, to suppress the principles of freedom, as well as to leave without the disturbance of moral influence the unjust system of slavery. The mob in Cincinnati in the summer of 1836, was nothing more nor less than a pro-slavery movement. The actual leading actors in destroying the press of Mr. Birney, were slaveholders from Kentucky, stirred up by the slaveholding interests. The merchants and influential citizens of Cincinnati who supported this outrage by their active co-operation, their presence at the mob, and their subsequent apologies for the proceedings, go to show, that for the sake of commercial gain, or political place and office, they fully sustained the pro-slavery mob, to keep on good commercial and political terms with slaveholders.

The great mob in Boston was instigated, and conducted, and apologized for, "by gentlemen of intelligence and property," all ready to conciliate the slaveholders of Charleston and other southern cities, in order to maintain advantageous commercial relations between them and their southern customers. The same was the case with most of the other mobs in which abolitionists have been assailed.

Nor is the plea of any weight, which goes to state, that the abolitionists have been sending incendiary tracts among the slaves, although this has been charged by such great names as Mr. Calhoun, Mr. Clay, and Mr. Madison. The abolitionists did no such thing. All their addresses, as a body and as antislavery associations, were directed to the slaveholders themselves and to the white free citizens, and never to the slaves. Besides, as slaves can not read, or, if they could, no publications addressed to them could reach them, the charge of addressing them is preposterous. (See a Statement to the Massachusetts Legislature, Note A: "Pacific Purposes of the Abolitionists.")

Nor is there any thing new in the fact, that the slaveholders of the south should have very great political and commercial support in the north. There are sprinklings every-where of northern residents, who are slaveholders in the south, and derive large profits from them. An additional sympathetic bond is the large number of persons residing in the north, whose relatives in the south are slaveholders. The profitable commercial relations maintained by rich merchants and mechanics, whose devotions to mammon are very faithfully performed, is a strong reason to keep on good terms with the oppressors; and it is notorious, that political considerations and the hope or enjoyment of offices have converted many cold northerners into warm advocates and supporters of slavery. Though these may be properly enough denominated dough-faces, or northern men with southern principles, the complaisant titles of prudent, conservative, or liberal patriots are assumed by them, awarded to them by their allies, and they are eulogized without stint by many able editors.

Such actually was the fact in England, during the reign of slavery in the British colonies, both while the African slave-trade was in operation and after its destruction, during the great contest in Parliament and out of it, till final emancipation took place in the West Indies. (See Life of Sharp, pp. 10–20.)

7. Slavery is in practical as well as theoretical antagonism to the great safeguards of national liberty, such as freedom of speech, freedom of the press, trial by jury, and the right of petition.

The Constitution of the United States says, "Congress shall make no law respecting an establishment of religion, or prohibiting the free exercise thereof, or abridging the freedom of speech or of the press, or the right of the people peaceably to assemble, and to petition for a redress of grievances." According to this, it is manifest, that liberty of conscience, or "the free exercise of religion," freedom of speech, freedom of the press, peaceable public discussion, the right of petition, and, we may add, trial by jury, are among the great safeguards of a free government, and are the principal guardians of American liberty; and every citizen of the United States has a right to worship God as he pleases—utter his thoughts—print them—provided he does not interfere with the rights of others. The Constitutions of New Hampshire and Massachusetts declare, that "the liberty of the press is essential to the security of freedom in a state." The Constitutions of Virginia and North Carolina affirm, "The freedom of the press is one of the great bulwarks of liberty." Similar language is employed in the constitutions of all or most of the states.

(1.) In the slaveholding states the *freedom of speech*, in regard to slavery, is laid under such unconstitutional embargo as greatly to intrench on the safety of liberty. Whoever would express in the south the sentiments respecting slavery which are generally adopted throughout the civilized world, would endanger his life, or be severely punished. On this great subject no philanthropist can speak his sentiments.

The ministers of religion must not treat of slavery in its purely moral characteristics, so as to bring the moral principles contained in the ten commandments to bear on it, without incurring heavy penalties. On the hostility between slavery and Christianity he dares not speak. The strong arm of the slave laws would punish him capitally, or popular rage would do it, according to the fashion of mobs or the rules of Lynch law.

In Congress, too, the unconstitutional restraint of *gag law* has been resorted to, or the fiery wrath of slaveholders, by noisy uproar, has thrown in its interference in Congress, whenever the subject of slavery has been introduced. Governor M'Duffie, in his address to the Legislature of South Carolina, declared: "As long as the halls of Congress shall be *open to the discussion* of this question, we can have neither peace nor security." The Charleston Mercury—very high authority on this subject—declared, in 1837, that "public opinion in the south would now, we are sure, justify an immediate resort to force by the southern delegation, even on the floor of Congress, were they forthwith to seize and drag from the hall any man who dared to insult them, as that eccentric old showman, John Quincy Adams, has dared to do." In the present session of Congress—winter of 1848 and 1849—because the subject of slavery has been introduced and treated with considerable freedom, the southern members have been highly offended, called a convention, and manifested the utmost alarm and dread.

The Columbus (South Carolina) Telescope says: "Let us declare, through the public journals of our country, that the question of slavery is not and shall not be open to discussion; that the system is too deep-rooted among us, and must remain forever; that the very moment any private individual attempts to lecture us upon its evils and immorality, and the necessity of putting means in operation to secure us from them, in the same moment his tongue shall be cut out and cast upon the dunghill."

Slavery brings the masters themselves under despotism. It takes away the liberty of speech, which all freemen prize as one of the essential guards of liberty. This, we are told, however, is necessary for the safety of the masters. But an institution imposing such a necessity can not be good. It must be exceedingly evil.

(2.) *Liberty of the press.* It is a well-known truth, that slavery has placed its prohibition on the liberty of the press, whenever it would undertake to censure or condemn slavery. In some states the laws of the United States have been set at naught, by statutes which are contrary to the Constitution of the United States, and of the state which made the enactment. This is the case in regard to Virginia especially, by whose statute the Christian Advocate and Journal, and the Western Christian Advocate, and other papers, have been proscribed, as incendiary publications. Where laws did not exist for this purpose, the public sentiment of slaveholders did the work by Lynch law. By mob violence Mr. Lovejoy's paper was driven from St. Louis to Alton. In Kentucky Mr. Birney would not be permitted to publish his paper; and after he commenced it in Ohio, the pro-slavery spirit and opposition followed it, and destroyed his press. Mr. Cassius M. Clay's paper was driven from Lexington, Kentucky, and his press conveyed to Cincinnati, by a mob of gentlemen. Many books, pamphlets, etc., have been expurgated from antislavery matter, to suit the sentiments of the south. In short, there are so many things so immoral in act and so unsound in principle, in the system of slavery, that it will not bear the light of discussion in books, papers, and pamphlets; for a faithful exposure of its sins and evil tendency would go far toward its destruction. Slavery will not come to the light, because its deeds are evil.

(3.) *Trial by jury.* In all governments, not despotic, trial by jury, or its equivalent, has been the remedy against injustice. The entire fabric of the federal Constitution, as well as the constitutions of the several states—the slave system excepted—is built on the basis which requires trial by jury, or one's peers, to be one of its chief corner-stones. But slavery comes in active subversion of this great privilege of freemen. In 1793 Congress passed a law authorizing the recovery of fugitive slaves, whereby any person in a free state may be seized as a fugitive from service and labor, and without a jury trial, upon proof oral or written to the satisfaction of such magistrate as the claimant may elect, may be hurried into endless slavery. Still, many contend, that the act of Congress, properly interpreted, does allow of the right of trial by jury, or its equivalent. But the practice, heretofore, has generally been to disregard any such trial, and on bare *accusation* or mere *claim* hurry the supposed fugitive into endless slavery, whether the person is free or a slave. For want of trial by jury thousands of free persons have been made slaves for life; and probably the number of free persons enslaved by this and other such means, has heretofore been fivefold, perhaps tenfold greater than the number of runaway slaves that have escaped into the free states and Canada from their masters in the slave states. So frequent and notorious have been the outrages committed on free persons by slaveholders in the United States, and their unprincipled hired aids in the free states, all along the borders of the slave states, that very few persons in the free states can now place any confidence in the claims laid in against fugitive slaves.

We can not place this in a clearer light than by quoting from the very able address of William Johnston, now Judge Johnston, in the case of the State of Ohio *vs.* Forbes and Armitage, before the Franklin Circuit Court, Kentucky, April 10, 1846. Mr. Johnston is intimately acquainted with the workings of slavery in this respect, having from youth resided on the border between the free and the slave states, and having every opportunity of being well acquainted in such matters. After contending for the right of a "judicial examination," in all such cases of claims, he declares:

"We in Ohio think such examination indispensable to the cause of justice and humanity. We see nothing but endless confusion, injustice, and oppression growing out of the right to drag men, women, and children from their homes, without such examination. We see encouragement given to a horde of pirates, who infest the waters of the Ohio on both its banks, and make man-catching a trade. I do not say these wretches are Kentuckians. They are to be found on both sides of the water, and do not deserve a name or local habitation on either. They are the enemies of the human race, without sympathy for any body—men who will steal your slave from you to-day and sell him to you to-morrow. There is a distinguished character now in the Ohio penitentiary, who made a fortune by first persuading slaves to run away from their masters, quartering them on credulous black people—who, on account of their color, could not be witnesses against him—till a reward should be offered, and then conveying them back again for the reward. There are unfortunately others out of the penitentiary, who follow the same calling; till, if you were on the southern line of Ohio, you would almost imagine you were on the slave coast of Africa. About eight years ago a free colored woman, born in Ohio, and residing in Brown county, in the absence of her husband was seized, and, without examination or any forms of law whatever, carried into Mason county, Kentucky, and lodged in jail, under pretense that she was the slave of Arthur Fox, high sheriff of Mason county. Mr. Fox disclaimed ownership in her; and then she was retained in prison, under pretense that she was the slave of Mrs. Johns of New Orleans. Mrs. Johns also disclaimed her; and then, being in prison as a runaway slave, she was subject to be sold, at the end of fourteen months, for jail fees. She was only set at large by executive interposition. I mention this case, not because it is a singular one, but because I happen to be familiar with it, and because it is a matter of record in both states. Cases far more aggravated, of which no record exists, have often occurred. Men, believed to be freemen, have been knocked down with a club in the streets in the night seasons—dragged into boats, and carried God only knows where. To prevent such outrages, the Legislature of Ohio have enacted two statutes against kidnapping: the one against seizing and carrying away free persons—the other against seizing and carrying away any person whatever, without a hearing. These statutes of Ohio in no way contravene the Constitution of the United States or the Act of 1793, nor embarrass the owners of fugitive slaves in recovering their property. Ought not these laws to be respected?"

(4.) *The right of petition.* The framers of the federal Constitution supposed the right of petition to be altogether too firmly established in the habits and affections of the people to need a constitutional guarantee. This omission roused some of the state conventions: the Virginia proposed, as an amendment, "that every freeman has the right of petition." Other state conventions substituted "person" for "freeman." The result of the whole was the amendment in the Constitution which we have quoted above, granting "the right of the people peaceably to assemble, and *to petition government* for a redress of grievances." When members of Congress swear to support the Constitution of the United States, they are as much bound by their oath to refrain from "*abridging* the right of petition," as they are to abstain from "prohibiting the free exercise of religion."

When the Declaration of Independence was proclaimed, and the Constitution of the United States formed, and for some time after, it was generally believed, north and south, that slavery would be of short continuance. But, in the addition of new slave states, and the increased demand for cotton and sugar, a new impulse was given to the advancement of slavery. The petitions on slavery have generally been sent in to Congress for the abolition of slavery in the District of Columbia, its extension in the territories, and the like. Were mere party to be silent, it would seem very clear, that Congress is invested by the Constitution with "exclusive jurisdiction, in all cases whatsoever," over the District, and that, therefore, it is palpably constitutional to abolish the slave-trade in the District, or emancipate the slaves. Even Congress, in 1816, appointed a committee to inquire into the expediency of doing away the slave-trade; and in 1829 another committee, on the "gradual abolition of slavery in the District," was appointed. Petitions, at different times, were sent to Congress on the subject of slavery, up to this time, without spreading much alarm in the south. But when Mr. Garrison established the Liberator in 1831, in Boston, and the Legislature of Georgia passed a law, offering $5,000 for his abduction and his delivery in Georgia, and southerners offered sums of $25,000, of $50,000, and of $100,000 for kidnapping certain abolitionists, the matter assumed a new form. In 1835 the President, in his message to Congress, foolishly or thoughtlessly charged the abolitionists with sending, by *mail*, inflammatory appeals to *slaves;* that is, sending printed papers to men who could not read them, and through a conveyance by which they could not receive them. The truth is, the papers were sent to the masters for their consideration, and the appeals were on the immorality of converting men, women, and children into chattels, depriving them of their rights, and inflicting wrongs on them. The masters in Charleston, fearing the moral influence of these appeals on the conscience of the slaveholding community, forced open the post-office and burned the papers. The Postmaster-General, with the sanction of the President, invaded the mail, and authorized every postmaster to become a censor of the press, so as to abstract from the mail every paper which *he* might think too favorable to the rights of man.

For more than twenty years, previous to 1836, petitions had been sent to Congress for the abolition of slavery in the District; but the increase of them alarmed the slaveholders, as they knew that discussion of any kind endangered their system. Hence, Mr. Pinckney's famous resolution, in 1836, declaring "that all petitions or papers, relating in any way or to any extent to the subject of slavery, shall, without being printed or referred, be laid on the table; and no further action whatever shall be had thereon." On January 18, 1837, Mr. Haine's gag law was passed. On February 11, following, on an inquiry from Mr. Adams whether a petition from slaves could be admitted, the two following resolutions were passed: "1. That this house can not receive the said petition without disregarding its own dignity, the rights of a large class of citizens of the south and west, and the Constitution of the United States." Yeas 160, nays 35. "2. That slaves do not possess the right of petition secured to the people of the United States by the Constitution." Yeas 162, nays 18. In the second resolution the house acknowledges that "the right of petition is secured to the people of the United States by the Constitution," and yet they passed a rule to cut off that constitutional right. They, also, by the first resolution contradict the second. Mr. Patton's gag law passed December, 1837, Mr. Atherton's in December, 1838, and Mr. Johnson's January, 1840. Mr. Johnson's motion made it a standing rule of the house, that "no petition, memorial, resolution, or other paper, praying the abolition of slavery in the District of Columbia, or any state or territory in the United States in which it now exists, shall be received by the house, or entertained in any way whatever."

It would seem to be a right which no man could doubt of, according to all, that each should be privileged to *peti-*

tion, *ask*, or *pray* for benefits or relief from grievances. This is even conceded to malefactors and criminals. God hears the poor publican, and even the ravens that cry. He hears sinners who have transgressed his law. The reception of petitions from the poorest and vilest of persons is an attribute or prerogative of the Almighty; and for *man* to deny it to a fellow-man, is the hight of arrogant and sinful assumption. The *right of petition*, and the corresponding reception or hearing it, is one thing; the disposition of it after reception is quite another, as the petition may or may not be granted, without injury to any one, or depriving him of any just right. But slavery confessedly has something in it inherently which shrinks from petition. A petition would involve the inquiry, is it right or wrong to grant the petition? An inquiry into the nature of *right* and *wrong*, of what man owes to man, and what God in his word declares to man, if applied to slavery would soon detect in the system injustice, wrong, oppression, and a long list of other sins, so that the result would be emancipation. The conscience of the south knows that slavery can not live under such an inquest. Their love of gain attaches them to slavery. This is the reason why gag laws have been passed, and the constitutional rights of citizens of the United States infringed upon by the acts and influence of the slave system of the south.

In a foregoing chapter we have shown how the slave system is antagonistic to Christianity, and infringes in several ways on the rights of conscience, thus "prohibiting the free exercise of religion." Here we have shown how slavery nullifies or counteracts the great safeguards of liberty, such as the freedom of speech, the freedom of the press, trial by jury, and the right of petition. Thus, slavery comes in collision with the very ramparts and barricades of freedom in a state. If it prevail and rule, all these safeguards of liberty must be suppressed. And then, when liberty of conscience is taken away,. when no man may utter his honest thoughts or speak of the evils around him, when the press will be thoroughly muzzled, no trials by jury to test wrong, and no right to petition for rights or against grievances, then will liberty be no more. All these are invaded and infringed on by slavery. But the contest is now up, and time will tell whether despotism or freedom will rule in these United States, after the victories of the Revolution and the adoption of the Declaration of Independence, and of the Constitution of the United States. Although there is now a contest, liberty will, in the end, gain the day.

8. Slavery impoverishes a country. Most travelers agree that the slave states are, at least, a century behind the free states in point of general improvement. The principal reason for this is, that a large proportion of the inhabitants are maintained in idleness; while in the free states they are employed in lawful industry.

(1.) Slaveholders are not industrious. They will not work. The children grow up in idleness, and in mature and advanced age it becomes a confirmed habit not to work. The white non-slaveholders partake, to a considerable degree, of the character of their neighbors. And sooner than be singular, many of them emigrate to the free states, where it is no disgrace for men to work with their own hands.

Slaveholders, also, are lacking in economy, and become addicted to wastefulness. The profits derived from slave labor are often squandered in gaming, intemperance, and other wasteful habits. Or, if these vices are not pursued, the slaveholder, to maintain his rank, deems the attendance of a slave indispensable. Hence, the expenses of living are usually much greater in slave than in free countries.

(2.) The slaves, too, are not producers equal to the freemen. They have not the same motives to industry which influence those who are free when they labor for themselves; hence, they do not perform labor generally equal to freemen. And, even when they are compelled to perform excessive labor, as they frequently are, especially on the sugar plantations, there are other drawbacks on the profits. Slaves will observe no modes of economy, but will waste unsparingly in every thing. So that the excess of labor taxed on them is mostly more than balanced by their deficiency in saving, and their habits of wastefulness.

(3.) The mechanics of the south are few and of inferior character. The negroes who are mechanics are of the coarsest kind, and rarely attempt perfection in the few mechanical arts with which they are acquainted. The sons of slaveholders, of course, will not stoop to the labors of the mechanic's shop. The enterprising mechanics of the south often leave for the free states, while the supply from the free states is deficient in number and qualifications.

(4.) The state of agriculture in the south is deplorable. The soil of the old northern slave states is very much reduced by corn and tobacco; and the principal profits in the grain-growing slave states arise from growing slaves for market. While the soil is thus reduced by a course of exhausting agriculture, the moral curse of making up losses by growing slaves for the far south, is producing moral ruin on the characters of men. The cotton and sugar crops of the extreme south are rapidly reducing its fertile lands to a state of sterility, equal to the condition of the exhausted corn and tobacco lands of Maryland, Virginia, and North Carolina. In brief, the soil of every country, in all ages, cultivated by the hands of slaves, has always deteriorated.

(4.) Indeed, there are numerous exhausting public *expenses* incurred by slavery, calculated to impoverish any country. The soil, by slovenly culture, becomes exhausted. To oversee and watch the slaves and keep them at work, the indolence of the masters, the standing army necessary to watch the slaves, as well as many other expenses of the slave system, go to show that it tends, in the issue, to poverty and ruin.

(5.) If the industry and enterprise of the free and slave states are compared, the result will be to prove the great superiority of freedom to slavery. The arts and sciences in a slave community are never cultivated to any extent, owing to the ignorance of the slaves, which diffuses itself among the masters. Hence, a general torpor rests on the industry and enterprise of the country. Cotton, the entire product of slave labor, affords a livelihood to but few white non-slaveholders. The tonnage, manufactures, and agricultural products of the free states far exceed those of the slave states; and the mere culture of cotton does not compensate for the deficiencies. Of four hundred and ninety-five patents granted in 1841 for new inventions, only seventy were received by citizens of the slave states. It would be too tedious to go through the details on this topic; we will content ourselves with the testimonies of a few witnesses, whose veracity and ability will not be questioned.

Mr. Clawney, of South Carolina, in his speech on the floor of Congress, thus describes the condition of his native state. He ascribes, however, the state of things to the tariff, rather than to the obvious cause that one-half of the population are poor, ignorant, degraded slaves, and the other half suffering by its incurable evils. Surely slavery is the cause why twenty thousand, six hundred and fifteen white citizens over twenty years of age do not know their letters; while Maine, with double her population, has only three thousand, two hundred and forty-one. Mr. Clawney says:

"Look at South Carolina now, with her houses deserted and falling to decay; her once fruitful fields worn out and abandoned, for want of timely improvement or skillful cultivation; and her thousands of acres of inexhaustible lands, still promising an abundant harvest to the *industrious* husbandman, lying idle and neglected. In the interior of the state where I was born, and where I now live, although a country possessing all the advantages of soil, climate, and health, abounding in arable land, unreclaimed from the first rude state of nature, there can now be found many neighborhoods where the population is too sparse to support a common elementary school for children. Such is the deplorable condition of one of the oldest members of this Union, that dates back its settlement more than a century and a half, while other states, born as it were but yesterday, already surpass what Carolina was, or ever has been, in the happiest and proudest day of her prosperity."

Mr. Preston, of South Carolina, in pleading in a speech for a railroad, says:

"No southern man can journey—as he had lately done—through the northern states, and witness the prosperity, the industry, the public spirit which they exhibit—the sedulous cultivation of all those arts by which life is rendered comfortable and respectable—without feelings of deep sadness and shame as he remembers *his own neglected and desolate home.* There, no dwelling is to be seen abandoned—not a farm uncultivated. Every person and every thing performs a part toward the grand result; and the whole land is covered with fertile fields, with manufactories, and canals, and railroads, and edifices, and towns, and cities. We of the south are mistaken in the character of these people, when we think of them only as peddlers in horn flints and bark nutmegs. Their energy and enterprise are directed to all objects, great and small, within their reach. The number of railroads and other modes of expeditious intercommunication knit the whole country into a closely-compacted mass, through which the productions of commerce and of the press, the comforts of life and the means of knowledge, are universally diffused; while the close intercourse of travel and of business makes all neighbors, and promotes a common interest and a common sympathy. How different the condition of these things in the south! *Here* the face of the country wears the aspect of premature old age and decay. NO IMPROVEMENT IS SEEN GOING ON, nothing is done for posterity. No man thinks of any thing beyond the present moment."

Hear Bentham:

"As soon as slavery is established, it becomes the lot of the greatest number. A master counts his slaves as his flocks, by hundreds, by thousands, by tens of thousands. The advantage is only on the side of a single person; the disadvantages are on the side of the multitude. If the evils of slavery were not great, its extent alone would suffice to make it considerable. Generally speaking, and every consideration apart, there can, therefore, be no ground for hesitation between the loss that would result to the masters from enfranchisement, and the gain which would result from it to the slaves.

"Another strong argument against slavery may be drawn from its influence upon the wealth and power of nations. A freeman produces more than a slave. Set at liberty all the slaves which a master possesses, this master would, without doubt, lose a part of his property; but slaves, taken together, would produce not only what he lost, but still more. But happiness can not be augmented with abundance, while public power increases in the same proportion.

"Two circumstances concur in diminishing the produce of slaves: the absence of the stimulus of reward, and the insecurity of their condition.

"It is easily perceived that the fear of punishment is little likely to draw from a laborer all the industry of which he is capable, all the work he can furnish. Fear leads him to hide his powers rather than to show them; to remain below rather than to surpass himself.

"By a work of supererogation, he would prepare punishment for himself; he would only raise the measure of his ordinary duties by displaying superior capacity. His ambition is the reverse of that of a freeman; and he seeks to descend in the scale of industry, rather than to ascend. Not only does he produce less; he consumes more, not in enjoyment, but lavishly, wastefully, and by bad economy. Of what importance to him are interests which are not his own? Every thing which saves his labor is a gain for him; every thing which he allows to be lost, is only the loss of his master. Why should he invent new methods of doing more or better? In making improvements he must think; and thinking is a labor to which no one gives himself without a motive. Degraded to a beast of burden, a slave never raises himself above a blind routine, and one generation succeeds another without any progress in improvement." (Jeremy Bentham's Principles of the Civil Code.)

The difference presented in the foregoing is not owing to tariffs, government patronage, or the like. The slave states have received their full share of the national domain. The area of the slave states is nearly double that of the free. New York, though the *empire* state, has less territory than Virginia, Missouri, Georgia, Louisiana, or North Carolina. The slave states, too, are older than the free states. In soil and climate, and other natural advantages, the southern states have the advantage of the northern. In 1790 the present free states and territories had only a little more than half a million over the slave territories and states. In 1840 the free states had nearly five million of inhabitants more than the slave states. Another fifty years will very much increase this preponderance.

Take Kentucky and Ohio. In 1840 Kentucky had five hundred and ninety-seven thousand, five hundred and seventy inhabitants, and Ohio one million, five hundred and nineteen thousand, four hundred and sixty-seven. Then

Louisville had twenty-one thousand, two hundred and ten population, and Cincinnati forty-six thousand, three hundred and thirty-eight. The difference now is greater.

The Louisville Journal, speaking of the two rival cities, remarks: "The most potent cause of the more rapid advancement of Cincinnati than Louisville is the ABSENCE OF SLAVERY. The same influences which made Ohio the young giant of the west, and is advancing Indiana to a grade higher than Kentucky, have operated in the *Queen* City. They have no *dead weight to carry,* and consequently have the advantage in the race."

In 1840 Mr. C. M. Clay wrote thus: "The world is teeming with improved machinery, the combined development of science and art. *To us it is all lost; we are comparatively living in centuries that are gone; we can not make it, we can not use it when made.* Ohio is many years younger, and possessed of fewer advantages than our state. Cincinnati has manufactories to sustain her; last year she put up one thousand houses. Louisville, with superior natural advantages, as all the world knows, wrote 'to rent' upon many of her houses. OHIO IS A FREE STATE, KENTUCKY A SLAVE STATE."

Mr. Thomas F. Marshall, of Kentucky, in a pamphlet published the same year and on the same subject, draws the following comparison between Virginia and New York. The statements were made before the results of the census of 1840 were known.

"In 1790 Virginia, with 70,000 square miles of territory, contained a population of 749,308. New York, upon a surface of 45,658 square miles, contained a population of 344,120. This statement exhibits in favor of Virginia a difference of 24,242 square miles of territory, and 408,188 in population, which is the *double* of New York and 68,600 more. In 1830, after a race of forty years, Virginia is found to contain 1,211,405 souls, and New York 1,918,608, which exhibits a difference in favor of New York of 607,203. The increase on the part of Virginia will be perceived to be 463,187, starting from a basis more than double as large as that of New York. The increase of New York, upon a basis of 340,120, has been 1,578,391 human beings. Virginia has increased in a ratio of 61 per cent., and New York in that of 566 per cent.

"The total amount of property in Virginia under the assessment of 1838, was $211,930,508. The aggregate value of real and personal property in New York, in 1839, was $654,000,000, exhibiting an excess in New York over Virginia, of capital, of $442,069,492.

"Statesmen may differ about policy, or the means to be employed in the promotion of the public good, but surely they ought to be agreed as to what prosperity means. I think there can be no dispute that New York is a greater, richer, a more prosperous and powerful state than Virginia. What has occasioned the difference? . . . There is but one explanation of the facts I have shown. The clog that has stayed the march of her people, the incubus that has weighed down her enterprise, strangled her commerce, kept sealed her exhaustless fountains of mineral wealth, and paralyzed her arts, manufactures, and improvement, is NEGRO SLAVERY."

The poverty arising from slavery in a state is a sinful poverty, because it is produced by indolence, wastefulness, and the exercise of wrong passions toward our fellow-men, inflicting injuries on them, as well as depriving them of their rights. Were a people to become poor by distributing their property to supply the wants of their more needy fellow-creatures, they would be innocently poor. But when they become poor by doing wrong, or refusing to do that which is right, such poverty is sinful. Add to this, that because men do wrong God withholds his blessings, and this leads to poverty. In this case it is a just punishment of God on men for their sins. In the slaveholding states, their poverty and want of prosperity may be traced to both these sources, so that they eat of the fruit of their own doings, and God visits them with his judgments as punishments for their sins. The south is, as a whole, this day, impoverished, ignorant, unstable in morals, depraved in religion, and corrupt in politics, notwithstanding their claims for respectability or chivalry.

9. Slavery weakens a state, and in proportion to its extent exposes it to easy conquest. Slaves are the natural enemy of the state. They derive no benefit from the government, but, on the other hand, are deprived of their inalienable rights, and endure many grievous wrongs. Hence, they want only an opportunity to overthrow the government. In some states, too, the slave population exceeds the free, and is still rapidly increasing, and must soon, without foreign aid, be able to overcome their oppressors. An enemy within a state is much more dangerous than one without.

Slaveholders in new countries occupy large bodies of land, and this leaves less room for free citizens; or, in the older countries, the slaveholders will purchase the land from the small farmers, and thus enlarge their plantations. This is commonly done. Hence, these emigrate mostly to the free states. And many of the best citizens, conscientiously opposed to slavery, as we have seen, emigrate to the free states. The slaveholders, raised in idleness, luxury, and unaccustomed to subordination, are not the proper materials for an army, and are ill prepared to endure the toils of the army.

Besides, in modern times, and in Christian countries, all slaveholding states have been united with countries that are free. Thus, the West Indian, Mexican, and South American slaveholding colonies were united to England, France, Spain, Portugal, and other free countries of Europe. If England, previous to the emancipation act, had withdrawn the protection of her *power* from the colonies, slavery would soon have been extinguished. As soon as Mexico and the South American colonies dissolved their connection with Spain, slavery was abolished in them. The free states of this Union are to the slave nearly in the same relation in which the European powers were to their slaveholding colonies. Slavery could not long exist in the south without the support of the northern states. Besides, the slaves in the United States, in regard to human rights, have intelligence superior to the West India or Mexican slaves; and in the West Indies, the power of the slaves to act was weakened by their insular condition, which prevented their acting in concert.

Slavery produces discord between the slaves and their masters; and it can not be otherwise, in the nature of things, because the interests of both are diametrically opposite. Slavery, with all its mortifying degradations, can not entirely divest man of the image of God, or of a knowledge, in some degree, of truth, justice, and the mutual duties and obligations of man to man. Although deprived of his freedom, he still sees, hears, tastes, and smells, and even thinks, reasons, reflects, independent of all restraints. Since the independence of the United States, slaves, by hearing the conversation of their masters upon civil liberty, are better acquainted with the rights of man than they could have been before that period; the effect of this is an increase of enmity between whites and blacks, which must lead to some tremendous irruption in the slave states, if their masters will persist in perpetuating slavery.

What would be the result now, in the case of war with any European power? A British army in the heart of South Carolina or Alabama, would soon rally the slaves around the standard of the enemy. Or, in case of a revolt of the slaves, what accessions of troops could they receive from the West Indies, in such wav as the citizens of the

United States invaded Texas, without the immediate acts of the imperial government authorizing it! But the appalling consequences of such an event are too alarming to write on; we therefore forbear to dilate on this point, except to beseech God that he would bestow his grace on those concerned, that those steps of just and right dealing between man and man might be resorted to in order to avoid such a catastrophe.

It is perfectly natural that we should fear those whom we have deeply injured; and fear is a cruel passion. Hence the shocking severity with which, in all slave states, attempts to escape from slavery have been punished. This is true, from Pharaoh and the Egyptians down to this day, and it must continue so, while slavery exists. As late as 1822, certain slaves in Charleston were *suspected* of an *intention* to rise and assert their freedom. A court consisting of two justices of the peace and five freeholders convened, and condemned them, and thirty-five were hanged. Many instances of the same character could be given within these last thirty years. A court which has not power to take away the land of the white man, hangs black men by dozens.

But as we might here be accused of mere northern prejudices, let us hear the southern men speak out on this topic. These will not be the declarations of "fanatics, abolitionists, or incendiaries," or other "treasonable" persons.

During the Revolutionary war, the secret journal of Congress, vol. i, p. 105, contains the following record:

"*March* 29, 1779.—The committee appointed to take into consideration the *circumstances of the southern states*, and the ways and means for *their* safety and defense, report, that the state of South Carolina—as represented by the delegates of the said state, and by Mr. Huger, who has come hither at the request of the Governor of said state, on purpose to explain the particular circumstances thereof—is UNABLE to make any effectual efforts with militia, by reason of the great proportion of citizens *necessary to remain at home to prevent insurrection among the negroes*, and to prevent the desertion of them to the enemy; that the state of the country, and the great number of these people among them, expose the inhabitants to *great danger* from the endeavors of the enemy to excite them to revolt or desert."

Governor Hayne, in his message of 1833, warned the South Carolina Legislature that "a state of *military preparation* must always be with us a state of perfect *domestic* security. A profound peace, and consequent apathy, may expose us to the danger of *domestic insurrection*."

The author of "A Refutation of the Calumnies inculcated against the Southern and Western States," himself a Carolinian, admonishes his countrymen thus: "Let it never be forgotten that our negroes are truly the Jacobins of the country; that they are the anarchists, and the domestic enemy, THE COMMON ENEMY OF CIVILIZED SOCIETY, AND THE BARBARIANS WHO WOULD, IF THEY COULD, BECOME THE DESTROYERS OF OUR RACE." Again: "Hatred to the whites, with the exception, in some cases, of attachment to the person and family of the master, is nearly universal among the black population. We have then a FOE cherished in our very bosoms; a foe WILLING TO DRAW OUR LIFE-BLOOD whenever the opportunity is offered; in the meantime intent on doing us all the mischief in his power." (Southern Religious Telegraph.)

In a debate in the Kentucky Legislature, in 1841, Mr. Harding opposing the repeal of the law prohibiting the importation of slaves from other states, and looking forward to the time when the blacks would greatly outnumber the whites, exclaimed:

"In such a state of things suppose an insurrection of the slaves to take place. The master has become timid and fearful, the slave bold and daring; the white men, overpowered with a sense of superior numbers on the part of the slaves, can not be embodied together; *every man must guard his own hearth and fireside.* No man would even dare for an hour to leave his own habitation; if he did, he would expect on his return to find his wife and children massacred. But the slaves, with but little more than the shadow of opposition before them, armed with the consciousness of superior force and superior numbers on their side, animated with the hope of liberty, and maddened with the spirit of revenge, embody themselves in every neighborhood and furiously march over the country, visiting every neighborhood with all the horrors of civil war and bloodshed. And thus the yoke would be transferred from the black to the white man, and the master fall a bleeding victim to his own slave."

"The negroes seduced and taken from the inhabitants of South Carolina, in the course of the war, remained subject to the disposal of the enemy. They were successively shipped to the West Indies; and it is asserted, on the authority of the best citizens of South Carolina, that more than twenty thousand slaves were lost to the state in consequence of the war." (Col. H. Lee's Memoirs of the Revotionary War in the Southern Department, vol. ii, p. 456.)

"The forces under the command of General Provost marched through the richest settlements of the state, where are the fewest white inhabitants in proportion to the number of slaves. The hapless Africans, allured with the hopes of freedom, forsook their owners, and repaired in great numbers to the royal army. They endeavored to recommend themselves to their new masters by discovering where their owners concealed their property, and were assisting in carrying it off." (Ramsay's History of South Carolina, vol. i, p. 312.)

"It has been computed by good judges that between the years 1775 and 1783, the state of South Carolina lost twenty thousand negroes." (Id., p. 475.)

The Maysville Intelligencer comments thus on the subject:

"We of the south are emphatically surrounded by a

dangerous class of beings—degraded and stupid savages—who, if they could but once entertain the idea, that immediate and unconditional death would not be their portion, would react the St. Domingo tragedy. But a consciousness, with all their stupidity, that a tenfold force, superior in discipline, *if not barbarity,* would gather from the *four corners of the United States,* and slaughter them, keeps them in subjection. But to the *non-slaveholding states,* particularly, are we indebted for a permanent safeguard against insurrection. Without their assistance the white population of the south would be *too weak* to quiet the innate desire for liberty which is ever ready to act itself out with every rational creature."

Mr. Underwood, of Kentucky, in 1842, in debate in Congress, said: "The dissolution of the Union will be the dissolution of slavery."

The military weakness of the south is a subject too delicate on which to expand. The Secretary of War, in his report for 1842, remarked: "The works intended for the more remote southern portion of our territory, particularly require attention. Indications are already made of designs of the worst character against that region in the event of hostilities from a certain quarter, to which we can not be insensible."

The Quartermaster-General, Mr. Jessup, a southern man, shows the same anxiety. He says: "In the event of a war with either of the great European powers possessing colonies in the West Indies, there will be danger of the peninsula of Florida being occupied by blacks from the islands. A proper regard for the security of our southern states requires that prompt and efficient measures be adopted to prevent such a state of things."

The Secretary of the Navy, a slaveholder, describes the prospective calamities as follows: "It would be a war of incursions aimed at revolution. The first blow would be struck to us through our institutions, in arraying what are supposed to be the hostile elements of our social system against each other. Even in the best event, war on our own soil would be the more expensive, the more embarassing, and the more horrible in its effects, by compelling us at the same time to oppose our enemy in the field, and to guard against all attempts to subvert our social system."

Indeed, the very idea of an armed negro awakens the fears of slaveholders. When a bill was introduced, in 1842, to regulate enlistments in the naval service, Mr. Calhoun proposed to amend the bill, so that negroes should be enlisted only as *cooks* and *stewards.* He thought it a matter of great consequence not to admit blacks into our vessels of national defense. Mr. Benton thought that *all arms,* whether on land or sea, should be borne by the whites. Mr. Bagley declared, "In the southern portion of the Union the great object was to keep arms and a knowledge of arms out of the hands of the blacks. The subject addressed itself to every southern heart. Self-preservation was the first law of nature, and the south must look to that."

The slaveholders, conscious of their weakness, and we trust, too, of their guilt, attempt to supply the place of strength by a bullying insolence, hoping to effect by intimidation what they well know can not be effected in any other way. This mode has long succeeded in Congress, and to such an extent as to call forth the following cutting but well-deserved reproach from Mr. Randolph, on the time-serving and servile souls of a class of northern members of Congress. He addresses the northern members thus: "We have conquered you, and will conquer you again; and we have not conquered you by the black slaves of the south, but by the WHITE SLAVES of the north." In 1835, when the Enterprise, a southern slaver, with a cargo of seventy-eight slaves, bound from Virginia to Charleston, was driven to Bermuda, and the slaves became freemen on their reaching

British territory, Mr. Stevenson and Mr. Forsyth employed some magisterial and threatening language to the British authorities. But when the matter was properly considered by our government, it was deemed best to pass over the matter as easily as possible. A war with Britain, then or now, because Britain would not aid the United States in upholding slavery, would certainly have no favorable influence in strengthening the bonds of slavery.

Again: when the case of the Creole was on the carpet, in 1841, the senate of the United States was made to resound to such speeches as the following:

"Mr. King, of Alabama, said: 'If such outrages continue, he solemnly believed nothing could prevent a collision. Unless that government should retrace her steps, war must inevitably come.'

"Mr. Calhoun, of South Carolina, held the liberation of the slaves of the Creole 'to be the most atrocious outrage ever perpetrated on the American people. As soon as they could get full information, they ought to demand that those who committed the piracy should be delivered to this government. If we can not obtain justice, every man with an American heart will be ready to raise his hand against oppression.'

"Mr. Barrow, of Louisiana, 'was not willing that those he represented should submit any longer to the insolence of a foreign power. He wished the committee to present to the people the true principles of national law, which we would maintain at all hazards. The people of the south would not submit to the British interpretations of the laws of nations, drawing a distinction between slaves and goods. The traffic of slaves from one state to another is a matter of every day's occurrence; and if these contemptible British subjects of Nassau are permitted to go on in this way, seizing by force of arms and liberating slaves belonging to American citizens, the south would be compelled to fit out armaments, and destroy Nassau and other British towns that trample on the laws and the rights of our citizens.' "

But when the British embassador arrived, and it came to the point, redress or war, the stipulation of making a "distinction between slaves and goods" was not insisted on. Southern men, as well as others, saw that the United States could not go to war with Britain, in order to sustain slavery, or rather restore fugitive slaves.

Now, the weakness of the states which entertain slavery arises principally, if not altogether, from the inherent moral evils contained in the system of American slavery. The slave is wronged and cruelly treated, however well he may be clothed, fed, housed, and exempted from punishment. The masters are the very persons who rob them of their rights and oppress them with innumerable wrongs. The constitutions and laws of the state authorize all this. The slave is aware of his wrongs, ignorant as he may be of science, art, or religion. The masters are ill qualified to resist in the time of trial. Besides, the God of heaven is against oppression; for "no attribute of God is on the side of slaveholders."

Slavery, therefore, provokes *insurrections*. Insurrections and slavery, whenever it is widely extended, are inseparable. Slavery is an unnatural state. The love of freedom inherent in the human constitution, is born with man, and can never be separated from him. The slave is sure to entertain an undying thirst and watchfulness to seize on the first opportunity to secure his liberty. According to what the master has taught him, by precept and example, he is misinformed about the nature of right and wrong. He, of course, will avail himself, without scruple, of whatever means he can employ, for accomplishing his end. Nor will his conscience smite him while urged on by the desire of freedom and the spirit of revenge for the injuries he has received, however indiscriminate the destruction he may scatter around him. Insurrections may have failed hitherto, but the danger is not over. The history of St. Domingo teaches what black men and slaves may do to obtain liberty.

10. Nor does the establishment of slavery by law make the system the less guilty in itself, the less injurious to its victims, or screen the enactors or upholders of these laws from the distributive justice of God.

Laws can not change the nature of things. There is an essential difference between right and wrong, justice and injustice, kindness and cruelty. Drunkenness, gambling, Sabbath-breaking, and prostitution are immoral in themselves, whether they are sanctioned or forbidden by human laws. Persecution is wrong, whether legalized or not. Clothing the naked, feeding the hungry, and the like, are right, whether they are authorized or forbidden by human laws. In short, God's laws are superior to all human laws.

Wrong done by law or society is as truly wrong as when done by an individual; and, according to Scripture, such wrong is condemned as well as wrong done by an individual. "Shall the throne of iniquity have fellowship with thee, which frame mischief by a law, and gather themselves together against the soul of the righteous, and condemn innocent blood," Psalm xciv, 20. "Woe unto them which decree unrighteous decrees," Isa. x, 1.

When the authority of law is quoted, it would be well to test the character of the slave statutes and principles of moral justice on which the true force of right laws depend. In the common law of England, adopted generally in this country, there are found a series of maxims, in harmony with the law of God, and which never have been excelled for wisdom, justice, and equity. The slave laws annul and break these maxims.

It is a maxim of the common law, "*sic utere tuo, ut alienum non lædas*"—we should so use our own rights, as not to injure those of others. (Vide 3 Blackstone Com., 217.) Or, as Blackstone interprets it, the "law enforces that rule of Gospel morality, of 'doing to others as we would they should do unto ourselves.'" The white people, who have had the power, have used or rather abused their powers, rights, and privileges, to the wrong and injury of the colored people. This conduct is the settled custom of the slave states, and is more or less exhibited in the free states. With the Bible and the just maxims of the common law in their hands, they have united to use their own rights and powers to enslave and oppress the colored people. The principal cause or pretext for this conduct seems to be the great slave maxim, that "slaves have no rights," not even to the benefit and protection of legal maxims. Legal justice has thus yielded to legal injustice or moral wrong, which has rendered the slaves, in the most material respects, *outlaws* in a professedly free and Christian country.

Another maxim of the common law is, "*that no man shall take advantage of his own wrong;*" that is, if he does one wrong to another, it is no reason why he should have a right to do him another wrong. But slaveholders take advantage of their own wrongs to perpetuate slavery. They deprive the slaves of freedom, and then, because they are thus deprived, continue to enslave them. They degrade, corrupt, and brutalize the slaves, and then, because they esteem them unfit for freedom, they say the slaves ought to remain in slavery. They deprive them of all literary knowledge, and then pronounce them too ignorant to make a proper use of rights, and that they ought, therefore, to remain deprived of them. They deprive them of the ordinary means of grace and correct knowledge of duty, and then pretend that they are too vicious to be trusted with liberty. They bind them, hand and foot, and then condemn them, because they can not use those hands and feet. Criminal necessity, or a kind of necessity produced by his own crimes, is every tyrant's plea. Slavery is one crime, and slave laws and customs are other crimes used to support man-stealing; and the only necessity they possess is in the facility and security they furnish for the commission of this great crime.

It is another maxim, "*that none are bound by contracts or laws but parties and privies to them.*" But slaves are never considered as parties to any law or contract, as they are deprived of all right to make either laws or contracts; nor are they allowed any privity to laws or contracts. Yet they are held responsible to the laws, and are bound by contracts made for them by others.

Another maxim is, "*that every wrong shall have its remedy.*" But all or the principal wrongs of slaves have no remedy by law. The slave has no legal redress for the daily civil and criminal wrongs he receives. He is not permitted to sue in a court of law, because he has no such right. The law which is a shield to others is a scourge to him. He is an *outlaw*, or without the protection of law, without crime on his part, and that, too, in his own native land. If he offends against laws which he had no agency in making, he is subjected to the most barbarous slave code that ever existed; but if others offend against him, so as to deprive him of personal liberty, the fruit of his labor or property, personal security, and such rights as are connected with these, he is without redress. Let no one call by the name of protection these scanty guards thrown around the life and limbs of slaves, in order to preserve them the better to be the productive property of their masters; for this protection is for the sake of the master, and not for the benefit of the slave.

We might proceed here to show how the slave code tramples on all subordinate rights of slaves, considered as men, and belonging to them at common law; such as the right to apply to courts of justice for redress of civil injuries, the right to petition for redress of grievances, the right to acquire education, the right of conscience, the right to bear arms, etc. These have been considered elsewhere in this treatise, and we need not now enlarge. Slavery is not only a great crime against the common law, but it is opposed to it both in its *spirit* and *genius*. The common law is republican in its principles; its general rules and maxims are in the highest degree equal, just, and right; while the slave code is unequal, unjust, and despotic. The common law naturally leads to improvement in the moral and social condition of mankind; while slavery tends to debase, degrade, and corrupt man, and to prevent his elevation in knowledge, morals, and social state. Wherever the common law prevails, wise and wholesome statute laws are made from time to time, to remedy its defects and improve the condition of those who are under its influence; but in the slave code the statutes relative to slaves are seldom made for any other purpose than to benefit or protect the master, or to degrade the slave, and prevent his improvement and elevation. The common law and the slave code, or *code noir*, are always antagonists, and wherever the one prevails the other falls.

Slavery at first was introduced into the United States by *custom*, and this custom prevailed in defiance of the common law. It is a *heathen* and wicked custom, originally adopted by Christians from the African negroes. Blackstone—vide 1 Black. Com., 76–79—lays down seven rules as criterions to test the rectitude or justice of all customs in general. The slave customs are violations of all or most of these rules to test the character of just customs. The great common law maxim, in regard to custom, is, "*Malus usus abolendus est*"—bad customs are to be abolished. Right customs, tested by the standard of Blackstone's criteria, are generally applied in deciding on the rights of white persons; but the rules which are customarily applied in the slave code are at variance with the criteria which test just customs.

By the common law all slavery is a usurpation of right, as is instantly felt whenever the rights of white persons are invaded. By that law no property in any thing stolen vests in the thief or his heirs, *as against the rightful owner.* Neither does the produce or increase of stolen property vest in the thief. The rightful owner or his heirs can, upon due proof, recover both at any time. So, if the thief *sells* the stolen property, neither the buyer nor his heirs acquires any title to it, *as against the lawful owner.* By the common law, too, as well as by the law of God, every man is, under God, his own owner; and whoever steals, kidnaps, purchases, or enslaves him, can acquire no title to him or his services, or to his posterity as slaves; and as "the receiver is as bad as the thief," slaveholding, knowingly and voluntarily entered into, is as criminal as slave-trading or kidnapping. By the common law, too, all the natural rights are inalienable. (Vide 1 Black. Com., 424.) Hence, all slave *titles* are mere usurpations, committed in defiance of common law. All slave laws, customs, and titles are *wrongs;* and all slave-traders and voluntary slaveholders are among the greatest criminals, according to the laws of God and all just laws of men.

11. Besides, slavery being fundamentally wrong in its principles and morally wrong in its practice, it even conflicts with the soundest principles which are acknowledged by the *laws of nations.* According to these laws, every sovereign state is entitled to the cultivated services, skill, and abilities of all its inhabitants, in order to preserve and perfect itself and its institutions, and promote its best interests. (Vide Vattel, xxii, 86–98.) And all its inhabitants have the right to perfect their skill to the utmost for the good of their country. But slavery prohibits this improvement, and thereby hinders the resources and weakens the defenses of

every country in which it exists. Free nations are much stronger than slave nations, as all history shows.

Mr. Fuller, in his reply to Wayland, presents the following inconsistent and sophistical pleas for slave laws; but they are the very best which so bad a cause will admit:

"It will be replied, that we must take slavery as it is embodied in the southern laws; and this, in fact, is the fruitful source of misconception. What I am writing about is slavery; but let no one suppose that I am defending all the slave laws. The statutes of a government for the regulation of slaves may be most oppressive and wicked. This, however, does not prove slavery a sin, any more than harsh and cruel enactments toward apprentices prove apprenticeship a sin; or than a law giving parents the power, or requiring them to abuse their children, would prove that it is criminal to have children. What my relation as master and parent gives me a right to do, is one thing; what the law may permit, or even enjoin, is another. The Roman law allowed masters to kill their slaves, and throw them into their ponds to feed fish; does it, therefore, follow that a Christian master has a right to do this? Most of the laws of South Carolina are virtually repealed by universal practice. The law, for example, forbidding slaves to assemble without the presence of so many white persons, is a dead letter, whenever the meeting is for religious purposes. Those laws which prohibit a discharge of the master's duty, are often notoriously inoperative. The most important law is that forbidding slaves being taught to read; yet, how many are taught!" (Fuller and Wayland's Letters, pp. 158–160.)

We barely notice a few of the gross mistakes of Mr. Fuller.

Christians, as we have seen, can as readily murder their slaves under the laws of the slave states, as Roman citizens could do under the Roman laws; although it must be done by the Christians with more privacy.

Slavery is the creature of law, and is contrary to nature, as the Roman law declares.

Mr. Fuller seems as little conversant with the principles of the Roman law, as he is with the principles of the Bible or of Christianity with regard to slavery.

How strange that Mr. Fuller can pronounce the gross immoralities, that enter into the very essence of slavery, no sin—such as theft, robbery, injustice, wrong! And this he does when he denies the essentially-sinful character of slavery.

The following declaration of Rev. Wm. Hague, in his reply to Dr. Fuller, p. 7, we fear has too much truth in it: "He [Dr. Fuller] has done greater disservice to the cause of religion and humanity, than could possibly be achieved by all the traffickers of human flesh, whom the laws of Christian nations now condemn as pirates."

CHAPTER VII.

WITNESSES.

1. WE present in this chapter the testimony of many of the wisest and best men the world ever saw, comprising the principal theologians, statesmen, moralists, and philanthropists of Great Britain and the United States, and other parts of the world.

The theologians are noted for their learning, piety, and love of liberty, whose study has been the word of God, and whose great work has been the benefit of the human race. These pronounce unhesitatingly against slavery, and furnish the most cogent reasons in showing its utter sinfulness.

The statesmen of Great Britain, taught first from the Bible, and then trained in the great Biblical, political principles of the British constitution, which secures to every man his inalienable rights of life, liberty, and the acquisition of property, express themselves in no doubtful terms. Their arguments are unanswerable; and, therefore, never have been answered, though often vilified and misrepresented.

Our own native statesmen, too, whose national motto is LIBERTY, whose Declaration of Independence asserts "ALL MEN ARE CREATED EQUAL, ENDOWED BY THEIR CREATOR WITH THE INALIENABLE RIGHTS OF LIFE, LIBERTY, AND THE PURSUIT OF HAPPINESS," and whose Constitution maintains "THE FREE EXERCISE OF RELIGION, UNABRIDGED FREEDOM OF SPEECH, FREEDOM OF THE PRESS, AND THE RIGHT OF PETITION"—our native statesmen, imbued with these holy principles, derived from their British parents, but divested of British hinderances and embarrassments, have spoken out in godlike strains in favor of liberty.

Surely, these voices, as the utterances of many waters, will be heard throughout the whole civilized world; and their very words will be civilizing talismans to the barbarous nations. Let us now hear them speak before the tribunal of the world; for there is no rebutting testimony, though often called for, since the mere clamor of prescriptive claims does not constitute any opposing testimony.

2. Testimonies of British clergymen, of different grades and denominations.

Among these may be found the most distinguished divines and theologians that the world ever saw—men eminent for their literature, their critical theological knowledge, and their correct moral principles. As far as they have had occcasion to speak of, or refer to slavery, they pronounce it a great moral evil, at variance with Scripture and the spirit of Christianity.

Rev. Morgan Godwyn, A. D., 1660.—He was a clergyman of Barbadoes, who wrote about the year mentioned above, and his book, entitled the Negro's and Indian's Advocate, was published in London in 1680. We are indebted to Watson's Sermons, vol. i, pp. 88, 89, for the following extract. He was among the first witnesses against slavery:

"Let us consider that we have no more dispensation for our silence than the apostles, with other succeeding holy bishops and priests, had, who first planted and watered the Church with their blood, and went about and preached every-where, when it was death to be a Christian; that faith is an active and prolific grace, and can not remain in idleness, but must operate and employ that heavenly heat which it receives from above, for the use of others; that there is no neutrality in this war; and that whoever is not actually in arms, prepared to fight against sin and infidelity, is to be reputed a conspirator with them; that there is the same heaven and salvation proposed for the conversion of slaves, as of more illustrious grandees; the whole being but the saving of souls; the effecting of which upon but a very few is worth the labor of many all their lives. Even we, no less than St. Paul, are debtors 'to the Greeks and barbarians, to the wise and to the unwise.' And God hath, by an extraordinary providence, brought these people to our very doors, to try our justice, and to see whether we will pay his debt, to which, if any ever did, each soul of us does stand most firmly obliged. Look upon them, and you can not but see in their countenances the lively effigies of St. Paul's Macedonian, imploring your help; and O! let not the blood of souls cry from the earth for vengeance against us. Reflect but upon the sad doom denounced against the fearful and unbelieving, (Rev., xxi,) and remember that the first great founders of our faith were no cowards. Think what shame it is, that we have given such just cause to the enemies of religion to reproach and triumph over our timidity, or, which is worse, our temporizing for filthy lucre. Nor let the opposition and peevishness of unreasonable men dishearten us; as knowing that our true portion is to be sent forth as sheep among wolves; and that success is, for the most part, the companion of a restless industry. Even so we, overlooking all difficulties, and pressing still forward to the mark, if we faint not, may obtain that prize for which we set forth, and accomplish a work greatly tending to the glory of God, and to the happiness of these poor people's souls, no less than of our own. And O, were our duty, as St. Chrysostom sweetly exhorteth of piety and a virtuous life, faithfully complied with, 'we might soon, and even without miracles, convert the world.' 'Wherefore, lift up the hands that hang down, and the feeble knees,' as saith the apostle. 'Let us be instant in season and out of season,' and keep back nothing of the whole counsel of God that is necessary for the souls of men."

Many of the English bishops, from 1711 to 1766, expressed themselves very strongly in reference to the irreligious and degraded condition of the slaves. But the most pointed declarations that we have met with, are from a sermon by Bishop Warburton, in 1766:

"From the free savages," he says, "I come now to the savages in bonds. By these I mean the vast multitude yearly stolen from the opposite continent, and sacrificed by the colonists to their great idol—the god of gain. But what, then, say these sincere worshipers of mammon? They are our own property which we offer up. Gracious God! to talk as of herds of cattle, of property in rational creatures—creatures endowed with all our faculties, possessing all our qualities but that of color—our brethren both by nature and grace—shocks all the feelings of humanity, and the dictates of common sense. But, alas! what is there in the infinite abuses of society which does not shock them? Yet, nothing is more certain in itself and apparent to all, than that the infamous traffic for slaves directly infringes both divine and human law. Nature created man free, and grace invites him to assert his freedom.

"In excuse of this violation, it hath been pretended that though, indeed, these miserable outcasts of humanity be torn from their homes and native country by fraud and violence, yet they thereby become the happier, and their condition the more eligible. But, who are you who pretend to judge of another man's happiness; that state which each man, under the guidance of his Maker, forms for himself, and not one man for another? To know what constitutes mine or your happiness, is the sole prerogative of Him who created us and cast us in so various and different molds. Did your slaves ever complain to you of their unhappiness amidst their native woods and deserts? Or, rather, let me ask, did they ever cease complaining of their condition under you, their lordly master, when they see, indeed, the accommodations of civil life, but see them all pass to others, themselves unbenefited by them? Be so gracious then, ye petty tyrants over human freedom, to let your slaves judge for themselves what it is which makes their own happiness, and then see whether they do not place it in return to their own country, rather than in the contemplation of your grandeur, of which their misery makes so large a part; a return so passionately longed for, that, despairing of happiness here—that is, of escaping the chains of their cruel taskmasters—they console themselves with feigning it to be the gracious reward of Heaven in their future state." (See Clarkson on the Slave-Trade, p. 63.)

JOHN WESLEY, IN 1776.—"That execrable sum of all villainies, commonly called the slave-trade, I read of nothing like it in the heathen world, whether ancient or modern. It infinitely exceeds every instance of barbarity, whatever Christian slaves suffer in Mohammedan countries." (Works, vol. iii, p. 341.)

"At Liverpool, many large ships are now laid up in the docks which had been employed for many years in buying or stealing Africans, and selling them in America for slaves. The men-butchers have now nothing to do at this laudable occupation. Since the American war broke out, there is no demand for human cattle; so the men of Africa, as well as Europe, may enjoy their native liberty." (Journal, of April, 1777.)

"May I speak plainly to you? I *must*. Love constrains me; love to you, as well as to those you are concerned with.

"Is there a God? You know there is. Is he a just God? Then there must be a state of retribution; a state wherein the just God will reward every man according to his works. Then what reward will he render to you? O think betimes! before you drop into eternity! Think now, 'He shall have judgment without mercy that showed no mercy.'

"Are you a man? Then you should have a human heart. But have you indeed? What is your heart made of? Is there no such principle as compassion there? Do you never feel another's pain? Have you no sympathy, no sense of human woe, no pity for the miserable? When you saw the flowing eyes, the heaving breasts, or the bleeding sides and tortured limbs of your fellow-creatures, were you a stone, or a brute? Did you look upon them with the eyes of a tiger? When you squeezed the agonizing creatures down in the ship, or when you threw their poor mangled remains into the sea, had you no relenting? Did not one tear drop from your eye, one sigh escape from your breast? Do you feel no relenting now? If you do not, you must go on, till the measure of your iniquities is full. Then will the great God deal with you as you have dealt with them, and require all their blood at your hands. And at 'that day it shall be more tolerable for Sodom and Gomorrah than for you!' But if your heart does relent, though in a small degree, know it is a call from the God of love. And 'to-day, if you will hear his voice, harden not your heart.' To-day resolve, God being your helper, to escape for your life. Regard not money! All that a man hath will he give for his life! Whatever you lose, lose not your soul: nothing can countervail that loss. Immediately quit the horrid trade: at all events, be an honest man.

"This equally concerns every merchant who is engaged in the slave-trade. It is you that induce the African villain to sell his countrymen; and in order thereto, to steal, rob, murder men, women, and children, without number, by enabling the English villain to pay him for so doing, whom you overpay for his execrable labor. It is your money that is the spring of all, that empowers him to go on: so that whatever he or the African does in this matter it is all your act and deed. And is your conscience quite reconciled to this? Does it never reproach you at all? Has gold entirely blinded your eyes, and stupefied your heart? Can you see, can you feel, no harm therein? Is it doing as you would be done to? Make the case your own. 'Master,' said a slave at Liverpool to the merchant who owned him, 'what, if some of my countrymen were to come here, and take away my mistress, and master Tommy, and master Billy, and carry them into our country, and make them slaves, how would you like it?' His answer was worthy of a man: 'I will never buy a slave more while I live.' O let his resolution be yours! Have no more any part in this detestable business. Instantly leave it to those unfeeling wretches, who

'Laugh at human nature and compassion!'

Be you a man, not a wolf, a devourer of the human species! Be merciful, that you may obtain mercy!

"And this equally concerns every gentleman that has an estate in our American plantations; yea, all slaveholders, of whatever rank and degree; seeing men-buyers are exactly on a level with men-stealers. Indeed you say, 'I pay honestly for my goods; and I am not concerned to know how they are come by.' Nay, but you are; you are deeply concerned to know they are honestly come by. Otherwise you are a partaker with a thief, and are not a jot honester than him. But you know they are not honestly come by; you know they are procured by means nothing near so innocent as picking of pockets, house-breaking, or robbery upon the highway. You know they are procured by a deliberate series of more complicated villainy—of fraud, robbery, and murder—than was ever practiced either by Mohammedans or Pagans; in particular, by murders, of all kinds; by the blood of the innocent poured upon the ground like water. Now, it is your money that pays the merchant, and through him the captain and the African butchers. You therefore are guilty, yea, principally guilty, of all these frauds, robberies, and murders. You are the spring that puts all the rest in motion; they would not stir a step without you; therefore, the blood of all these wretches who die before their time, whether in their country or elsewhere, lies upon your head. 'The blood of thy brother'—for, whether thou wilt believe it or no, such he is in the sight of Him that made him—'crieth against thee from the earth,' from the ship, and from the waters. O, whatever it costs, put a stop to its cry before it be too late: instantly, at any price, were it the half of your goods, deliver thyself from blood-guiltiness! Thy hands, thy bed, thy furniture, thy house, thy lands, are at present stained with blood. Surely it is enough; accumulate no more guilt; spill no more the blood of the innocent! Do not hire another to shed blood; do not pay him for doing it! Whether you are a Christian or no, show yourself a man! Be not more savage than a lion or a bear!

"Perhaps you will say, 'I do not buy any negroes; I only use those left me by my father.' So far is well; but is it enough to satisfy your own conscience? Had your father, have you, has any man living, a right to use another as a slave? It can not be, even setting revelation aside. It can not be, that either war, or contract, can give any man such a property in another as he has in his sheep and oxen. Much less is it possible that any child of man should ever be born a slave. Liberty is the right of every human creature, as soon as he breathes the vital air; and no human law can deprive him of that right which he derives from the law of nature.

"If, therefore, you have any regard to justice—to say nothing of mercy, nor the revealed law of God—render to all their due. Give liberty to whom liberty is due; that is, to every child of man, to every partaker of human nature. Let none serve you but by his own act and deed, by his own voluntary choice. Away with all whips, all chains, all compulsion! Be gentle toward all men; and see that you invariably do to every one as you would he should do to you." (Thoughts on Slavery in the year 1774, Wesley's Works, vol. vi, pp. 291–293.)

Dr. Primatt.—"It has pleased God to cover some men with white skins, and others with black; but as there is neither merit nor demerit in complexion, the white man, notwithstanding the barbarity of custom and prejudice, can have no right by virtue of his color to enslave and tyrannize over the black man. For whether a man be white or black, such he is by God's appointment, and, abstractly considered, is neither a subject for pride nor an object of contempt." (Dissertation on the Duty of Mercy, and on the Sin of Cruelty to Brute Animals.)

Dr. Peckard.—"Now, whether we consider the crime with respect to the individuals concerned in this most barbarous and cruel traffic, or whether we consider it as patronized and encouraged by the laws of the land, it presents to our view an equal degree of enormity. A crime founded on a dreadful pre-eminence in wickedness—a crime which, being both of individuals and the nation, must sometime draw down upon us the judgment of almighty God, who made of one blood all the sons of men, and who gave to all equally a natural right to liberty, and who, ruling all the kingdoms of the earth with equal providential justice, can not suffer such deliberate, such monstrous iniquity to pass long unpunished." (Sermon before the Cambridge University.)

William Robertson, D. D.—"In the ancient world . . . . the persons, the goods, the children of these slaves, were the property of their masters, disposed of at pleasure, and transferred, like any other possession, from one hand to another. No inequality, no superiority in power, no pretext of consent can justify this ignominious depression of human nature, or can confer upon one man the right of dominion over another. But not only doth reason condemn this institution as unjust; experience proved it to be pernicious both to masters and slaves. The elevation of the former inspired them with pride, insolence, impatience, cruelty, and voluptuousness; the dependent and hopeless state of the latter dejected the human mind, and extinguished every generous and noble principle in the heart." (Sermon.)

George Whitfield.—"As I lately passed through your provinces in my way hither, I was sensibly touched with a fellow-feeling for the miseries of the poor negroes. Whether it be lawful for Christians to buy slaves, and thereby encourage the nations from whom they are bought to be at perpetual war with each other, I shall not take upon me to determine. Sure I am it is sinful, when they have bought them, to use them as bad as though they were brutes, nay worse; and whatever particular exceptions there may be—as I would charitably hope there are some—I fear the generality of you, who own negroes, are liable to such a charge; for your slaves, I believe, work as hard, if not harder, than the horses whereon you ride. These, after they have done the work, are fed and taken proper care of; but many negroes, when wearied with labor on your plantations, have been obliged to grind their corn after their return home. Your dogs are caressed and fondled at your table; but your slaves, who are frequently styled dogs or beasts, have not an equal privilege. They are scarce permitted to pick up the crumbs which fall from their master's table. Not to mention what numbers have been given up to the inhuman usage of cruel taskmasters, who, by their unrelenting scourges have plowed their backs, and made long furrows, and at length brought them even to death. When passing along I have viewed your plantations cleared and cultivated, many spacious houses built, and the owners of them faring sumptuously every day, my blood has frequently almost run cold within me, to consider how many of your slaves had neither convenient food to eat nor proper raiment to put on, notwithstanding most of the comforts you enjoy were solely owing to their indefatigable labors." (Letter to the Inhabitants of Maryland, Virginia, North and South Carolina, 1739.)

ARCHBISHOP SHARP, the grandfather of Granville Sharp, in a sermon preached before the British house of commons, *one hundred and fifty-six years ago,* used the following remarkable language:

"That Africa, which is not now more fruitful of monsters than it was once for excellently-wise and learned men—that Africa, which formerly afforded us our Clemens, our Origen, our Tertullian, our Cyprian, our Augustin, and many other extraordinary lights in the Church of God—that famous Africa, in whose soil Christianity did thrive so prodigiously, and could boast of so many flourishing Churches—alas! is now a wilderness. 'The wild boars have broken into the vineyard, and ate it up, and it brings forth nothing but briers and thorns,' to use the words of the prophet. And who knows but God may suddenly make this Church and nation, this our England, which, Jeshurun-like, is waxed fat and grown proud, and has kicked against God, *such another example of vengeance of this kind!*"

ROWLAND HILL.—"Slavery is made up of every crime that treachery, cruelty, and murder can invent; and men-stealers are the very worst of thieves. The most knavish tricks are practiced by these dealers in human flesh; and if slaves think of our general character, they must suppose that Christians are devils, and that Christianity was forged in hell."

DR. BURGESS, BISHOP OF SALISBURY, IN 1789.—We make the following extracts from the Bishop's pamphlet, entitled, "Considerations on the Abolition of Slavery and the Slave-Trade, upon Grounds of Natural. Religious, and Political

Duty." We are indebted for this extract to the London Antislavery Reporter, vol. ii, pp. 433–437.

To those who prate about the reciprocal duties of slaves, the Bishop replies: "Reciprocal duties!" he exclaims, "reciprocal duties! To have an adequate sense of the propriety of these terms, we must forget the humane provisions of the Hebrew law, as well as the indulgence of Roman slavery, and think only of West India slavery—of unlimited, uncompensated, brutal slavery—and then judge what reciprocity there can be between absolute authority and absolute subjection, and how the divine rule of Christian charity can be said to enforce the reciprocal duties of the West India slave and his master. Reciprocity is inconsistent with every degree of real slavery. . . . Slavery can not be called one of the species of civil subordination. A slave is a nonentity in civil society. . . . Law and slavery are contradictory terms."

"Such oppression," says the Bishop—meaning the state of slavery—"and such traffic [meaning the slave-trade] must be swept away at one blow. Such horrid offenses against God and nature can admit of no medium. Yet some of the more moderate apologists of slavery think that a medium may be adopted. They think that slavery ought not to be abolished, but modified and meliorated by good laws and regulations.

The Bishop proceeds to observe, that "all the laws hitherto made have produced little or no benefit to the slaves. But there are many reasons why it is very improbable that such provisions should produce any effectual benefit. The power which is exercised over the slaves, and the severe coercion necessary to keep an immense superiority of numbers in absolute obedience to a few, and restrain from insurrection, are incompatible with justice or humanity, and are obnoxious to abuses which no legal regulations can counteract. The power which a West Indian master has over his slave it is impossible for the generality of masters or managers not to abuse. It is too great to be intrusted in the hands of men subject to human passions and infirmities: the best principles and most generous natures are perverted by the influence of passion and habit."

"Many attacks," says his lordship, "have been made on the authority of Scripture, but nothing would more effectually subvert its authority than to prove that its injunctions are in opposition to the common principles of benevolence, and are inimical to the general rights of mankind. It would degrade the sanctity of Scripture; it would reverse all our ideas of God's paternal attributes, and all arguments for the Divine origin of the Christian religion, drawn from its precepts of universal charity and benevolence; that any custom so repugnant to the natural rights of mankind as the slave-trade—or slavery, the support and source of the slave-trade—should be thought to be consonant to the principles of natural and revealed religion, is a paradox which it is difficult to reconcile with the reverence due to the records of our holy religion." (See further extracts in the Reporter, vol. ii, pp. 435–437.)

Bishop Porteus.—He declared in the house of lords, in 1806, in answering certain Scriptural arguments in behalf of slavery, "there was no such thing as perpetual slavery under the Old or New Testament;" and he showed that all Hebrew servants were set at liberty every seventh year, and all others at the jubilee. He says: "The Christian religion is opposed to slavery, in its spirit and in its principles; it classes men-stealers among murderers of fathers and of mothers, and the most profane criminals upon earth."

Archbishop Sutten, in 1797.—"Christianity hath left all temporal governments as it found them, without impeachment of any form or description whatever, instilling only into the minds of the governors and governed the love of order, of justice, of mercy, of forgiveness, of mutual good-will, of universal charity. If all or any of these be incompatible with slavery, doubtless slavery is incompatible with the Christian religion. It can not be a question with Christians, whether the propagation of the Gospel or the system of slavery shall be preferred."

BISHOP HORSLEY, IN 1813.—"What can the utmost humanity of the master do for the slave? He may feed him well, clothe him well, work him moderately; but, my lords, nothing that the master can do for his slave, short of manumission, can reinstate him in the condition of man. But the negro slave in the West Indies! my lords, you may pamper him every day with the choicest viands; you may lay him to repose on beds of roses; but, with all this, he is not in the condition of man; he is nothing better than a well-kept horse. This is my notion of slavery." And again, says Horsley: "No such slavery as that in the West Indies is to be found in Grecian or Roman history—so stolen, so transported. Who can sanction it? Slavery is injustice, which no consideration of policy could extenuate; impolicy equal in degree to its injustice." (See Two Letters, etc., p. 6.)

The Bishop proves, in his discussion, that *man-stealers*, or slaveholders, or slave-dealers (1 Tim. i, 9, 10) are to be ranked with murderers and criminals of the worst kind. (See a large extract in a Letter to the Archbishop of Canterbury, by the Rev. John Rilard, M. A., pp. 11, 12.)

SAMUEL WILBERFORCE, BISHOP OF OXFORD, IN 1839.—"Never, in the history of any people, was the righteous retribution of the holy and living God more distinctly marked than in the manifold evils which now trouble America for her treatment of the African race. Like all other sinful courses, it has brought in, day by day, confusion and entanglement into all the relations of those contaminated by it. It is the cause which threatens to disorganize the Union; it is the cause which upholds the power of mobs and Lynching;

it is the occasion of bloodshed and violated law; it is, throughout the south, the destroyer of family purity, the hinderance to the growth of civilization and refinement; it is the one weak point of America, as a nation, exposing her to the deadliest internal strife, that of an internecine war, whenever a foreign enemy should find it suit his purpose to arm the blacks against their masters. Further: like all other great and established evils, it is most difficult to devise any escape out of the evils which it has already wound around every civil and social institution, while every day of its permitted continuance both aggravates the evil and increases the difficulty of its ultimate removal. This, then, is exactly one of those sore evils of which the Church of Christ is the appointed healer. She must, in his name, rebuke this unclean spirit; she who has been, at all times, the best adjuster of the balance between the rich and the poor—between those who have and those who want; she who has redressed the wrongs of those who have no helper; she who, wherever he has settled, has changed slaves or serfs, by whatever title they are known, into freemen and peasants. She must do this in the west, or the salt of the earth hath lost its savor, and is given over, with all things around, to the wasting of that utter and extreme corruption which she should have averted." (Reproof of the American Church, by the Bishop of Oxford, pp. 44, 45.)

Dr. Adam Clarke.—"I here record my testimony against the unprincipled, inhuman, antichristian, and diabolical *slave-trade*, with all its *authors, promoters, abettors*, and *sacrilegious gains*, as well as against the great devil, the father of it and them." (Concluding Remarks on 1 Cor., vii.)

"In heathen countries slavery was in some sort excusable; among Christians it is an enormity for which perdition has scarcely an adequate state of punishment." (Note on Ephesians vi, 5.)

At the last anniversary meeting of the Wesleyan Missionary Society, previous to his death, Dr. Clarke, on the platform, declared: "Slavery—that infernal system—it is cursed at both ends, and blasted in the middle, by the malediction of almighty God." Dr. Newton, at a missionary meeting at Thirsk, Yorkshire, England, repeated with approbation the above sentence uttered by Clarke in his hearing. It was uttered in reference to the West India missions. The Rev. Thomas Harrison, now in this country, an intimate friend, and a man of the most strict veracity, was present at the meeting where Dr. Newton repeated and indorsed the denunciation of Dr. Clarke against slavery.

REV. RICHARD WATSON said, "If it was wrong to steal men from Africa and reduce them to a state of bondage, it is for the same reason wrong to retain them in a state of slavery. If you condemn the first thief and the first receiver of stolen goods, how will you justify those, who, knowing them to be stolen, continue to retain them? I confess I can not see how the perpetuation of an injury can cause it to cease to be an injury, or by what process an acknowledged wrong can be transmuted into a right by continuing it. My argument, then, is, that if it is wrong to enslave the negroes, it is wrong to keep them in hopeless bondage; and it follows that, after this country had renounced the African slave-trade, it was bound, by the very principles on which that wretched traffic was repudiated, to have taken measures for the liberation of all who had been thus wickedly reduced to a state of captivity, . . . and long before this time to have converted them into a free, industrious, and happy peasantry." (Watson's Life, p. 380.)

"Slavery was man-stealing in its origin, and with this vicious origin it remains tainted to this day. It would be as hopeless a task to wash it out of us as it would be to wash the Ethiop white. Characterized as a crime against God and man, the thin gauze of sophistry can not conceal its hateful aspect; and the attempt to find a palliation for it in the New Testament, only makes more audible those thunders which are lanched against it, as one of the most odious crimes, both in the law and in the Gospel. But the advocates of slavery take us to the New Testament as well as to the Old. I am sure we can have no objection to follow them. It is, indeed, surprising enough, that, with the fact before them that Christianity has abolished slavery in all the ancient countries where it obtained predominant influence, any persons should dream that in its earliest period, when it glowed with all that warmth of charity with which it burst from that fountain of divine compassion, it should enter into any alliance with it. To hold property in men is a thing agreeable enough to human nature, as we have proof in the present day. It flatters man's pride, it gratifies his love of power, to see his fellow-creatures tremble before him, and to be absolute lord of their life and happiness.

"They tell us that the apostles did not command Pagan governments to loose their slaves, and they take shelter here as though they could plead this black privilege of Pagan despotism; but we hold them to their profession: they profess Christianity; therefore, they must be tried by its laws, and by one of these laws we are content that the whole question of the consonancy of Christianity with slavery shall be tried. 'Whatsoever ye would that men should do unto you, so do ye also unto them.' St. Paul sets freedom before the Christian slave, as a good after which he ought to aspire by all lawful means: 'If thou mayest be free, choose it rather.' I believe this language would have conducted him to a jail in Jamaica; but it is his language, and it proves that he regarded slavery as an evil, and liberty as a good to be sought by every Christian slave. If the apostle were a friend to slavery, why did he thus exhort the slaves? And, if he thus urges them to seek their liberty, then in vain do our Scripture-quoting slaveholders plead apostolical authority." (Watson's Life, pp. 380, 381.)

Rev. Jabez Bunting, D. D., in 1836.—The following sentiment was expressed by this distinguished divine, before the British conference, in 1836, in reference to the acts of the General conference of the Methodist Episcopal Church the May preceding: "Slavery is always wrong—essentially, eternally, and incurably wrong. Die it must; and happy should I have been had they passed sentence of death upon it." On this we may remark, that the Methodist Episcopal Church, at its organization, did pronounce this sentence on slavery, and officially recorded the sentence; and that sentence has been maintained by the same Church down to this day.

Rev. James Dixon, D. D., in 1849.—"Slavery in itself is one thing, and the relations of men to it another. As to slavery, in its own nature, nothing can be said, but that it is the grossest evil existing under the sun. It is, in truth, every possible personal wrong in one. Rob a man of his watch, his clothes, his purse, his house, his lands—is not this a moral evil, a sin? If not, what of the laws of civilized communities, jails, and the gallows? But is it not a greater crime to rob man of himself, than to strip him of his coat, to pull down his house, and to drive him from his home? The degrees of evil in each case can bear no comparison. Slavery is robbery in its highest possible enormity. But it is a lingering injury. It is inflicted for life—a life of conscious wrong; for, to imagine that these wretches are not sensible of their condition, is to add calumny to injury. It is robbery, torture, degradation, misery, mental and physical, dealt out by the moment, the livelong day, the whole period of existence. It is as if, by some infernal contrivance, existence were sustained—as with the damned—while the operations of the whip, the iron, the fangs, of slavery, were constantly at work upon their tortured and lacerated limbs. This is not all. The wretched slave is obliged to bequeath his inheritance to his offspring. That which was pronounced a blessing, the ties of family, the relations of wedded life, the parental state, is by this system perverted into an unmitigated curse. All the political, all the social, all the municipal laws of civilized society, are perverted. That cruel code which makes a man a thing, identifies him with the beast, classes him with farm-stock, places him among lumber, reduces him to the condition of household furniture, treats him as the canes, the tobacco, the cotton, the indigo, which his hands cultivate, then buys and sells him in the market like any other stock or goods, is—but we are afraid to call it by its true name.

"To say that villainy like this can in any way be identical with Christianity, is to degrade our holy religion to a copartnership, or a connivance, with man's greatest, most concentrated, and unmitigated crimes against his fellow. There is not a truth, a doctrine, a principle, a precept, of the Gospel, which, if fairly carried out, would not annihilate slavery. The very existence of the Church is fundamentally opposed to the spirit and injustice of this evil. How can a slaveholder make his servants his property, and then meet them in the Church, at the Lord's table, as his brethren? It would be a curious thing to see one of these gentlemen receiving the Lord's supper, the emblem of Christian brotherhood, with one of his slaves on the Sabbath, and then on Monday morning selling him as a log of wood." (Dixon's Tour in America.)

3. American clergymen.

The most learned, the wisest, and most pious of the American clergy furnish their strong testimony against slavery. We select a few out of the many who might be brought forward:

Rev. E. Styles, 1791.—"Slavery is unjust in its nature."

The Quakers.—The testimony and action of the Quakers

are well known to the world, and need not be repeated here.

THE METHODIST EPISCOPAL CHURCH.—This Church has maintained one unbroken and unwavering testimony against slavery, from its organization down to this day.

In 1785 the Church declared: "We do hold in the deepest abhorrence the practice of slavery, and shall not cease to seek its destruction by all wise and prudent means."

The general rule on slavery forbids "the buying and selling of men, women, and children, with an intention to enslave them." The purchase or sale of slaves, either to originate slavery or to continue it, is considered by the general rule *such*, or the same in moral guilt, as profane swearing, Sabbath-breaking, drunkenness, fighting, etc. This rule concerns all the members of the Church as Christians.

The following is the present testimony of the Church:

"*Question.* What shall be done for the extirpation of the evil of slavery?

"*Answer.* We declare we are as much as ever convinced of the great evil of slavery; therefore, no slaveholder shall be eligible to any official station in our Church hereafter, where the laws of the state in which he lives will admit of emancipation, and permit the liberated slave to enjoy freedom."

This regulation relates to all bearing office in the Church: while the declaration that slavery is a great moral evil concerns all, whether lay or official members.

This testimony has been continued without faltering, and maintained even at the expense of unity. And so deeply did the sentiment imbue the southern mind, that on the organization of a new Church, to favor pro-slavery sentiment, the old doctrine of the Church was so dominant, that the new Church, thus far, dared not venture to give up the testimony.

PRESBYTERIAN SYNOD OF NEW YORK AND PHILADELPHIA, 1787.—"The synod of New York and Philadelphia, (1787,) do highly approve of the general principles in favor of universal liberty that prevail in America, and the interest which many of the states have taken in promoting the abolition of slavery. They earnestly recommend it to all the members belonging to their communion, to give those persons who are at present held in servitude, such good education as to prepare them for the better enjoyment of freedom. And they moreover recommend that masters, whenever they find servants disposed to make a just improvement of the privilege, would give them a *peculium,* or grant them sufficient time, and sufficient means of procuring their own liberty at a moderate rate; that thereby they may be brought into society with those habits of industry that may render them useful citizens. And finally, they recommend it to all their people to use the most prudent measures, consistent with the interests and the state of civil society in the countries where they live, to procure eventually the final abolition of slavery in America.

"*Advice given by the Assembly, in relation to Slavery in* 1815.—The General Assembly have repeatedly declared their cordial approbation of those principles of civil liberty which appear to be recognized by the federal and state governments, in these United States. They have expressed their regret that the slavery of the Africans and of their descendants still continues in so many places, and even among those within the pale of the Church; and have urged the presbyteries under their care, to adopt such measures as will secure, at least to the rising generation of slaves, within the bounds of the Church, a religious education; that they may be prepared for the exercise and enjoyment of liberty, when God, in his providence, may open a door for their emancipation.

"*A full expression of the Assembly's views of slavery, in*

1818.—We consider the voluntary enslaving of one part of the human race by another, as a gross violation of the most precious and sacred rights of human nature; as utterly inconsistent with the law of God, which requires us to love our neighbor as ourselves; and as totally irreconcilable with the spirit and principles of the Gospel of Christ, which enjoins that 'all things whatsoever ye would that men should do to you, do ye even so to them.' Slavery creates a paradox in the moral system—it exhibits rational, accountable, and immortal beings in such circumstances as scarcely to leave them the power of moral action. It exhibits them as dependent on the will of others, whether they shall receive religious instruction; whether they shall know and worship the true God; whether they shall enjoy the ordinances of the Gospel; whether they shall perform the duties and cherish the endearments of husbands and wives, parents and children, neighbors and friends; whether they shall preserve their chastity and purity, or regard the dictates of justice and humanity. Such are some of the consequences of slavery; *consequences not imaginary*, but which connect themselves with its very existence. The evils to which the slave is *always* exposed, often take place in their *very worst degree and form;* and where all of them do not take place, still the slave is deprived of his natural rights, degraded as a human being, and exposed to the danger of passing into the hand of a master who may inflict upon him all the hardships and injuries which inhumanity and avarice may suggest.

"We enjoin it on all Church sessions and presbyteries to discountenance, and as far as possible to prevent all cruelty, of whatever kind, in the treatment of slaves; especially the cruelty of separating husband and wife, parents and children; and that which consists in selling slaves to those who will either themselves deprive those unhappy people of the blessings of the Gospel, or who will transport them to places where the Gospel is not proclaimed, or where it is forbidden to slaves to attend upon its institutions. The manifest violation or disregard of this injunction, ought to be considered as just grounds for the discipline and censures of the Church. And if it shall ever happen that a Christian professor in our communion shall sell a slave who is also in communion with our Church, contrary to his or her will and inclination, it ought immediately to claim the particular attention of the proper Church judicature; and unless there be such peculiar circumstances attending the case as can but seldom happen, it ought to be followed, without delay, by a suspension of the offender from all the privileges of the Church, till he repent and make all the reparation in his power to the injured party." (Digest of the General Assembly, p. 341.)

Samuel Hopkins, D. D.—"Are you sure your slaves have a sufficiency of good food, in season; and that they never want for comfortable clothing and bedding? Do you take great care to deal as well by them in these things, as you would wish others would treat your own children, were they slaves in a strange land? If your servants complain, are you ready to attend to them? Or do you in such cases frown upon them, or do something worse, so as to discourage their ever applying to you, whatever they may suffer, having learned that this would only be making bad worse? Do you never fly into a passion, and deal with them in great anger, deciding matters respecting them, and threatening them, and giving sentence concerning them, from which they have no appeal, and perhaps proceed to correct them, when to a calm bystander you appear more fit to be confined in a bedlam, than to have the sovereign, uncontrollable dominion over your brethren, as the sole lawgiver, judge, and executioner? Do not even your children domineer over your slaves? Must they not often be at the beck of an ungoverned, peevish child in the family; and if they do not run at his or her call, and are not all submission and obedience, must they not expect the frowns of their masters, if not the whip?

"If none of these things, my good sir, take place in your family, have we not reason to think you a most singular instance? How common are things of this kind, or worse, taking place between masters and their slaves? In how few instances, if in any, are slaves treated, as the masters would wish to have their own children treated, in like circumstances? How few are fit to be masters? To have the sovereign dominion over a number of their fellow-men, being his property, and wholly at his disposal; who must abide his sentence and orders, however unreasonable, without any possibility of relief?

"But are we at the same time making slaves of many thousands of our brethren, who have as good a right to liberty as ourselves, and to whom it is as sweet as it is to us, and the contrary as dreadful! Are we holding them in the most abject, miserable state of slavery, without the least compassionate feeling toward them or their posterity, utterly refusing to take off the oppressive, galling yoke! O, the shocking, the intòlerable inconsistency! And this gross, barefaced inconsistency is an open, practical condemnation of holding these our brethren in slavery; and in these circumstances the crime of persisting in it becomes unspeakably greater and more provoking in God's sight; so that all the former unrighteousness and cruelty exercised in this practice, is innocence, compared with the awful guilt that is now contracted. And in allusion to the words of our Savior, it may with great truth and propriety be said, 'If he had not thus come in his providence, and spoken to us, [comparatively speaking,] we had not had sin, in making bond-slaves of our brethren; but now we have no cloak for our sin.'" (Dialogue on African Slavery, 1776, republished 1785, by the New York Manumission Society, whose President was John Jay.)

JONATHAN EDWARDS.—"The eradication, or even the diminution of compassion, tenderness, and humanity, is certainly a great depravity of heart, and must be followed with correspondent depravity of manners. And measures which lead to such depravity of heart and manners, can not but be extremely hurtful to the state, and consequently are extremely impolitic.

"African slavery is exceedingly impolitic, as it discourages industry. Nothing is more essential to the political prosperity of any state than industry in the citizens. But in proportion as slaves are multiplied, every kind of labor becomes ignominious; and in fact, in those of the United States in which slaves are the most numerous, gentlemen and ladies of any fashion disdain to employ themselves in business, which in other states is consistent with the dignity of the first families and first offices. In a country filled with negro slaves, labor belongs to them only, and a white man is despised in proportion as he applies to it. Now how destructive to industry in all of the lowest and middle classes of citizens, such a situation, and the prevalence of such ideas will be, you can easily conceive. The consequence is, that some will nearly starve, others will betake themselves to the most dishonest practices, to obtain the means of living.

"As slavery produces indolence in the white people, so it produces all those vices which are naturally connected with it; such as intemperance, lewdness, and prodigality. These vices enfeeble both the body and the mind, and unfit men for any vigorous exertions and employments, either external or mental; and those who are unfit for such exertions, are already a very degenerate race; degenerate, not only in a moral, but a natural sense. They are contemptible, too, and will soon be despised even by their negroes themselves.

"Slavery has a most direct tendency to haughtiness also, and a domineering spirit and conduct in the proprietors of the slaves, in their children, and in all who have the control of them. A man who has been bred up in domineering over negroes, can scarcely avoid contracting such a habit of haughtiness and domination, as will express itself in his general treatment of mankind, whether in his private capacity, or in any office, civil or military, with which he may be vested. Despotism in economics naturally leads to despotism in politics, and domestic slavery in a free government is a perfect solecism in human affairs." (The Injustice and Impolicy of the Slave-Trade and of the Slavery of the Africans—a Sermon in New Haven, September 15, 1791.)

FREEBORN GARRETSON.—"As I stood with a book in my hand, in the act of giving out a hymn, this thought powerfully struck my mind: 'It is not right for you to keep your fellow-creatures in bondage; you must let the oppressed go free.' I knew it to be that same blessed voice which had spoken to me before. Till then I had suspected that the practice of slave-keeping was wrong; I had not read a book on the subject, nor been told so by any. I paused a minute, and then replied, 'Lord, the oppressed shall go free.' And I was as clear of them in my mind, as if I had never owned one. I told them they did not belong to me, and that I did not desire their services without making them a compensation. I was now at liberty to proceed in worship. After singing, I kneeled to pray. Had I the tongue of an angel, I could not fully describe what I felt: all my dejection, and that melancholy gloom which preyed upon me, vanished in a moment, and a divine sweetness ran through my whole frame.

"It was God, not man, that taught me the impropriety of holding slaves: and I shall never be able to praise him enough for it. My very heart has bled, since that, for slaveholders, especially those who made a profession of religion; for I believe it to be a crying sin."

Rev. Robert J. Breckenridge.—"Just and equal! What care I, whether my pockets are picked, or the proceeds of my labor are taken from me? What matters it whether my horse is stolen, or the value of him in my labor be taken from me? Do we talk of violating the rights of masters and depriving them of their property in their slaves? And will some one tell us if there be any thing in which a man has or can have so perfect a right of property, as in his own limbs, bones, and sinews? Out upon such folly! The man that can not see that involuntary domestic slavery, as it exists among us, is founded upon the principle of taking by force that which is another's, has no moral sense.

"Nature, and reason, and religion unite in their hostility to this system of folly and crime. How it will end time only will reveal; but the light of heaven is not clearer than that it must end." (African Repository, January, 1834.)

4. Testimony of British jurists, statesmen, patriots, and philanthropists.

The declarations of holy Scripture are most clear and pointed against slavery—in no case either tolerating, sanctioning, or permitting it; and even regulating servitude so as effectually to prevent it from terminating in, or even countenancing slavery. The British common law, in adopting Scriptural principles as the guide in all matters of right and wrong between men, adopted, also, the antislavery element. And the great Scriptural political principles of liberty in the British Constitution, at the breaking up of the feudal system, became the elements of general liberty, first in America, and then in Europe. This is fully acknowledged by that extraordinary man, Daniel O'Connel, who contended for liberty, but did very little, if any thing, to promote it, in any efficient or practical way. In a speech before the British Antislavery Society, June 30, 1825, he says, speaking of slavery: "Who could doubt that the people of this land would lend their support to put down a system so atrocious? Who could doubt of the effect which the example of England must have on the world in general? It has had that influence universally, and every page of its history confirmed it. Who could imagine that there could be, at the present moment, one spark of liberty on continental Europe—from the frozen regions of Russia to the rock of Gibraltar—if, when feudal power was merging into despotism, England had not struggled for and gained her free Constitution, giving to all the earth her glorious example, and showing how easy it was for a nation to be free if she willed freedom? What was it but her example that had placed France under a new constitution? What was it which revolutionized Spain and Portugal? And, though fortune might for a time frown upon their efforts, yet many a gallant heart now glowed with the hope that they might yet be able to follow that example and triumph at last over their oppressors. Nor was the example of this country confined to Europe. That example had passed the Atlantic and expanded itself over America; but the example must go farther even than America. Who could be so absurd as to think, that, when the negro saw warriors and statesmen of his race, he would not make a desperate exertion for freedom? Could any man say, that, when that time came in which we should see the poet and the hero of the same cast and color, slavery could exist a moment longer?" (Speech of O'Connel before the London Antislavery Society, April 30, 1825. See Report, p. 66.)

BLACKSTONE.—We quote from this great jurist the following principles, deduced from Scripture, and incorporated into the British Constitution:

"Those rights which God and nature have established,

and are, therefore, called natural rights—such as life and liberty—need not the aid of human laws to be more effectually invested in every man than they are; neither do they receive any additional strength when declared by the municipal laws to be inviolable. On the contrary, no human legislature has power to abridge or destroy them, unless the owner himself shall commit some act which amounts to a forfeiture." (Commentaries, Introduction, section 2, p. 54.)

"The first and primary end of all human laws is, to maintain and regulate those absolute rights of individuals. The absolute rights of man, considered as a free agent, endowed with discernment to know good from evil, and with power of choosing those measures which appear to him most desirable, are usually summed up in one general appellation, and denominated the natural liberty of mankind. This natural liberty consists, properly, in a power of acting as one thinks fit, without any restraint or control, unless by the law of nature, being a right inherent in us by birth, and one of the gifts of God to man at his creation, when he endued him with the faculty of free will. But every man, when he enters into society, gives up a part of his natural liberty, as the price of so valuable a purchase; and, in consideration of receiving the advantages of mutual commerce, obliges himself to conform to those laws which the community has thought proper to establish." (Commentaries, book i, p. 125.)

"These rights and liberties are no other than either that *residuum* of natural liberty which is not required by the laws of society to be sacrificed to public convenience, or else those civil privileges which society hath engaged to provide in lieu of the natural liberties so given up by individuals. These are the right of personal security, the right of personal liberty, and the right of private property." (Commentaries, book i, p. 129.)

"And this spirit of liberty is so deeply implanted in our

Constitution, and rooted even in our very soil, that a slave or a negro, the moment he lands in England, falls under the protection of the laws, and so far becomes a freeman; though the master's right to his services may, *possibly*, still continue." (Id., p. 127.)

JOHN PHILPOT CURRAN.—" *Universal Emancipation.*—I speak in the spirit of the British law, which makes liberty commensurate with, and inseparable from, the British soil—which proclaims, even to the stranger and the sojourner, the moment he sets his foot upon British earth, that the ground on which he treads is holy, and consecrated by the genius of universal emancipation. No matter in what language his doom may have been pronounced; no matter what complexion incompatible with freedom, an Indian or an African sun may have burnt upon him; no matter in what disastrous battle his liberty may have been cloven down; no matter with what solemnities he may have been devoted upon the altar of slavery; the first moment he touches the sacred soil of Britain, the altar and the god sink together in the dust; his soul walks abroad in her own majesty; his body swells beyond the measure of his chains, that burst from around him, and he stands redeemed, regenerated, and disinthralled, by the irresistible genius of UNIVERSAL EMANCIPATION."

HENRY GRATTAN.—"Liberty—and is this subject a matter of indifference? Liberty, which, like the Deity, is an essential spirit best known by its consequences—liberty, which now animates you in your battles by sea and land, and lifts you up proudly superior to your enemies—liberty, that glorious spark and emenation of the Divinity, which fired your ancestors, and taught them to feel like a Hampden, that it was not life, but the condition of living! An Irishman sympathizes in these noble sentiments—wherever he goes—to whatever quarter of the earth he journeys—whatever wind blows his poor garments, let him but have the pride, the glory, *the ostentation of liberty!*"

Dr. Lushington.—"It has never been given by God to man to hold his fellow-man in bondage. Every thing short of a total abolition of slavery he considered as unsatisfactory, and ending only in disappointment and discontent. The supporters of the abolition of slavery took their stand upon the eternal principles of truth and justice, and it would be next to blasphemy to doubt their success."

Andrew Thompson.—"Slavery is the very Upas tree of the moral world, beneath whose pestiferous shade all intellect languishes, and all virtue dies. It must be cut down and eradicated; it must be, root and branch, cast into the consuming fire, and its ashes scattered to the four winds of heaven. It is thus you must deal with slavery. You must annihilate it—annihilate it now, and annihilate it for ever."

Lord Mansfield.—"Slavery is so odious that nothing but positive law can sustain it."

Oglethorpe, 1776.—"Sir,—Being at Woolston Hall, Dr. Scott's home, he showed me your 'Law of Retribution.' I was greatly rejoiced to find that so laborious and learned a man had appeared as champion for the rights of mankind, against avarice, extortion, and inhumanity; that you had, with a heroic courage, dared to press home on an infidel, luxurious world, the dreadful threats of the Lord. The ruins of Babylon, Memphis, and Tyre, are strong mementoes to a Lisbon, a London, and a Paris, of the recompense paid to those who fat their luxuries on the labor of wretched slaves.

"The Portugese were the first of the western Christians who allowed slavery; their adventurers stole men from Guinea and sold them as slaves. On Lisbon, the judgment has fallen. An unnatural war between us and America seems to denote the second. You fairly open up the third, etc. James Oglethorpe."

"My friends and I settled the colony of Georgia, and, by charter, were established trustees, to make laws, etc.

We determined not to suffer slavery there. But the slave-merchants and their adherents occasioned us not only much trouble, but, at last, got the then government to favor them. We would not suffer slavery—which is against the Gospel, as well as the fundamental law of England—to be authorized under our authority. We refused, as trustees, to make a law permitting such a horrid crime. The government, finding the trustees resolved, firmly, not to concur with what they believed unjust, took away the charter, by which no law could be passed without our consent.

"This cruel custom of a *private man* being supported in exercising *more power* over the man whom he *affirms to have bought as his slave,* than the *magistrate* has *over the master,* is a solecism in politics. This, I think, was taken from the Romans. The horrid cruelty which that proud nation showed in all they did, gave such power to the masters of slaves, that they confused even the state. Decius Brutus, by the gladiators, his slaves, defended the conspirators that killed the Dictator, Cæsar. The cruelty of the slave-masters occasioned the slaves to join Spartacus, who almost overturned Rome, etc. I find in Sir Walter Raleigh's History of the Saracens, that *their* success, and the destruction of the Grecian and Persian empires, were chiefly owing to the Greeks and Persians having such vast numbers of slaves, by whom all labor and husbandry were carried on. And on the Saracens giving freedom to all who professed their law, the multitude, in every conquered province, joined them.

"The Christian emperors would have qualified the laws of slavery; but the senate of Rome, in whom the old leaven of idolatry still prevailed, stopped such good designs. St. Austin, in his "*De Civitate Dei,*" mentions that idolatry was sunk into the marrow of the Romans; that the destruction of Rome by the Goths seemed necessary to root out idolatry. The Goths and all the northern nations, when converted to

Christianity, abolished slavery. The husbandry was performed by men under the protection of the laws. Though some tenures of villenage were too severe, yet the villain had the protection of law; and their lords could not exact more than was by the laws regulated." (See Life of Sharp, by C. Stuart, pp. 24–26.)

Mr. Fox, in 1791.—"Personal freedom is the first right of every human being. It is a right, of which he who deprived a fellow-creature was absolutely criminal in so depriving him, and which he who withheld was no less criminal in withholding. Why is this race of our fellow-beings to be carried away by force, and subjected to the will, and caprice, and tyranny of oppression of other human beings for their whole natural lives, and their posterity for ever? It is necessary to abolish slavery for the credit of our jurisprudence, and of our character as Christians. Why should that wrong be tolerated in the West Indies, for which a man would be hanged in England? Make the cause of the slaves your own, and judge of it by this Christian rule. Wherever Christianity has extended its influence, slavery has been abolished; it has produced this glorious triumph by teaching us that, in the sight of their Maker, all mankind are equal. The whole country, the whole civilized world, must rejoice in the abolition of slavery, not merely as a matter of humanity, but as an act of justice." (See Negro Slavery, p. 132.)

Charles James Fox.—"Some had considered this question as a question of political, whereas it was a question of personal freedom. Political freedom was undoubtedly a great blessing; but, when it came to be compared with personal, it sunk to nothing. To confound the two served, therefore, to render all arguments on either perplexing and unintelligible. Personal freedom was the first right of every human being. It was a right, of which he who deprived a fellow-creature was absolutely criminal in depriving him, and which he who withheld was no less criminal in withholding. He would say that if the house, knowing what the trade was by the evidence, did not by their vote mark to all mankind their abhorrence of a practice so savage, so enormous, so repugnant to all laws, human and divine, they would consign their characters to eternal infamy.

"But what was our motive in the case before us? To continue a trade which was a wholesale sacrifice of a whole order and race of our fellow-creatures; which carried them away by force from their native country, in order to subject them to the mere will and caprice, the tyranny and oppression, of other human beings, for their whole natural lives, them and their posterity for ever! O, most monstrous wickedness! O, unparalleled barbarity!

"Let them remember that humanity did not consist in a squeamish ear. It did not consist in shrinking and starting at such tales as these; but in a disposition of the heart to remedy the evils they unfolded. Humanity belonged rather to the mind than to the nerves. But, if so, it should prompt men to charitable exertion.

"Let them make the case their own. This was the Christian rule of judging; and, having mentioned Christianity, he was sorry to find that any should suppose that it had given countenance to such a system of oppression. So far was this from being the case, that he thought it one of the most splendid triumphs of this religion, that it had caused slavery to be so generally abolished on its appearance in the world. It had done this by teaching us, among other beautiful precepts, that, in the sight of their Maker, all mankind were equal. He knew, however, that what he had been ascribing to Christianity had been imputed by others to the advances which philosophy had made. Each of the two parties took the merit to itself. The philosopher gave it to philosophy, and the divine to religion. He should not then dispute with either of them; but as both coveted the praise, why should they not emulate each other by promoting this improvement in the condition of the human race?"

William Pitt, in 1804.—"With the improvement of internal population, the condition of every negro will improve also; his liberty will advance, or at least he will be approaching to a state of liberty. Nor can you increase the happiness or extend the freedom of the negro, without adding in an equal degree to the safety of the islands and of all their inhabitants. Thus, sir, in the place of slaves, who naturally have an interest directly opposite to that of their master, and are therefore viewed by them with an eye of constant suspicion, you will create a body of valuable citizens and subjects, forming a part of the same community, having a common interest with their superiors in the security and prosperity of the whole. Gentlemen talk of the diminution of labor. But if you restore to this degraded race the true feelings of men; if you take them out from among the order of brutes, and place them on a level with the rest of the human species, they will then work with that energy which is natural to men, and their labor will be productive in a thousand ways above what it has yet been, as the labor of a man must be more productive than that of a brute." (Hansard's Parliamentary History, vol. xxix, p. 1138. See A Review of Some Arguments against Parliamentary Interference with the Negro Slaves, p. 27.)

Mr. Pitt elsewhere says: "Slavery is incurable injustice. Why is injustice to remain a single hour?"

Lord Glenville, in 1806.—"Personal freedom was a blessing granted by God, and could not with justice be violated." Again: "It is of great consequence that we should look attentively to that period, when the disgrace of slavery, in any form, shall no longer be suffered within the territories of this free country. While we are advocates for the liberties of Europe, while we raise the standard of freedom against the common enemy of order, virtue, and humanity, it behooves us peculiarly to preserve that freedom unpolluted within the pale of the British empire. I recommend this measure as the most safe and effectual means of the ultimate emancipation of the slaves in the West Indies. By this expedient you will abundantly ameliorate their condition, so that they may be fitted for the enjoyment of that liberty which, in every region of the earth, IS THE COMMON RIGHT OF HUMAN NATURE." (See Review of Some Arguments, etc., pp. 28, 29.)

EARL OF WESTMORELAND, IN 1807.—"If slavery was contrary to justice and humanity, it was also contrary to justice and humanity to keep the negroes, who had been procured by means of the trade, in a state of perpetual slavery." (Id., p. 31.)

EARL OF LIVERPOOL, IN 1807.—"The same principle on which the noble lord condemned the slave-trade, applied with equal force to the state of slavery itself." (Id., p. 31.)

MR. WINDHAM, IN 1806.—"That the slave-trade is contrary to justice, humanity, and sound policy, nobody can doubt; and I would add slavery, too: for that is the first character of slavery. Slavery is that which every one must wish to see abolished. And, certainly, I had rather see it abolished by law than wait for the process of civilization. What gentlemen say of the slave-trade, I say of slavery, that it is a great evil; they are each *malum in se.* Although slavery has so long subsisted, I have no hesitation in saying it is a state not fit to subsist, because it gives to one human being a greater power over another than it is fit for any human being to possess. Man is not fit to have such power over his fellow-creatures." (Id., p. 31.)

EDMUND BURKE.—"Nothing makes a slave but a degraded man. In proportion as the mind grows callous to its degradation, and all sense of manly pride is lost, the slave feels comfort. In fact, he is no longer a man. If he were to define a man, he would say with Shakspeare,

> 'Man is a being, holding large discourse,
> Looking before and after.'

But a slave was incapable of looking before and after. He had no motive to do it. He was a mere passive instrument in the hands of others, to be used at their discretion. Though living, he was dead as to all voluntary agency; though moving amidst the creation with an erect form, and with the shape and semblance of a human being, he was a nullity as a man.

"The slave-trade was directly contrary to the principles of humanity and justice; and the state of slavery which followed it, however mitigated, was a state so improper, so degrading, and so ruinous to the feelings and capacities of human nature, that it ought not to be suffered to exist."

Granville Sharp.—"If such laws are not absolutely necessary for the government of slaves, the law-makers must unavoidably allow themselves to be the most cruel and abandoned tyrants upon the earth, and, perhaps, that ever were on earth. But, on the other hand, if it be said that it is impossible to govern slaves, without such inhuman severity and detestable injustice, the same is an invincible argument against the least toleration of slavery among Christians; because temporal profits can not compensate the forfeiture of everlasting welfare—that the cries of these much injured people will certainly reach heaven—that the Scriptures denounce a tremendous judgment against the man who shall offend one little one—that it were better for the nation that their American dominions had never existed, or even that they had sunk in the sea, than that the kingdom of Great Britain should be loaded with the horrid guilt of tolerating such abominable wickedness.

"The same benevolent principles, namely, universal love

and charity, founded on the great commandment, 'Thou shalt love thy neighbor as thyself,' which obliges the true Christian most disinterestedly to forgive all personal injuries, and pass over every affront offered to his own person, will necessarily engage him on the other hand, as disinterestedly to oppose every danger of oppression and injustice, which affects his brother, and neighbors, when he has a fair opportunity of assisting them. From hence arises the zeal of good men for just and equitable laws, as being the most effectual means of preserving the peace and happiness of the community, by curbing the insolence and violence of wicked men."

Resolutions of the Antislavery Society of Great Britain, April 23, 1831:

"5. That this assembly consider it incumbent on them to renew the declaration of their decided conviction, that slavery is not merely an abuse to be mitigated, but an enormity to be suppressed; that it involves the exercise of severities on the part of the master, and the endurance of sufferings on the part of the slave, which no laws can effectually prevent; and that to impose on the British people the involuntary support of a system so essentially iniquitous, is an injustice no longer to be endured.

"6. That the experience of the last eight years has not only furnished additional evidence of THE CRIMINALITY AND INCURABLE INHUMANITY OF SLAVERY, but has also demonstrated incontrovertibly, that it is only by the direct intervention of Parliament that any effectual remedy can be applied to this enormous evil; and that it is the unalterable determination of this meeting to leave no lawful means unattempted for obtaining, by Parliamentary enactment, the total abolition of slavery throughout the British dominions." (London committee—T. F. Buxton, S. Gurney, W. Wilberforce, W. Smith, Z. Macaulay, D. Wilson, R. Watson, S. Lushington, and T. Clarkson; Secretary, Thos. Pringle.

With these were associated the leading men of moral and religious worth in Great Britain and Ireland.)

5. Testimonies of British philosophers, moralists, literary men, and poets:

JAMES THOMSON.

"Kind equal rule, the government of laws,
And all-protecting freedom, which alone
Sustains the name and dignity of man:
These are not theirs. The parent sun himself
Seems o'er this world of slaves to tyrannize.
Here dwells the direful shark, lur'd by the scent
Of steaming crowds, of rank disease and death:
He, from the partners of that cruel trade,
Which spoils unhappy Guinea of her sons,
Demands his share of prey—demands themselves.
The stormy fates descend: one fate involves
Tyrants and slaves." (The Seasons.)

"O great design,
Ye sons of mercy! O complete your work;
Wrench from oppression's hand the iron rod,
And bid the cruel feel the wounds they give.
Man knows no master save creating Heaven,
Or those whom choice and common good ordain."
(The Poem of Liberty.)

JOHN BOWRING.

"Liberty for the white, the few,
From the oppressor's thrall;
Nay! but liberty, liberty, too,
For the blacks, for ALL!
Slavery shall not stamp her ban
On any men or man.

Despised there is none, degraded none—
Each holds its ordered place;
But 'tis man, usurping man alone,
Who hath stigmatized his race;
Who hath given his fellow—O shame! O shame!
A *slave's* ignoble name."

JOHN LOCKE.—"Slavery is so vile and miserable an estate of man, and so directly opposite to the generous temper and courage of our nation, that it is hard to be conceived that an Englishman, much less a gentleman, should plead for it. The natural liberty of man is to be free from any superior power on earth, and not to be under the will of legislative authority of man, but to have only the law of nature for his rule. The liberty of man, in society, is to be under no other legislative power, but that established, by consent, in the commonwealth; nor under the dominion of any will, or restraint of any law, but what that legislature shall enact, according to the trust put in it. Every body has a property in his own person that nobody has any right to but himself. The labor of his body and the work of his hands we may say are properly his." (Treatise on Government.)

Adam Smith.—"Though the wear and tear of a free servant be equally at the expense of his master, it generally costs him much less than that of a slave. The fund destined for replacing or repairing, if I may say so, the wear and tear of the slave, is commonly managed by a negligent master or careless overseer. That destined for performing the same office with regard to the free man, is managed by the free man himself. The disorders which generally prevail in the economy of the rich, naturally introduce themselves into the management of the former; the strict frugality and parsimonious attention of the poor, as naturally establish themselves in that of the latter. Under such different management, the same purpose must require very different degrees of expense to execute it. If great improvements are seldom to be expected from great proprietors, they are least of all to be expected when they employ slaves for their workmen. The experience of all ages and nations, I believe, demonstrates that the work done by slaves, though it appears to cost only their maintenance, is in the end the dearest of any. A person who can acquire no property, can have no interest but to eat as much, and to labor as little as possible. Whatever work he does beyond what is sufficient to purchase his own maintenance, can be squeezed out of him by violence only, and not by any interest of his own. In ancient Italy how much the cultivation of corn degenerated, how unprofitable it became to the master, when it fell under the management of slaves, is remarked by both Pliny and Columella. In the time of Aristotle it had not been much better in ancient Greece.

"As the profit and success of the cultivation which is carried on by means of cattle, depend very much upon the good management of those cattle, so the profit and success of that which is carried on by slaves must depend equally upon the good management of those slaves; and in the good management of their slaves, the French planters, I think it is generally allowed, are superior to the English. The law, so far as it gives some weak protection to the slave against the violence of his master, is likely to be better executed in a colony where the government is in a great measure arbitrary, than in one where it is altogether free. In every country where the unfortunate law of slavery is established, the magistrate, when he protects the slave, intermeddles in some measure in the management of the private property of the master; and, in a free country, where the master is, perhaps, either a member of the colony assembly or an elector of such a member, he dares not do this, but with the greatest caution and circumspection. The respect which he is obliged to pay to the master, renders it more difficult for him to protect the slave. But in a country where the government is in a great measure arbitrary, where it is usual for the magistrate to intermeddle even in the private property of individuals, and to send them, perhaps, a *lettre de catchet*, if they do not manage it according to his liking, it is much easier for him to give some protection to the slave; and common humanity naturally disposes him to do so. The protection of the magistrate renders the slave less contemptible in the eyes of his master, who is thereby induced to consider him with more regard, and to treat him with more gentleness. Gentle usage renders the slave not only more faithful, but more intelligent, and therefore, upon a double account, more useful. He approaches more to the condition of a free servant, and may possess some degree of integrity and attachment to his master's interest—virtues which frequently belong to free servants, but which can never belong to a slave, who is treated as slaves commonly are, in countries where the master is perfectly free and secure. That the condition of a slave is better under an arbitrary than under a free government, is, I believe, supported by the history of all ages and nations." (Wealth of Nations.)

William Paley.—"I define slavery to be 'an obligation to labor for the benefit of the master, without the contract or consent of the servant.' This obligation may arise, consistently with the law of nature, from three causes: 1. From crimes; 2. From captivity; 3. From debt. In the first case the continuance of the slavery, as of any other punishment, ought to be proportioned to the crime; in the second and third cases, it ought to cease, as soon as the demand of the injured nation or private creditor is satisfied.

"The slave-trade upon the coast of Africa is not excused by these principles. When slaves in that country are brought to market, no questions, I believe, are asked about the origin or justice of the vender's title. It may be presumed, therefore, that this title is not always, if it be ever, founded in any of the causes above assigned.

"But defect of right in the first purchase is the least crime with which this traffic is chargeable. The natives are excited to war and mutual depredation, for the sake of supplying their contracts or furnishing the market with slaves. With this the wickedness begins. The slaves, torn away from parents, wives, children, from their friends and companions, their fields and flocks, their home and country, are transported to the European settlements in America, with no other accommodation on ship-board than what is provided for brutes. This is the second stage of cruelty, from which the miserable exiles are delivered only to be placed, and that for life, in subjection to a dominion and system of laws, the most merciless and tyrannical that ever were tolerated upon the face of the earth; and from all that can be learned by the accounts of the people upon the spot, the inordinate authority, which the plantation laws confer upon the slaveholder, is exercised, by the English slaveholder especially, with rigor and brutality.

"But necessity is pretended—the name under which every enormity is attempted to be justified. And, after all, what is the necessity? It has never been proved that the land could not be cultivated there, as it is here, by hired servants. It is said that it could not be cultivated with quite the same conveniency and cheapness, as by the labor of slaves; by which means a pound of sugar, which the planter now sells for sixpence, could not be afforded under sixpence half-penny; and this is the *necessity!*" (Principles of Moral and Political Philosophy.)

James Beattie.—"It is well observed, by the wisest of poets—as Atheneus, quoting the passage, justly calls Homer, who lived when slavery was common, and whose knowledge of the human heart is unquestionable—that 'when a man is made a slave, he loses from that day the half of his virtue.' And Longinus, quoting the same passage, affirms, 'Slavery, however mild, may still be called the poison of the soul and a public dungeon.' And Tacitus remarks, that 'even wild animals lose their spirit when deprived of their freedom.' All history proves, and every rational philosopher admits, that as liberty promotes virtue and genius, slavery debases the understanding and corrupts the heart of both the slave and the master, and that in a greater or less degree, as it is more or less severe; so that in this plea of the slave-monger we have an example of that diabolical casuistry, whereby the tempter and corrupter endeavors to vindicate or gratify himself, by accusing those whom he himself has tempted or corrupted.

"Slavery is inconsistent with the dearest and most essential rights of man's nature; it is detrimental to virtue and to industry; it hardens the heart to those tender sympathies which form the most lovely part of human character; it involves the innocent in hopeless misery, in order to procure wealth and pleasure for the authors of that misery; it seeks to degrade into brutes beings whom the Lord of heaven and earth endowed with rational souls, and created for immortality; in short, it is utterly repugnant to every principle of reason, religion, humanity, and conscience. It is impossible for a considerate and unprejudiced mind to think of slavery without horror. That a man—a rational and immortal being—should be treated on the same footing with a beast or a piece of wood, and bought and sold, and entirely subjected to the will of another man, whose equal he is by nature, and whose superior he may be in virtue and understanding, and all for no crime, but merely because he was born in a certain country, or of certain parents, or because he differs from us in the shape of his nose, the color of his skin, or the size of his lips—if this be equitable, or excusable, or pardonable, it is in vain to talk any longer of the eternal distinctions of right and wrong, truth and falsehood, good and evil. It has been said that negroes are animals of a nature inferior to man, between whom and the brutes, they hold, as it were, the middle place. But though this were true, it would not follow that we have a right either to debase ourselves by a habit of cruelty, or to use them ill; for even beasts, if inoffensive, are entitled to gentle treatment; and we have reason to believe that they who are not merciful will not obtain mercy.

"The same sentiments are found in Pliny and Columella,

who both impute the decay of husbandry, in their time, not to any deficiency in the soil, but to the unwise policy of leaving to the management of slaves those fields which, says Pliny, 'had formerly rejoiced under the laureled plowshare and the triumphant plowman.' Rollin, with good reason, imputes to the same cause the present barrenness of Palestine, which in ancient times was called the land flowing with milk and honey." (Elements of Moral Science.)

JONATHAN DYMOND.—"That any human being, who has not forfeited his liberty by his crimes, has a right to be free, and that whosoever forcibly withholds liberty from an innocent man, robs him of his right, and violates the moral law, are truths which no man would dispute or doubt, if custom had not obscured our perceptions, or if wickedness did not prompt us to close our eyes.

"The whole system is essentially and radically bad; injustice and oppression are its fundamental principles. Whatever lenity may be requisite in speaking of the agent, none should be shown, none should be expressed for the act. I do not affirm or imagine that every slaveholder is therefore a wicked man; but if he be not, it is only upon the score of ignorance. If he is exempt from the guilt of violating the moral law, it is only because he does not perceive what it requires. Let us leave the deserts of the individual to Him who knoweth the heart: of his actions he may speak; and we should speak in the language of reprobation, disgust, and abhorrence.

"Although it could be shown that the slave system is expedient, it would not affect the question whether it ought to be maintained; yet it is remarkable that it is shown to be impolitic as well as bad. We are not violating the moral law because it fills our pockets. We injure ourselves by our own transgressions. The slave system is a costly iniquity, both to the nation and to individual men. It is matter of great satisfaction that this is known and proved; and yet it is just what, antecedently to inquiry, we should have reason to expect. The truth furnishes one addition to the many evidences, that even with respect to temporal affairs, that which is right is commonly politic; and it ought, therefore, to furnish additional inducements to a fearless conformity of conduct, private and public, to the moral law." (Essay on Morality.)

The Poet Cooper, in 1788.—"Laws will, I suppose, be enacted for the more humane treatment of the negroes; but who shall see to the execution of them? The planters will not, and the negroes can not. In fact, we know that laws of this tendency have not been wanting, enacted even among themselves, but there has been always a want of prosecutors or virtuous judges, deficiences which will not be very easily supplied. The newspapers have lately told us that these merciful masters have on this occasion been occupied in passing ordinances, by which the lives and limbs of their slaves are to be secured from cruelty hereafter. But who does not immediately detect the artifice, or can give them a moment's credit for any thing more than a design, by this show of lenity, to avert the storm which they think hangs over them. On the whole, I fear there is reason to wish, for the honor of England, that the nuisance had never been troubled, lest we eventually make ourselves justly chargeable with the whole offense, by not removing it. The enormity can not be palliated; we can no longer plead that we were not aware of it, or that our attention was otherwise engaged, and shall be inexcusable, therefore, ourselves, if we leave the least part of it unredressed. Such arguments as Pharaoh might have used to justify his destruction of the Israelites, substituting sugar for bricks—ye are idle, ye are idle—may lie ready for our use also; but I think we can find no better." (Letter of April, 1788. See Antislavery Reporter, vol. ii, p. 434.)

MONTGOMERY.

"The negro, spoiled of all that nature gave
The freeborn man, thus shrunk into a slave;
His passive limbs to measur'd tasks confined,
Obeyed the impulse of another mind—
A silent, secret, terrible control,
That ruled his sinews and repressed his soul.
Not for himself he waked at morning light,
Toil'd the long day, and sought repose at night;
His rest, his labor, pastime, strength, and health,
Were only portions of his master's wealth.
His love—O, name not *love* where Britons doom
The fruit of love to slavery from the womb.
Thus spurned, degraded, trampled, and oppressed,
The negro exile languished in the west,
With nothing left of life but hated breath,
And not a hope, except the hope, in death,
To fly forever from the creole-strand,
And dwell a freeman in his Father's land.
Is he not *man*, though knowledge never shed
Her quickening beams on his neglected head?
Is he not *man*, though sweet Religion's voice
Ne'er bade the mourner in his God rejoice?
Is *he* not man by sin and suffering tried?
Is *he* not man for whom the Savior died?
Belie the negro's *powers*—in headlong will,
Christian! *thy* brother thou shalt prove him still.
Belie his virtues—since his wrongs began
His follies and his crimes have stamped him man."
(Montgomery's West Indies.)

SAMUEL TAYLOR COLERIDGE.

"We have offended, O! my countrymen!
We have offended very grievously,
And been most tyrannous. From east to west
A groan of accusation pierces heaven!
The wretched plead against us; multitudes
Countless and vehement, the sons of God,
Our brethren! Like a cloud that travels on
Steam'd up from Cairo's swamps of pestilence,
Even so, my countrymen! have we gone forth
And borne to distant tribes slavery and pangs,
And deadlier far our vices, whose deep taint
With slow perdition murders the whole man,
His body and his soul!" (Sibylline Leaves.)

"There are truths so self-evident, or so immediately and palpably deduced from those that are, or are acknowledged for such, that they are at once intelligible to all men who possess the common advantages of the social state; although by sophistry, by evil habit, by the neglect, false persuasions, and impostures of an antichristian priesthood joined in one conspiracy with the violence of tyrannical governors, the understandings of men have become so darkened, and their consciences so lethargic, that there may arise a necessity for the republication of these truths, and this, too, with a voice of loud alarm and impassioned warning. Such were the doctrines proclaimed by the first Christians to the Pagan world; such were the lightnings flashed by Wickliff, Huss, Luther, Calvin, Zuinglius, Latimer, etc., across the Papal darkness; and such in our time the truths with which Thomas Clarkson, and his excellent confederates, the Quakers, fought and conquered the legalized banditti of men-stealers, the numerous and powerful perpetrators and advocates of rapine and murder, and—of blacker guilt than either—slavery. Truths of this kind being indispensable to man, considered as a moral being, are above all *expediency*, all accidental consequences; for, as sure as God is holy, and man immortal, there can be no evil so great as the ignorance or disregard of them. It is the very madness of mock prudence to oppose the removal of a poisonous dish on account of the pleasant sauces or nutritious viands which would be lost with it! The dish contains destruction to that, for which alone we wish the palate to be gratified or the body to be nourished." (The Friend, pp. 49, 50.)

James Stephen, Esq.—"Enough was known before; more than enough was incontrovertibly proved; nay, enough was always admitted or undenied, to make the legislative toleration of this slavery a disgrace to the British and Christian name. Iniquity, indeed, of every kind, loses in human detestation what it gains in mischief, by wide, unreproved diffusion, and by age. We sin remorselessly, because our fathers sinned, and because multitudes of our own generation sin, in the same way, without discredit. But if ever those most flagitious crimes of Europe—slave-trade and colonial slavery—shall cease to be tolerated by human laws, and live in history alone, men will look back upon them with the horror they deserve, and wonder as much at the depravity of the age that could establish or maintain them, as we now do at the murderous rites of our Pagan ancestors, or the ferocious, cannibal manners of New Zealand.

"There is enough in the simplest conception of personal, hereditary slavery, to revolt every just and liberal mind, independently of all aggravations to be found in its particular origin, or in abuses of the master's powers. But how much should sympathy and indignation be enhanced, when the cruel, perpetual privation of freedom, and of almost every civil and human right, is the punishment of no crime, nor the harsh consequence of public hostility in war, but imposed upon the innocent and helpless, by the hand of rapacious violence alone, and maintained for no other object but the sordid one of the master's profit, by the excessive labor to which they are compelled?

"Were our merchants to send agents to buy captives from the bandits in the forests of Italy, or from the pirates on the Barbary coast, and sell them here as slaves, to work for our farmers or manufacturers; and were the purchasers to claim, in consequence, a right to hold these victims of rapine and avarice, with their children, in bondage forever, and to take their work without wages; what would it be but the same identical case we are contemplating, except that the captives were of a different complexion? Yet the bandits and pirates are hanged; and their vendees, in the case supposed, would have less to apprehend from actions or indictments for false imprisonment, than from the vengeance of indignant multitudes. It certainly, at least, would not be necessary, for the purpose of their deliverance, to prove to the British Parliament or people, that the poor captives were overworked, underfed, driven with whips to their work, punished in a brutal way for every real or imputed fault, and, by such complicated oppressions, brought in great numbers prematurely to their graves." (Stephen's Slavery in the British West India Colonies Delineated, pp. 387, 388.)

"And now I will answer the other question, which my readers were supposed likely to put. 'Do I contend that no general improvement in the treatment of slaves has yet actually taken place?' Yes; speaking of the temporal lot of the field negroes, in all the most important points, and of their spiritual wants, too, with few and slight exceptions, I verily and conscientiously do. Different degrees of severity there are, and always have been, on different estates, according to the various dispositions and circumstances of their managers and owners; but in those grand articles, and main sources of ordinary oppression, under which the field negroes suffer and die; in the fatal excess of labor, and with some local and accidental exceptions, in the penury of maintenance, also, the case in general is little, if at all better than it was forty years ago. This I maintain, and this I undertake to establish." (Id., pp. 40, 41, A. D. 1830.)

JOHN MILTON.

"O execrable son, so to aspire
Above his brethren, he himself assuming
Authority usurped from God, not given.
Man over men
He made not lord; such title to *himself*
Reserving, human left from human free."

"In all things that have beauty, there is nothing to man more comely than liberty.

"Give me the liberty to know, to utter, and to argue freely, above all liberties."

ALEXANDER POPE.

"Some safer world in depths of wood embraced,
Some happier island in the watery waste;
Where slaves once more their native land behold,
No fiends torment, no Christians thirst for gold."
(Essay on Man.)

"God fixed it certain, that, whatever day
Makes man a slave takes half his worth away."
(Homer's Odyssey.)

JOSEPH ADDISON.

"O, *Liberty*, thou goddess heavenly bright,
Profuse of bliss, and pregnant of delight!
Eternal pleasures in thy presence reign,
And smiling plenty leads thy wanton train:
Eas'd of her load, subjection grows more light,
And poverty looks cheerful in thy sight;
Thou mak'st the gloomy face of nature gay,
Giv'st beauty to the sun, and pleasure to the day."

ROBERT BURNS.

"If I'm designed yon lordling's slave,
By nature's laws design'd,
Why was an independent wish
E'er planted in my mind?
If not, why am I subject to
His cruelty or scorn?
Or why has man the will and power
To make his fellow mourn?

Then let us pray that come it may,
As come it shall for a' that,
That sense and worth o'er all the earth
Shall bear the gree, an' a' that.
For a' that, an' a' that,
It's coming yet, for a' that,
When man to man, the warld all o'er,
Shall brothers be, an' a' that."

TOBIAS SMOLLETT.

"Thy spirit, INDEPENDENCE! let me share,
Lord of the lion-heart and eagle-eye—
Thy steps I'll follow, with my bosom bare,
Nor heed the storm that howls along the sky."

S. J. PRATT.

"Tyrants o'er brutes with ease extend their plan,
Then rise in cruelty from beast to man;
Their sordid policy each crime allows,
The flesh that quivers, and the blood that flows,
The furious stripes that murder in a day,
Or torturing arts that kill by dire delay;
The fainting spirit and the bursting vein,
All, all, are reconciled to Christian gain."
(The Rights of Nature.)

WILLIAM COWPER.

"Man finds his fellow guilty of a skin
Not colored like his own; and having power
T' enforce the wrong, for such a *worthy cause*
Dooms and devotes him as his lawful prey.
Thus man devotes his brother and destroys;
And worse than all, and most to be deplor'd,
As human nature's broadest, foulest blot,
Chains him, and tasks him, and exacts his sweat
With stripes that mercy, with a bleeding heart,
Weeps when she sees inflicted on a beast.
Then what is man? And what man, seeing this,
And having human feelings, does not blush
And hang his head, to think himself a man?
I would not have a slave to till my ground,
To carry me, to fan me while I sleep,
And tremble when I wake, for all the wealth
That sinews bought and sold have ever earned.
No! dear as freedom is, and in my heart's
Just estimation prized above all price,
I had much rather be myself the slave,
And wear the bonds, than fasten them on him."

"The tender ties of parent, husband, friend,
All bonds of nature, in that moment end.
O, most degrading of all ills that wait
On man—a mourner in his best estate!—
All other sorrows virtue may endure,
And find submission more than half a cure,
But SLAVERY! Virtue dreads it as her grave;
Patience itself is meanness in a slave.
Wait, then, the dawning of a brighter day,
And snap the chain the moment when you may.
Nature imprints upon whate'er we see
That has a heart and life in it, 'BE FREE.'"

WILLIAM ROSCOE.

"Form'd with the same capacity of pain,
The same desire of pleasure and of ease,
Why feels not man for man! When nature shrinks
From the slight puncture of an insect's sting,
Faints, if not screen'd from sultry suns, and pines
Beneath the hardship of an hour's delay
Of needful nutriment; when liberty
Is prized so dearly, that the slightest breath
That ruffles but her mantle, can awake
To arms unwarlike nations, and can rouse
Confed'rate states to vindicate her claims:
How shall the suff'rer, man, his fellow doom
To ills he mourns or spurns at; tear with stripes
His quiv'ring flesh; with hunger and with thirst
Waste his emaciate frame; in ceaseless toils
Exhaust his vital powers, and bind his limbs
In galling chains!"

HANNAH MORE.

"See the dire victim torn from social life,
The shrieking babe, the agonizing wife!
She! wretch forlorn, is dragg'd by hostile hands
To distant tyrants, sold to distant lands,
Transmitted miseries and successive chains,
The sole sad heritage her child obtains!
E'en this last wretched boon their foes deny,
To live together, or together die.
By felon hands, by one relentless stroke,
See the fond links of feeling nature broke!
The fibers twisting round a parent's heart,
Torn from their grasp, and bleeding as they part."

JAMES MONTGOMERY.

"Lives there a reptile baser than a slave,
Loathsome as death, corrupted as the grave?
See the dull creole at his pompous board,
Attendant vassals cringing round their lord;
Satiate with food, his heavy eyelids close,
Voluptuous minions fan him to repose;
Prone on the noonday couch he lolls in vain,
Delirious slumbers rack his maudlin brain;
He starts with horror from bewildering dreams,
His bloodshot eye with fire and frenzy gleams,
He stalks abroad; through all his wonted rounds
The negro trembles, and the lash resounds,
And cries of anguish shrilling through the air."

ROBERT SOUTHEY.

"O, he is worn with toil! the big drops run
Down his dark cheek! Hold—hold thy merciless hand,
Pale tyrant! for beneath thy hard command
O'er-wearied nature sinks. The scorching sun,
As pitiless as proud Prosperity,
Darts on him his full beams; gasping as he lies,
Arraigning with his looks the patient skies,
While that inhuman trader lifts on high
The mangling scourge. O! ye who at your ease
Sip the blood-sweetened beverage, thoughts like these
Haply ye scorn. I thank thee, gracious God!
That I do not feel upon my cheek the glow
Of indignation, when beneath the rod
A sable brother writhes in silent woe."

THOMAS CAMPBELL.

"And say, supernal powers, who deeply scan
Heav'n's dark decree, unfathom'd yet by man,
When shall the world call down, to cleanse her shame,
That embryo spirit, yet without a name—
That friend of Nature, whose avenging hands
Shall burst the Lybian's adamantine bands?
Who, sternly marking on his native soil
The blood, the tears, the anguish, and the toil,
Shall bid each righteous heart exult, to see
Peace to the slave and vengeance on the free!

Yet, yet, degraded man, th' expected day
That breaks your bitter cup is far away;
Trade, wealth, and fashion, ask you still to bleed,
And holy men give Scripture for the deed;
Scourg'd and debas'd, no Briton stoops to save
A wretch, a coward; yes, because a slave!"

ERASMUS DARWIN.

"Wrench'd the red scourge from proud Oppression's hands,
And broke, curs'd Slavery! thy iron bands.
E'en now, e'en now, on yonder western shores
Weeps pale Despair, and writhing Anguish roars.
E'en now, in Afric's groves, with hideous yell,
Fierce Slavery stalks and slips the dogs of hell;
From vale to vale the gathering cries rebound,
And sable nations tremble at the sound.
Who right the injured, and reward the brave,
Stretch your strong arm, for ye have power to save!

Throned in the vaulted heart, his dread resort,
Inexorable Conscience holds his court;
With still small voice the plots of guilt alarms,
Bares his masked brow, his lifted hand disarms;
But, wrapp'd in night, with terrors all his own,
He speaks in thunders when the deed is done.
Hear him, ye senates! hear this truth sublime,
He who allows oppression shares the crime."

(Botanic Garden.)

ROBERT POLLOK.

"Who blushed alike to be, or have a slave.
Unchristian thought! on what pretense soe'er
Of right inherited, or else acquired;
Of loss, or profit, or what plea you name,
To buy or sell, to barter, whip, and hold
In chains, a being of celestial make—
Of kindred form, of kindred faculties,
Of kindred feelings, passions, thoughts, desires;
Born free, and heir of an immortal hope!
Thought villainous, absurd, detestable!
Unworthy to be harbored in a fiend!"

(Course of Time.)

"LIBERTY." (United States coins.)

THE DECLARATION OF INDEPENDENCE.—"We hold these truths to be self-evident, that all men are created equal, that they are endowed by their Creator with certain inalienable rights; that among these are life, liberty, and the pursuit of happiness. That to secure these rights, governments are instituted among men, deriving their powers from the just consent of the governed," etc. (See the whole Declaration, signed by the delegates of all the original states, and adopted as the basis of all the state constitutions.)

THE UNITED STATES CONSTITUTION.—"*Amendment* 1. Congress shall make no law respecting an establishment of religion, or prohibiting the free exercise thereof; or abridging the freedom of speech or of the press; or the right of the people peaceably to assemble and petition the government for a redress of grievances."

VIRGINIA.—"The freedom of the press is one of the great bulwarks of liberty, and can never be restrained but by despotic governments."

THE SLAVE-TRADE DECLARED TO BE PIRACY BY THE LAW OF THE UNITED STATES, 1820.—"If any citizen of the United States, being of the crew or ship's company of any foreign ship or vessel engaged in the slave-trade, or any person whatever, being of the crew or ship's company of any ship or vessel owned in the whole or part, or navigated for, or in behalf of, any citizen or citizens of the United States, shall land, from any such ship or vessel, and on any foreign shore seize any negro or mulatto, not held to service or labor by the laws of either of the states or territories of the United States, *with intent to make such negro or mulatto a slave, or shall decoy, or forcibly bring or carry, or shall receive such negro or mulatto on board any such ship or vessel*, with intent as aforesaid, such citizen or person *shall be adjudged a* PIRATE, and on conviction thereof, before the circuit court of the United States, for the district wherein he may be brought or found, shall suffer DEATH."

PREAMBLE TO THE PENNSYLVANIA ACT, 1780.—"We conceive that it is our duty, and we rejoice that it is in our power, to extend a portion of that freedom to others which has been extended to us, and relieve from that state of thralldom, to which we ourselves were tyrannically doomed, and from which we have now every prospect of being delivered. It is not for us to inquire why, in the creation of mankind, the inhabitants of the different parts of the earth were distinguished by a difference of feature and complexion. It is sufficient to know, that all are the work of an almighty Hand. We find in the distribution of the human species, that the most fertile, as well as the most barren parts of the earth are inhabited by men of different complexions from ours, and from each other; from whence we may reasonably, as well as religiously infer, that He, who placed them in their various situations, hath extended equally his care and protection to all, and that it becometh not us to counteract his mercies. We esteem it a peculiar blessing, granted to us, that we are this day enabled to add one more step to universal civilization, by removing, as much as possible, the sorrows of those who have lived in undeserved bondage, and from which, by the assumed authority of the kings of Great Britain, no effectual legal relief could be obtained. Weaned by a long course of experience from those narrow prejudices and partialities we had imbibed, we find our hearts enlarged with kindness and benevolence toward men of all conditions and nations; and we conceive ourselves, at this particular period, extraordinarily called upon by the blessing which we have received, to manifest the sincerity of our profession, and to give a substantial proof of our gratitude.

"And whereas, the condition of those persons who have heretofore been denominated negro and mulatto slaves, has been attended with circumstances which not only deprived them of the common blessing they were by nature entitled to, but has cast them into the deepest afflictions, by an unnatural separation and sale of husband and wife from each other, and from their children; an injury, the greatness of which can only be conceived by supposing that we were in the same unhappy case. In justice, therefore, to persons so unhappily circumstanced, and who, having no prospect before them, wherein they may rest their sorrows and their hopes, have no reasonable inducement to render the service to society which they otherwise might, and also, in grateful commemoration of our own happy deliverance from that state of unconditional submission, to which we were doomed by the tyranny of Britain, Be it enacted, That no child hereafter born shall be a slave," etc.

"*To the Senate and House of Representatives of the United States:* From a persuasion that equal liberty was originally the portion, and is still the birthright of all men, and influenced by the strong ties of humanity and the principles of their institution, your memorialists conceive themselves bound to use all justifiable endeavors to loosen the bands of slavery, and promote a general enjoyment of the blessings of freedom. Under these impressions, they earnestly entreat your serious attention to the subject of slavery; that you will be pleased to countenance the restoration of liberty to those unhappy men, who alone, in this land of freedom, are degraded into perpetual bondage, and who amidst the general joy of surrounding freemen, are groaning in servile subjection—that you will devise means for removing this inconsistency from the character of the American people—that you will promote mercy and justice toward this distressed race—and that you will step to the very verge of the power vested in you for discouraging every species of traffic in the persons of our fellow-men.

"BENJAMIN FRANKLIN, *President.*

"*Philadelphia, February* 3, 1790."

GEORGE WASHINGTON.—"The benevolence of your heart, my dear Marquis, is so conspicuous on all occasions, that I never wonder at fresh proofs of it; but your late purchase of an estate in the colony of Cayenne, with a view of emancipating the slaves, is a generous and noble proof of your humanity. Would to God, a like spirit might diffuse itself generally into the minds of the people of this country! But I despair of seeing it. Some petitions were presented to the assembly at its last session, for the abolition of slavery; but they could scarcely obtain a hearing." (Letter to Lafayette.)

"I hope it will not be conceived from these observations, that it is my wish to hold the unhappy people who are the subject of this letter in slavery. I can only say, that there is not a man living, who wishes more sincerely than I do to see a plan adopted for the abolition of it; but there is only one proper and effectual mode by which it can be accomplished, and that is, by the legislative authority; and this, as far as my suffrage will go, shall not be wanting." (Letter to Robert Morris.)

"I never mean, unless some particular circumstance should compel me to it, to possess another slave by purchase; *it being among my first wishes to see some plan adopted by which slavery in this country may be abolished by law.*" (Letter to John F. Mercer.)

"Because there are, in Pennsylvania, laws for the gradual *abolition of slavery,* which neither Maryland nor Virginia has at present; but which nothing is more certain than that they must have, and at a period not remote." (Reasons for Depreciation of Southern Lands in a Letter to Sir John Sinclair.)

"Upon the decease of my wife, it is my will and desire that all my slaves, which I hold, *in my own right,* shall receive their freedom. To emancipate them during her life, would, though earnestly wished, be attended with such unspeakable difficulties, on account of their intermixture by marriages with the dower negroes, as to create the most fearful sensation, if not disagreeable consequences from the latter, while both descriptions are in the occupancy of the same proprietor, it not being in my power, under the tenure by which the dower negroes are held, to manumit them." (Washington's Will.)

THOMAS JEFFERSON.—"The whole commerce between master and slave is a perpetual exercise of the most boisterous passions; the most unremitting despotism on the one part and degrading submissions on the other. Our children see this and learn to imitate it; for man is an imitative animal. This quality is the germ of all education in him. From his cradle to his grave he is learning to do what he sees others do. If a parent could find no motive, either in his philanthropy or his self-love, for restraining the intemperance of passion toward his slave, it should always be a sufficient one that his child is present. But generally it is not sufficient. The parent storms, the child looks on, catches the lineaments of wrath, puts on the same airs in the circle of smaller slaves, gives loose to his worst passions, and thus nursed, educated, and daily exercised in tyranny, can not but be stamped by it with odious peculiarities. The man must be a prodigy who can retain his manners and morals undepraved by such circumstances. And with what execration should the statesman be loaded, who, permitting one half of the citizens thus to trample on the rights of the other, transforms those into despots, and these into enemies, destroys the morals of the one part, and the *amor patriæ* of the other! For if the slave can have a country in this world, it must be any other in preference to that in which he is born to live and labor for another: in which he must lock up the faculties of his nature, contribute as far as depends on his individual endeavors to the evanishment of the human race, or entail his own miserable condition on the endless generations proceeding from him. With the morals of the people, their industry also is destroyed. For in a warm climate no man will labor for himself who can make another labor for him. This is so true, that of the proprietors of slaves, a very small proportion indeed are ever seen to labor. And can the liberties of a nation be thought secure when we have removed their only firm basis, a conviction in the minds of the people that these liberties are of the gift of God? That they are not to be violated but with his wrath? Indeed, I tremble for my country when I reflect that God is just; that his justice can not sleep forever; that considering numbers, nature, and natural means only, a revolution of the wheel of fortune, an exchange of situation, is among possible events; that it may become probable by supernatural interference! The Almighty has no attribute which can take side with us in such a contest.

"What an incomprehensible machine is man! Who can endure toil, famine, stripes, imprisonment, and death itself, in vindication of his own liberty, and the next moment be deaf to all those motives whose power supported him through his trial, and inflict on his fellow-men a bondage, one hour of which is fraught with more misery than ages of that which he rose in rebellion to oppose. But we must wait with patience the workings of an overruling Providence, and hope that that is preparing the deliverance of these our suffering brethren. When the measure of their tears shall be full—when their tears shall have involved heaven itself in darkness—doubtless a God of justice will awaken to their distress, and by diffusing a light and liberality among their oppressors, or at length by his exterminating thunder manifest his attention to things of this world, and that they are not left to the guidance of blind fatality.

"I am very sensible of the honor you propose to me, of becoming a member of the society for the abolition of the slave-trade. You know that nobody wishes more ardently to see an abolition, not only of the trade, but of the condition of slavery; and certainly nobody will be more willing to encounter every sacrifice for that object. But the influence and information of the friends to this proposition in France will be far above the need of my association." (Letter to M. Warville, Paris, February, 1788.)

"*Dear Sir,*—Your favor of July 31st was duly received, and was read with peculiar pleasure. The sentiments breathed through the whole do honor to both the head and heart of the writer. Mine, on the subject of the slavery of negroes, have long since been in possession of the public, and time has only served to give them stronger root.

The love of justice and the love of country plead equally the cause of these people; and it is a moral reproach to us that they should have pleaded it so long in vain, and should have produced not a single effort—nay, I fear, not much serious willingness to relieve them and ourselves from our present condition of moral and political reprobation.

"It is an encouraging observation, that no good measure was ever proposed which, if duly pursued, failed to prevail in the end. We have proof of this in the history of the endeavors in the British Parliament to suppress that very trade which brought this evil on us. And you will be supported by the religious precept, 'be not weary in well-doing.' That your success may be as speedy and complete, as it will be honorable and immortal consolation to yourself, I shall as fervently and sincerely pray as I assure you of my great friendship and respect." (Letter to Edward Cole, Esq., August 25, 1814.)

Lafayette.—"While I am indulging in my views of American prospects, and American liberty, it is mortifying to be told that in that very country a large portion of the people are slaves! It is a dark spot on the face of the nation. Such a state of things can not always exist."

"I see in the papers, that there is a plan of gradual abolition of slavery in the District of Columbia. I would be doubly happy of it, for the measure in itself, and because a sense of American pride makes me recoil at the observations of the diplomatists, and other foreigners, who gladly improve the unfortunate existing circumstances into a general objection to our republican, and—saving that deplorable evil—our matchless system."

Benjamin Rush.—"The [cruel] master's wealth can not make him happy. The sufferings of a single hour in the world of misery, for which he is preparing himself, will overbalance all the pleasures he ever enjoyed in this life—

and for every act of unnecessary severity he inflicts on his slaves, he shall suffer tenfold in the world to come.

"His unkind behavior is upon record against him. The gentle spirits in heaven, whose happiness consists in expressions of gratitude and love, will have no fellowship with him. His soul must be melted with pity, or he can never escape the punishment which awaits the hard-hearted, equally with the impenitent, in the regions of misery." (Paradise of Negro Slaves.)

"About the year 1775 I read a short essay, with which I was much pleased, in one of Bradford's papers, against the slavery of the Africans in our country, and which, I was informed, was written by Thomas Paine. This excited my curiosity to become better acquainted with him. We met soon afterward at Mr. Aitkens' bookstore, where I did homage to his principles and his pen on the subject of the enslaved Africans. He told me it was the first piece he had ever published here. I possess one of his letters written to me from France on the subject of the abolition of the slave-trade." (Letter to Cheetham, July 17, 1809.)

ANTHONY BENEZET.—"I can with truth and sincerity declare, that I have found among the negroes as great variety of talents, as among a like number of whites; and I am bold to assert, that the notion entertained by some that the blacks are inferior in their capacities, is a vulgar prejudice founded on the pride or ignorance of their lordly masters, who have kept their slaves at such a distance as to be unable to form a right judgment of them."

JAMES MONROE.—"We have found that this evil has preyed upon the very vitals of the Union, and has been prejudicial to all the states in which it has existed." (Speech in the Virginia Convention.)

JOHN JAY.—"The state of New York is rarely out of my mind or heart, and I am often disposed to write much respecting its affairs; but I have so little information as to its present political objects and operations, that I am afraid to attempt it. An excellent law might be made out of the Pennsylvania one, for the gradual abolition of slavery. Till America comes into this measure, her prayers to Heaven will be impious. This is a strong expression, but it is just. Were I in your legislature, I would present a bill for the purpose with great care, and I would never cease moving it till it became a law, or I ceased to be a member. I believe God governs the world, and I believe it to be a maxim in his as in our court, that those who ask for equity ought to do it." (Letter from Spain, 1780.)

Thomas F. Marshall.—"I have said that I considered negro slavery as a political misfortune. The phrase was too mild. It is a cancer—a slow, consuming cancer—a withering pestilence—an unmitigated curse. I speak not in the spirit of a puling and false philanthropy. I was born in a slave state—I was nursed by a slave—my life has been saved by a slave. To me, custom has made the relation familiar, and I see nothing horrible in it. I am a Virginian by descent. Every cross in my blood, so far as I can trace it, in the paternal or maternal line, is Virginian."

Abigail Adams, (*the Mother of John Quincy Adams.*)—"I wish, most sincerely, there was not a slave in the province; it always appeared a most iniquitous scheme to me, to fight ourselves, for what we are daily robbing and plundering from those who have as good a right to freedom as we have. You know my mind on this subject." (Letter to her husband, John Adams, dated Boston, Garrison, September 22, 1774.)

"Is it not amazing, when the rights of humanity are defined with precision, in a country above all others fond of liberty—that in such an age, and in such a country, we find men, professing a religion the most humane and gentle, adopting a principle as repugnant to humanity as it is inconsistent with the Bible, and destructive to liberty? Believe me, I honor the Quakers for their noble efforts to abolish slavery. Every thinking, honest man rejects it in speculation; yet how few in practice from conscientious motives! Would any man believe that I am master of slaves of my own purchase? I am drawn along by the general inconvenience of living without them. I will not, I can not justify it. For, however, culpable my conduct, I will so far pay my devoir to virtue, as to own the excellence and rectitude of her precepts, and to lament my own want of conformity to them."

"It is a debt we owe the purity of our religion, to show that it is at variance with that law which warrants slavery." (Letter to Anthony Benezet.)

Patrick Henry.—"Is life so dear, or peace so sweet, as to be purchased at the price of chains and slavery? Forbid it, almighty God! I know not what course others may take; but, as for me, give me liberty or give me death."

"Another thing will contribute to bring general emancipation about. Slavery is detested. We feel its fatal effects. We deplore it with all the pity of humanity. I repeat it again, that it would rejoice my very soul that every one of my fellow-beings was emancipated. As we ought with gratitude to admire the decree of Heaven, which has numbered us among the free, we ought to lament and deplore the necessity of holding our fellow-men in bondage."

Henry Clay.—"As a mere laborer, the slave feels that he toils for his master, and not for himself; that the laws do not recognize his capacity to acquire and hold property, which depends altogether upon the pleasure of his proprietor, and that all the fruits of his exertions are reaped by others. He knows that, whether sick or well, in times of scarcity or abundance, his master is bound to provide for him by the all-powerful influence of self-interest. He is generally, therefore, indifferent to the adverse or prosperous fortunes of his master, being contented if he can escape his displeasure or chastisement, by a careless and slovenly performance of his duties.

"That labor is best, in which the laborer knows that he will derive the profits of his industry, and his employment depends upon his diligence, and his reward upon his assiduity. He then has every motive to excite him to exertion, and to animate him in perseverance. He knows that if he is treated badly, he can exchange his employer for one who will better estimate his service; and that whatever he earns is *his*, to be distributed by himself as he pleases among his wife and children, and friends, or enjoyed by himself. In a word, he feels that he is a free agent, with rights, and privileges, and sensibilities.

"Wherever the option exists to employ, at an equal hire, free or slave labor, the former will be decidedly preferred, for the reasons already assigned. It is more capable, more diligent, more faithful, and in every respect more worthy of confidence.

"It is believed that no where in the *farming* portion of the United States would slave labor be generally employed, if the proprietor were not tempted to raise slaves by the high price of the southern market, which keeps it up in his own."

Speaking of an attempt more than thirty-five years ago, to adopt gradual emancipation in Kentucky, Mr. Clay says:

"We were overpowered by numbers, and submitted to the decision of the majority with the grace which the minority, in a republic, should ever yield to such a decision. I have nevertheless never ceased, and never shall cease, to regret a decision, the effects of which have been, to place us in the rear of our neighbors, who are exempt from slavery, in the state of agriculture, the progress of manufactures, the advance of improvement, and the general prosperity of society." (Address before the Colonization Society.)

"I consider slavery as a curse—a curse to the master—a wrong, a grievous wrong to the slave. In the abstract it is all wrong, and no possible contingency can make it right." (Colonization speech in 1836.)

WILLIAM WIRT.—"Slavery is contrary to the laws of nature and of nations. That slavery is an evil, it would be more than idle for any human being to doubt or deny."

JOHN RANDOLPH.—"Dissipation, as well as *power* or prosperity, hardens the heart, but avarice deadens it to every feeling but the thirst for riches. Avarice alone could have produced the slave-trade. Avarice alone can drive, as it does drive, this infernal traffic, and the wretched victims, like so many post-horses whipped to death in a mail-coach. Ambition has its cover-sluts, in the pride, pomp, and circumstance of glorious war; but where are the trophies of avarice? The handcuff, the manacle, and the blood-stained cowhide! *What man is worse received in society for being a hard master? Who denies the hand of a sister or daughter to such monsters?*—nay, they have even appeared in 'the abused shape of the vilest of women.' I say nothing of India or Amboyna—of Cortez or Pizarro." (Southern Literary Messenger.)

"*Resolved,* That a committee be appointed, to inquire into the existence of an *inhuman* and illegal traffic of slaves, carried on in and through the District of Columbia, and to report whether any, and what measures are necessary for putting a stop to the same." (Resolution presented by John Randolph in Congress, March, 1816.)

"Virginia is so impoverished by the system of slavery, that the tables will sooner or later be turned, and the slaves will advertise for runaway masters."

"Sir, I neither envy the head nor the heart of that man from the north, who rises here to defend slavery upon principle." (Rebuke of Edward Everett, in Congress, 1820.)

"I give to my slaves their freedom, to which my conscience tells me they are justly entitled. It has a long time been a matter of the deepest regret to me, that the circumstances under which I inherited them, and the obstacles thrown in the way by the laws of the land, have prevented my emancipating them in my lifetime, which it is my full intention to do in case I can accomplish it." (Extract from John Randolph's will.)

Thomas Jefferson Randolph.—"I agree with gentlemen in the necessity of arming the state for internal defense. I will unite with them in any effort to restore confidence to the public mind, and to conduce to the sense of the safety of our wives and our children. Yet, sir, I must ask, upon whom is to fall the burden of this defense? not upon the lordly masters of their hundred slaves, who will never turn out except to retire with their families when danger threatens. No, sir; it is to fall upon *the less wealthy class of our citizens; chiefly upon the non-slaveholders.* I have known patrols turned out where *there was not a slaveholder among them,* and this is the practice of the country. I have slept in times of alarm quietly in bed, without having a thought of care, while the individuals owning none of this property themselves, were patrolling under a compulsory process, for a pittance of seventy-five cents for twelve hours, the very curtilage of my house, and guarding that property, which was alike dangerous to them and myself. After all, this is but an expedient. As this population becomes more numerous, it becomes less productive. Your guard must be increased, till finally its profits will not pay for the expense of its subjection. Slavery has the effect of lessening the free population of a country.

"The gentleman has spoken of the increase of the female slaves being a part of the profit; it is admitted; but no great evil can be averted, no good attained, without some inconvenience. It may be questioned, how far it is desirable to foster and encourage this branch of profit. It is a practice, and an increasing practice in parts of Virginia, to rear slaves for market. How can an honorable mind, a patriot, and a lover of his country, bear to see this ancient dominion, rendered illustrious by the noble devotion and patriotism of her sons in the cause of liberty, converted into one grand menagerie, where men are to be reared for the market, like oxen for the shambles. Is it better, is it not worse, than the slave-trade; that trade which enlisted the labor of the good and wise of every creed, and every clime, to abolish it? The trader receives the slave, a stranger in language, aspect, and manner, from the merchant who has brought him from the interior. The ties of father, mother, husband, and child, have all been rent in twain; before he receives him, his soul has become callous. But here, sir, individuals, whom the master has known from infancy, whom he has seen sporting in the innocent gambols of childhood, who have been accustomed to look to him for protection, he tears from the mother's arms, and sells into a strange country, among strange people, subject to cruel taskmasters.

"He has attempted to justify slavery here, because it exists in Africa, and has stated that it exists all over the world. Upon the same principle, he could justify Mohammedanism, with its plurality of wives, petty wars for plunder, robbery, and murder, or any other of the abominations and enormities of savage tribes. Does slavery exist in any part of civilized Europe? No, sir, in no part of it." (Speech in the Virginia Legislature.)

Governor Randolph.—"The deplorable error of our ancestors in copying a civil institution from savage Africa, has affixed upon their posterity a depressing burden, which nothing but the extraordinary benefits conferred by our happy climate, could have enabled us to support. We have been far outstripped by states, to whom nature has been far less bountiful. It is painful to consider what might have been, under other circumstances, the amount of general wealth in Virginia, or the whole sum of comfortable subsistence and happiness possessed by all her inhabitants." (Address to the Legislature of Virginia, in 1820.)

Hon. Thomas H. Benton.—"'My opinions.' They are wanted. Very good: they shall know my opinions. And first, they may see them in my public acts—in my proposals for the admission of Texas five years ago, in which I proposed to limit the western extension of slavery by a longitudinal line; I believe the one hundredth degree of west longitude. Next, in my votes upon the Oregon bill, in which *I opposed the introduction of slavery there;* and, again, in my letter to the people of Oregon, in which I declared myself to be no propagandist of slavery. These were public acts. But you want public declarations of personal sentiments; very good, you shall have them. My personal sentiments, then, are *against the institution of slavery, and against its introduction into places in which it does not exist.* If there was no slavery in Missouri to-day, I should oppose its coming in; if there was none in the United States, I should oppose its coming into the United States. As there is none in New Mexico or California, I am against sending it to those territories, and could not vote for such a measure—a declaration which costs me but little, the whole dispute now being about the abstract right of carrying slaves there, without the exercise of the right. No one asks for the exercise of the right, and can not ask it in the face of the dogma which denies the power to grant it. States do as they please. These are my principles." (Benton's speech to the people of Missouri, May 25, 1849.)

De Witt Clinton.—"*Patria cara, carior libertas*—Dear is my country, liberty is dearer." (Motto for his library.) As Governor of the state of New York, in his speech to the Legislature, January 4, 1820, alluding to the Missouri question, he says: "Nor can I conceal on this occasion, the deep anxiety which I feel on a subject now under the consideration of the General government; and which is, unfortunately, calculated to produce geographical distinctions. Highly important as it is to allay feelings so inauspicious, yet I consider the interdiction of the extension of slavery a paramount consideration. Morally and politically speaking, slavery is an evil of the first magnitude; and whatever may be the consequences, it is our duty to prohibit its progress in all cases where such prohibition is allowed by the Constitution. No evil can result from its inhibition more pernicious than its toleration; and I earnestly recommend the expression of your sense on this occasion, as equally due to the character of the state and the prosperity of the empire."

6. Testimonies of distinguished men, neither American nor English:

Grotius.—"Those are *men-stealers,* who abduct, keep, sell, or buy slaves or free men. To steal a man is the highest kind of theft."

Pope Leo X.—"Not only the Christian religion, but nature herself cries out against a state of slavery."

Montesquieu.—"Slavery is not useful either to the master or to the slave; to the slave, because he can do nothing by virtue; to the master, because he contracts with his slaves, all sorts of evil habits, inures himself insensibly to the neglect of every moral virtue, and becomes proud, passionate, hard-hearted, violent, voluptuous, and cruel. The slave sees a society happy whereof he is not even a part; he finds that security is established for others, but not for him; he perceives that his master has a soul capable of self-advancement, while his own is violently and forever repressed. Nothing puts one nearer the condition of the beasts than always to see freemen and not to be free. *Such a person is the natural enemy of the society in which he lives.* It is impossible to allow the negroes are men, because if we allow them to be men, it will begin to be believed that we are not Christians.

"Slavery not only violates the laws of nature and of civil society; it also wounds the best forms of government; in a democracy, where all men are equal, slavery is contrary to the spirit of the constitution."

JEAN JAQUES ROUSSEAU.—"To renounce our liberty is to renounce our quality of man, and with it all the rights and duties of humanity; and no adequate compensation can possibly be made for such a sacrifice; as it is in itself incompatible with the nature of man, whose actions, when once he is deprived of his free will, must be destitute of all morality. In a word, a convention which stipulates for absolute authority on one side, and unlimited obedience on the other, must always be considered as vain and contradictory. What right can my slave have that is not mine, since every thing that he has belongs to me; and to speak of the right of me against myself is absolute nonsense.

"Thus, in whatever light we view things, the right of slavery is found to be null; not only because it is illegal, but because it can have no existence; for the terms *slavery* and *right* contradict and exclude each other; and be it from man to man, or from a man to a nation, it would be equally nonsensical to say—'I make a covenant with you entirely at your expense, and for my benefit; I will observe it as far as my inclination leads me, and you shall observe it as far as I please.'" (On the Social Contract.)

BUFFON.—"Upon the whole, it is apparent that the unfortunate negroes are endowed with excellent hearts, and possess the seeds of every human virtue. I can not write their history, without lamenting their miserable condition. Is it not more than enough to reduce men to slavery, and to oblige them to labor perpetually, without the capacity of acquiring property? To these, is it necessary to add cruelty, and blows, and to abuse them worse than brutes? Humanity revolts against those odious oppressions which result from avarice, and which would have been daily renewed, had not the laws given a friendly check to the brutality of masters, and fixed limits to the sufferings of their slaves. They are forced to labor; and yet the coarsest food is dealt out to them with a sparing hand. 'They support,' say their obdurate taskmasters, 'hunger without inconvenience; a single European meal is sufficient provision to a negro for three days; however little they eat or sleep, they are always equally strong and equally fit for labor.' How can men, in whose breasts a single spark of humanity remains unextinguished, adopt such detestable maxims? How dare they, by such barbarous and diabolical arguments, attempt to palliate those oppressions which originate solely from their thirst of gold? But let us abandon those hardened monsters to perpetual infamy, and return to our subject." (Natural History.)

H. Gregoire.—"If ever negroes, bursting their chains, should come—which Heaven forbid—on the European coast, to drag whites of both sexes from their families—to chain them and conduct them to Africa, and mark them with a hot iron—if whites stolen, sold, purchased by crimes, and placed under the guidance of merciless inspectors, were immediately compelled, by the stroke of the whip, to work in a climate injurious to their health, where, at the close of each day, they could have no other consolation than that of advancing another step to the tomb—no other perspective than to suffer and to die in all the anguish of despair—if devoted to misery and ignominy, they were excluded from all the privileges of society, and declared legally incapable of judicial action, their testimony would not have been admitted even against the black class—if driven from the sidewalks, they were compelled to mingle with the animals in the middle of the street—if a subscription were made to have them *lashed* in a mass, and their backs, to prevent gangrene, covered with pepper and with salt—if the forfeit for killing them were but a trifling sum—if a reward were offered for apprehending those who escape from slavery—if those who escape were hunted by a pack of hounds, trained to carnage—if, blaspheming the Divinity, the blacks pretended, that, by their origin, they had permission of Heaven to preach passive obedience and resignation to the whites—if greedy, hireling writers published, that, for this reason, just reprisals may be exercised against the *rebellious* whites, and that white slaves are happy, more happy than the peasants in the bosom of Africa—in a word, if all the arts of cunning and calumny, all the strength and fury of avarice, all the inventions of ferocity were directed against you, by a coalition of dogs, merchants, priests, kings, soldiers, and colonists, what cry of horror would resound through these countries! To express it, new epithets would be sought; a crowd of writers, and particularly of poets, would exhaust their eloquent lamentations, provided that, having nothing to fear, there was something to gain. Europeans, reverse this hypothesis, and see what you are!" (Faculties of Negroes.)

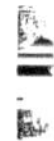

The Abbe Raynal.—"Will it be said that he who wants to make me a slave does me no injury, but that he only makes use of his rights? Where are those rights? Who hath stamped upon them so sacred a character as to silence mine?

"He who supports the system of slavery is the enemy of the whole human race. He divides it into two societies of legal assassins—the oppressors and the oppressed. It is the same thing as proclaiming to the world, 'If you would preserve your life, instantly take away mine, for I want to have yours.'

"But the negroes, they say, are a race born for slavery;

their dispositions are narrow, treacherous, and wicked; they themselves allow the superiority of our understandings, and almost acknowledge the justice of our authority. Yes; the minds of the negroes are contracted, because slavery destroys all the springs of the soul. They are wicked, but not equally so with you. They are treacherous, because they are under no obligation to speak truth to their tyrants. They acknowledge the superiority of our understandings, because we have abused their ignorance. They allow the justice of our authority, because we have abused their weakness.

"I shall not be afraid to cite to the tribunal of reason and justice those governments which tolerate this cruelty, or which even are not ashamed to make it the basis of their power.

"But these negroes, it is further urged, were born slaves. Barbarians! will you persuade me that a man can be the property of a sovereign, a son the property of a father, a wife the property of a husband, a domestic the property of a master, a negro the property of a planter?"

Jaques Pierre Brissot.—"When you run over Maryland and Virginia, you conceive yourself in a different world; and you are convinced of it, when you converse with the inhabitants.

"They speak not here of projects for freeing the negroes; they praise not the societies of London and America; they read not the works of Clarkson; no, the indolent masters behold with uneasiness the efforts that are making to render freedom universal.

"*God has created men of all nations, of all languages, of all colors, equally free; slavery, in all its forms, in all its degrees, is a violation of the Divine laws, and a degradation of human nature.*" (Travels in the United States, 1788.)

7. Testimony of pro-slavery advocates, apologists, and prudent men.

If slavery were supported either by Scripture or reason, it could certainly be sustained by Scriptural proofs, or rational arguments.

When we examine the reasons given by the statesmen and the swarm of politicians who are the representatives of the true slaveholders, we find no argument, of any kind, in their pleas. The sum of the whole is comprised in a few set phrases—"southern institutions," "domestic institution," "our property," "patriarchal institution," and the like. These are the arguments of the philosophers who are the mouthpieces for the slaveholders, to meet the arguments of antislavery men. But the Bowie-knife heroes, who treat the subject very differently, prove slavery to be right by dint of Lynch law, hanging, burning, shooting, and dirking.

The good, religious people, whether minister, Church judicatories, or members, generally seem to satisfy their consciences by declaring that slavery is a civil institution, with which the Church has nothing to do. This is all their argument, in a word. Yet they seem to be as forward, generally, as their neighbors, to buy, sell, trade in negroes, and hold them as slaves. And if a word is uttered against slavery, the outcry of abolitionist, incendiary, is a sufficient argument to silence the declarations of Scripture and the arguments of reason.

8. In this chapter we have adduced a cloud of witnesses against slavery. The greatest divines the world ever saw—the leaders of the mighty phalanx of British and American Protestant theologians—taught by God's word, and imbued with the true spirit of Christianity, pronounce against slavery, not only by protest, but by invincible reasons. The statesmen, philanthropists, and literary men of Britain, nursed in the cradle of British liberty—Britain herself the apostle of liberty to the modern world—utter their protests, and furnish their reasons, against slavery. Our own great statesmen, of every name, slaveholders and non-slaveholders,

utter their heartiest amen to what the voices of all good men have uttered before them against this crying sin of slavery; and to all this there is no reply, except the soft words of the prudent men, begging for a truce; or the lifted up deadly weapons of the Lynch-law men; or the sophistical, unmeaning phrases of the special pleaders, who exclaim, "*Our institutions! our property!*"

CHAPTER VIII.

OBJECTIONS AGAINST THE FOREGOING VIEWS STATED, CONSIDERED, AND CONFUTED.

1. In the foregoing chapters we have pointed out the moral evils, or sinful character, of slavery, by a great variety of argument, which, we are persuaded, can never be overturned, or even weakened, although they may be evaded, through the perverseness or weakness of human nature. Through this weakness, if not perverseness, a number of specious pleas have been mustered up and arrayed against the evidence which proves the sinfulness of slavery. And it is beyond doubt that some, at least, have satisfied their consciences, so far, that they have concluded they may enter on, or continue in, the practice of slaveholding, without sin against God, or, at any rate, that their salvation will not be frustrated by their becoming slaveholders, or by continuing such, if they are now slaveholders. A brief reply to these pleas will serve as a subject for the present chapter.

2. It is argued that the negroes are by nature *inferior* to the whites, and may therefore be justly held as slaves.

If the argument mean that they are a *different race* from the whites, it is the reasoning of an infidel, and not of a believer in divine revelation, which asserts that God "made of one blood all nations of men for to dwell on all the face of the earth," Acts xvii, 26.

If it mean that some men are intended by nature to be slaves, and that the Author of nature has given some men a license to enslave others, this is denied, and the denial must be persisted in till the express Divine warrant can be shown, a thing never yet done, though often attempted.

If it mean that God has made their capacities inferior to others, and that the last have a right to enslave the first, this argument will prove, that some of the citizens of every country have a right to enslave other citizens of the same country; nay, that some have a right to enslave their own brothers and sisters.

If the argument have a reference to their alleged *intellectual* inferiority to the white race, which we may admit, for the sake of disposing of the objection, without deciding such a difficult subject, it would prove entirely too much. It would prove that any white nation which had made greater advances in civilization, knowledge, and wisdom, than another white nation, would have a right to reduce the latter to slavery. Besides, as the argument is as applicable to individuals as to nations, then the wisest man in the world might make slaves of all the rest.

If the argument mean to say that because God, in the exercise of his government, suffers some men to be enslaved, he therefore, from the beginning, intended they should be enslaved, the answer is, that because he suffers some men to be murdered, he intended and made them to be murdered, which is too absurd to be believed, or to need confutation.

But if the whites do indeed possess this intellectual superiority, they should be thankful to God, who bestowed it on them, and they ought to fulfill all the obligations, and perform all the duties which it imposes. And these obligations require them not to subjugate or deal unjustly with those who are less blessed than they are, but to instruct, improve, and elevate them. If the whites are strong, they ought to be merciful, not unjust and cruel. They who are strong ought to bear with the infirmities of the weak.

But, setting the Bible aside, it remains to be proved that the African race is inferior by nature to the white race. Augustine, Tertullian, and Cyprian, will favorably compare with the highest intellects of any age. Hannibal and other African generals, stand among the foremost of their race. And there are not wanting examples of intellectual capacity among the negroes, even the slaves, that will advantageously compare with the capacity of the whites. Besides, this plea is very unbecoming in the mouths of the descendants of the ancient aboriginal inhabitants of Ireland, England, Scotland, France, Spain, and Germany. Let any one read the Germania of Tacitus, the Commentaries of Cæsar, and the writings of some others, and he will find that it would be difficult to decide whether the ancient forefathers of the white inhabitants of America were more enlightened, civilized, or elevated than the African negroes, especially before they became demoralized by the Christian merchants of Britain, Spain, and Portugal, who carried on all the damning degradations of the slave-trade.

3. It is pretended that none but negroes can endure labor in the hot climates of the West Indies and the southern states; and as they will not labor in a state of freedom, in the cultivation of cotton and sugar, it is necessary to enslave them and compel them to work.

It is allowed that the black man can work more than the white man, in warm climates; but he can not, without great injury to health, work as much as an Englishman, of the same bodily strength, can in his own native climate. But the Creator's works abound with compensatory and equalizing provisions. The same heat which renders arduous and continued labor irksome, lessens the need of it, by promoting more fruitfulness than in the temperate zones. In these man finds vigorous, bodily action, rather pleasant than irksome; but in the torrid zone, his instincts are very strongly on the side of rest and ease. This disposition, or, rather, instinct, if not carried to a vicious excess, conduces to their physical welfare. This compensatory arrangement of God, by the teachings of the slave system, is produced as a reason for enslaving man. Because, from the exuberance of the soil, they need not work hard for themselves, it is inferred, that they may be justly enslaved, and whipped into hard work for the benefit of others. The very bounty of God is thus made a plea for the tyranny of man.

Among the sophisms resorted to by the apologists of slavery, is that, in the driving system, they confound moral with physical force. They maintain that the free laborer is compelled to work for the subsistence of himself and family. A sufficient answer to the sophism is, that the instinct of self-preservation is too strong to be easily subdued, either by the love of comfort or the fear of want, as in the case of the free laborer. Yet it yields to present pain, or nearly-impending torture, as in the case of the slave. We do not find that free laborers work themselves to death, however high the wages; but in the sugar and cotton plantations, thousands of thousands of slaves have been worked to death, under the rigor necessary to maintain slavery, in view of the great, leading object of the system—the emolument of the master, at the expense of the liberty, comfort, and life of the slave.

Besides, it is strange reasoning, and stranger morality, to maintain, that because you are feeble and can not labor, you have a right to enslave your robust neighbor. As in all other cases, the feeble and those who choose not to labor, and yet wish to have their lands cultivated, are necessitated to hire the robust to labor for them, so no reason can be given why the inhabitants of hot climates should not either perform their own labor or hire those who can perform it, whether negroes or others.

4. It is objected against the charges brought and proved against slavery, "that the slaves are happy and contented in their condition, and, therefore, they had better remain slaves."

If the slaves are so well satisfied with their condition, why are such severe laws made against their running away? Why are the newspapers in the south stuffed with advertisements for runaway slaves? If free negroes are so much worse off than those in bondage, that the laws bestow freedom on any slave "who saves his master's or mistress' life, or performs any meritorious service to the state," it is strange, indeed, that *meritorious* actions shall be rewarded by making a man more unhappy than he was before.

Every man has a right to judge concerning his own happiness, and to choose the means of obtaining or promoting it. To deprive him of this right, is to enslave him. Because we judge the negroes are more happy in slavery than in freedom, we have no more right to enslave them than we have to enslave any of our neighbors, who, we judge, would be more happy in being our slaves than in being freemen. Would we ourselves be willing to be slaves, because others think that we would be happier on that account?

It seems to have been an old plea with the apologists for slavery, that the happiness of slavery was very great, indeed. As early as 1790, Admiral Barrington, in his testimony before the British house of Parliament, speaks highly of the happiness of slavery. Being asked, "What have you observed of the behavior of masters toward their negro slaves in those islands where you have commanded?" he answered, "Always the greatest humanity;" and afterward added, "They seemed so happy that he had wished himself a negro." (Commons' Report on the Slave-Trade, 1790, p. 405. See Stephen's Delineation, ii, 22.)

A good, slaveholding lady, who contended that freedom would be a great curse to her slaves, and that they were happier than if they were free, was asked, what would be their condition after her death, answered, "If they will be good and faithful servants, they will find, at my death, that papers of manumission had been duly prepared." She was reminded by a friend, "You told me that freedom was the greatest curse that could be bestowed on a slave. How is it possible that you would leave, as your dying legacy to good and faithful servants, the greatest curse you could bestow?"

The happiness of slavery may be illustrated by the following: "James Walker has been one of the most respectable and one of the most wealthy of slaves in the island of Jamaica. He has been blessed with prosperity and length of days; he has lived to see his children and his grandchildren rise to maturity around him; and he has lived to see every female among them drop, one after another, into the abyss of colonial sin. With a heart imbued with the feelings of the Christian religion, he has looked around on the females of his family, and has beheld them all the prostitutes—some the reluctant prostitutes—of the profligate white men in authority over and around them! What must be the feelings of this Christian parent? Such is the happiness of this opulent slave!" (Antislavery Reporter, p. 268, London, 1832.)

Some, indeed, say the slaves have no wish to change their condition. Take an illustration from the history of West India slavery, which, in all its essential elements, was one with that in this country. Thomas Burton, a slave of Jamaica, redeemed his wife Sophy, also a slave, and her four children, begotten in concubinage to a white overseer, before her marriage to Thomas, who generously preferred the freedom of his wife and her mulatto children to his own, as his means did not allow him to redeem himself, his wife, and her children; and as he was old, he considered it of less importance to have his own freedom than the freedom of his wife and her children. Mr. Barclay, in his vindication of the slave system of Jamaica, p. 18, quotes the case as follows: "Here was a wealthy slave purchasing the manumission of a woman with a large family, not even of his own caste, for they were mulattoes, who had yet no wish to change his own condition." In most cases where the slave seems to prefer slavery, there will be found something similar to the case of Joseph Mariat. (Antislavery Reporter, pp. 265–268.)

There are few, indeed, who believe, or can believe, what they say, when they declare that slaves are happier than freemen. Indeed, as slavery is considered to be a punishment for capital offenses, no man who understands himself would prefer slavery to freedom. Governor Giles, of Virginia, in 1827, speaking of punishing free blacks by selling them for slaves, declares: "Slavery must be admitted to be a punishment of the highest order; and according to every just rule for the apportionment of punishment to crimes, it would seem that it ought to be applied to crime of the highest order."

But allowing that slaves are happy in their condition, it would only prove that slavery so brutalizes and demoralizes man that, under its influences, he no longer sustains the true character of an intelligent and accountable being. When the slave can see his daughters and those of his kind reduced to prostitution, and be happy under the pressure of such moral degradation, who can think such happiness to be other than hellish? Or, when the slave can be happy, deprived of freedom, and writhing under the lash, he must be considered below the brute.

The favorable accounts that most travelers give concerning the happiness of slaves have no weight. They are received from the masters or overseers, who are interested persons; or when received from the slaves, they are the utterances of suppressed discontent, in the place of expressions of real enjoyment.

It is said, however, that the negroes are bettered in their condition by having the privileges of Christianity. To this we reply: 1. We are not to do evil that good may come; to commit a crime more aggravated than theft or robbery—enslavement of children—that we may make proselytes to Christianity. Neither Christ nor his apostles taught this mode of propagating the Christian faith. 2. The enslaving of men is one of the greatest barriers to the spread of true Christianity among the slaves; as they see, if they see any thing, the greatest repugnancy between Christianity and the practice of slavery. 3. Men, while slaves, in many cases, can not be Christians at all, in the full sense of the word, because the slave laws prohibit them from exercising the duties and enjoying the privileges of Christians. And even when they become Christians, in the very limited sense in which they can, they labor under disabilities which prevent them from enjoying the entire chartered privileges of our holy religion.

But suppose the happiness of individual slaves, or whole gangs of them, be real for the time being, the argument derived from it is void. Masters and overseers may have been kind and indulgent, and the slaves, for a time, may have experienced few of the evils of slavery; but an overseer may be dismissed, or the estate may fall into the hands of a minor or a mortgagee, and then the whole scene may be changed. Harshness may succeed to indulgence; severity to mildness; privation to plenty; brutal outrage to considerate kindness; excessive exaction to moderate labor; a contempt of the domestic relation to a solicitude to cherish and protect these richest springs of worldly enjoyment; a bitter spirit of persecution and intolerance to a Christian zeal to impart to them the privileges of religion; and all the horrors of unbridled lust, rioting in the despotism of unmeasured power, may succeed to a fatherly care over the moral purity and chastity of the young female slave. Every one must see that a condition of life daily liable to such vicissitudes is illy calculated to promote real happiness. Nor are these evils imaginary. They are every-day occurrences in all slave communities.

5. It is also said, that the negroes in this country are in a better condition than they were in Africa. If this be the case, they certainly owe none of their improved state to those who enslaved them, whether those who originally

purchased them in Africa, those who conveyed them across the ocean in ships, those who purchased them here, or those who constantly are originating slavery in reducing to bondage innocent children. Whatever advantages the slaves have had in the way of improvement, they have not received it through the influence of the slave system, but in spite of it. Hence, slavery has nothing to claim on this score; but it has to receive a heavy sentence of condemnation for *preventing* the improvement of the slaves.

6. It is said, "when they are *willing* or *prefer* to be slaves, it is lawful to enslave them." We reply: 1. If man is willing to become the property of another, it is because slavery has greatly debased him. It is an instinct of human nature to love liberty. Hence, no one in whom the man has not been degraded, can be willing to become a slave. 2. If it is right to enslave those who are willing to be slaves, and no others, then as often as the slave may change his views, so often would the duty of the master change with it. 3. If it is right to hold those only in slavery who are willing to be slaves, no one is justified in *enforcing* the laws of slavery. The laws which declare one man to be the *property* of another, thus sanctioning his *forcible detention* as a chattel, are all wrong; and the *enforcing* of such laws is wrong. Slaveholding could not survive the practical adoption of the principle, that the willingness of the man to be a slave is the only thing that can justify his enslavement.

7. It is a very common apology used by slaveholders, and others for them, "The good treatment of slaves—that they are well clothed, fed, housed, and mercifully dealt with." We reply:

(1.) It is impossible to treat innocent persons well, and at the same time deprive them of their liberty and rights. Deprivation of liberty is next in cruelty to murder. We all feel it to be so in our own cases; and slaves feel it as much as others. It is impossible to enslave a human being, and at the same time treat him well. Properly speaking, no slave was ever well treated.

(2.) The most humane treatment of the master, reaching to clothing, feeding, housing, and mildness, is not the principal thing entering into good treatment. The culture of the moral and intellectual powers of man is the principal part of good treatment. A sufficient supply of food and other comforts may be rendered for the vilest purposes.

(3.) Even when humane and religious masters do their very best—as many of them doubtless do—the system of slavery does not allow them to deal either justly or mercifully with the slave to the proper extent. The system constantly throws obstacles in the way of the benevolent that they are unable to remove. If the master desires to free the slave, he rarely can do it. If the master sends him to school, or teaches him himself, the system forbids it.

(4.) Hence, all the good treatment that slavery proper either uses or allows, in clothing, food, etc., is such as is awarded to beasts. The good treatment of slaves, according to its code, has for its end the benefit of the master, and not the good of the slave.

(5.) And when masters treat their slaves better than the slave laws allow, they virtually protest against the sinfulness of slavery; because their consciences lead them to dissent from the system, and practice contrary to it.

8. It is sometimes said that we may hold slaves for their good.

If the tenure of the slaveholder be continued barely for the benefit of the slave, in view of giving him liberty after educating him, and at the same time acknowledging the *right* of the slave to liberty, and that freedom is a blessing, the mere legal relation of master may be sustained for a time.

If the master can not emancipate him where he lives, he can give him a pass to a free state, and thus put the man in possession of his liberty.

But in most cases, at least in very many, where the plan is made for keeping men slaves for their good, there is a very dangerous principle adopted; namely, that those who are wise in their own estimation may rightfully exercise despotic power for the good of the ignorant, or that the powerful may hold absolute dominion, at their private discretion, for the benefit of such as they deem incapable of taking care of themselves. The good of the people is th' general plea of despots; and yet a despotism is so bad a form of government that no people willingly submit to it. The slaveholding power, being of this absolute description, is an unsafe deposit in the hands of man. As the slave is stolen property, the holder of it is to retain it, not for his own use, but for the owner, till the owner be found; and the rightful owner of a slave is the slave himself. While the slaveholder denies the right of the slave to leave him, while he recovers runaways, while he refuses them free papers, what he does for their comfort may be viewed only in the light of an indulgence.

His refusing to sell them, his paying them wages, is not a legal or permanent arrangement. If he holds them subject to all the liabilities of his other property, and to all the probable caprices of his own mind, he is nothing but a slaveholder. Let him acknowledge all the rights of his slaves, and hold them as such only till he can get legally and morally rid of the forbidden tenure.

Indeed, some would teach that all the laborers of a country ought to be slaves; and they place them virtually in that rank. But this is such an outrage on common sense and good principles, and has been so fully rebutted by the enlightened principles of the times, that we need not stop here to confute it.

9. It is objected, "We do not enslave them; we found them enslaved. We can not deprive a person of a thing of which he is not in possession." As all are born free, every one reduced to slavery, whether in infancy or in mature age, is deprived of liberty. There is a right to freedom, and also the power of enjoying it. Africans have the right to freedom with all mankind, but they possess not the power; for the power is on the side of their oppressors.

10. Some who think it wrong to steal or buy slaves, think it right to hold them when they receive them by gift or inheritance. But it does not follow that because a slave is bequeathed, he must be received. A slaveholder, morally considered, is one who *enforces* the laws of slavery. Others can confer on him only the *power* of enslaving men; to be a slaveholder, he must claim the power and exercise it. A man can refuse all such gifts, or he may exercise his legal power to set the captive at liberty. If he holds man as a slave he is a sinner.

11. It is affirmed "that some slaves have very cruel masters, and, therefore, it is an act of benevolence in the humane to buy and hold them in bondage, in order to better their condition." Mr. Rankin, in his Letters, p. 106, answers the objection thus: "This is a very plausible excuse for the practice of slavery, and has, no doubt, had a powerful influence upon many well-meaning people; but it is as false as it is plausible. Every man readily supposes himself to be humane; hence, every man, on the same principle, would think himself authorized to purchase and hold slaves; and thus the widest door would be opened to the practice of what we admit, in itself, to be unjust. If all the humane would refuse to hold slaves, the evil of slavery would be banished from the world. The example of the humane encourages the cruel, by giving countenance to their oppressions, and their kindness to their slaves keeps out of view many of the worst evils of slavery, and causes

it to assume a mild and tolerable aspect; thus, their partial benevolence becomes universal cruelty.

"If slavery is unjust, it must be criminal to sanction it by our example. Again: suppose we were to purchase from the Algerines an unfortunate captive, whom they were determined to enslave during life, do you suppose that their determination to deprive him of liberty would justify you in subjecting him to similar bondage, with some mitigations of suffering? Certainly you would never so much as think of subjecting such a person to slavery for life, unless his skin were black. But the color of the skin does not in the least alter the nature of the case; the law of love knows no distinction in colors; it binds us alike to regard the natural rights of all men; whatever is naturally due from us to a white man, is equally so to one that is black."

12. Some suppose that slaveholding may be justified by the ignorance, or early prejudices of the slaveholder, and that it is wrong to charge him with guilt because he may know no better. On the foregoing we remark:

(1.) Nothing is more plain in morals than that slavery is wrong. What is plainer than that stealing a man, or seizing him by violence, whether by law, war, or individual force, depriving him of his liberty, his labor, and his rights, is wrong? Is it doubtful that it is wrong to prevent, annul, or violate marriage, beat a man cruelly, etc.?

(2.) He who has inquired into the moral character of slavery, must have a mind of singular inconsistency, if his honest conclusion is that he serves God by becoming or continuing a slaveholder. If slavery is sinful, as this plea of ignorance supposes, it is absurd to think that honest inquiry will not detect it. The slaveholder can not but know, if he reflects, that every man has rights which he is bound to respect, and that slavery is a violation of them.

(3.) The usages of society and a long familiarity with a practical denial of plain moral precepts, may have drowned reflection, perverted the understanding, and stupefied conscience. The truth, however, must still remain in possession of his mind, ready to assert its existence and claims as soon as the question of duty is agitated.

(4.) No man can be a willing slaveholder, without doing violence to his conscience. At best he must *doubt* as to its morality. He that doubteth is condemned.

(5.) What is the cause of his ignorance? What else is it but his slaveholding spirit. It is a covetous, proud, selfish disposition, which leads to the subjection of a fellow-man to a state of slavery. The temper and disposition of Joseph's brethren, when they sold him, compose the temper and spirit of all who engage in slavery. The character of Pharoah and the Egyptians, in enslaving the Israelites, is the character of all slaveholders. They come not to the light because their deeds are evil.

(6.) We do not consign all slaveholders to perdition any more than all bigamists, robbers, thieves, and liars; yet, bigamy, robbery, theft, and lying are sins plainly declared to be such in the word of God, yet not more plainly than slavery is.

13. It is objected, "The laws prohibit the liberation of the slaves, and, therefore, the crime of slavery falls upon the state and not upon the individual." We reply:

(1.) It is not morally right to do every thing that the laws of the land authorize. Otherwise, the manufacture, sale, and use of intoxicating drinks would be right. Licensed gambling, Sabbath-breaking, and prostitution would be right. Human laws can not change the nature of things, otherwise there would be no difference between right and wrong, justice and injustice, kindness and cruelty.

(2.) The fundamental principle of the Declaration of Independence is at variance with the system of slavery: "We hold these truths to be self-evident: that all men are created equal, and that they are endowed by their Creator with certain inalienable rights; that among these are life, liberty, and the pursuit of happiness." So that slavery is condemned by the Constitution, and is only permitted by the administration.

(3.) Although laws have been passed to protect citizens in holding slaves, yet no one is bound either to purchase slaves or to hold them in possession. And although the civil authority did oblige the people to hold them, it would be no reason why they should obey; for the law of God, which expressly forbids slavery, is superior to any human enactment. If a civil legislature has a right and power to overturn the obligations of God's law in one case, it must have the same in all points of moral obligation. It is the doctrine of passive obedience, that we may innocently obey any unjust laws which the legislature may enact. Obedience to civil authority is required of Christians in all matters which are indifferent, or which do not plainly contravene the laws of God. But holding men in unmerited, involuntary, hereditary bondage, is not a matter of indifference, but is directly condemned by the moral law.

(4.) Slaveholders made the laws which prohibit emancipation, and they are the men who prevent the repeal of these laws. They made the government and may alter it at pleasure. Hence, they are the sole cause of the evil.

(5.) In those states in which no slave can be legally freed without the act of the legislature, a master may be unable to emancipate his slaves, and being a slaveholder by necessity he may be one innocently. Such a one may be unable to give his slaves *legal* emancipation on the soil. But he can tell them, that as far as he is concerned they are free; he can refuse to enforce the laws of slavery; he can let them go where they please, he can pay them wages for services rendered to him; he can make them absolutely free, unless others interfere; and for their interference he is not responsible. By doing this, if he can do no more, he ceases to hold or use man merely as property for his own use, or treat the image of God as a thing, although he may be a slave-owner or slaveholder in a legal point of view.

14. It is objected that the negroes are doomed, by the curse of God, to perpetual slavery. "Cursed be Canaan; a servant of servants shall he be unto his brethren," Gen. ix, 25. On the foregoing we observe:

(1.) Before this threatening can be adduced as a warrant for American slavery, it will be necessary to prove that the negroes in America are the descendants of Canaan; that every slaveholder is descended from Shem or Japheth; that each descendant of Shem or Japheth has a right to reduce to bondage any descendant of Canaan; that a prediction is a warrant for its accomplishment. Not one of these can be established.

(2.) We have no ground to believe that the curse respected any particularly than the posterity of Canaan, which is remote from the great slave regions of Africa. We have particular account that the sons of Canaan settled in the land of Canaan, as may be seen from Gen. x, 15–20. The posterity of Canaan settled the land of Canaan, and its neighboring countries. Nor have we any account that any of them settled Africa, except the Carthaginians. The other sons of Ham, Mizraim and Cush, settled Africa. So that the negroes are the descendants of Cush or the Ethiopians, and of Mizraim or the Egyptians.

(3.) The history of Canaan's descendants, for more than three thousand years, records the fulfillment of the prophecy. First, they were made tributary to the Israelites; then to the Medes and Persians; then to the Macedonians, Grecians, and Romans, successively; and finally to the Ottoman dynasty, where they remain.

(4.) The doom did not refer to individual slavery, but to national subjection. There were so few of the posterity of Canaan reduced to individual slavery, that we can not reasonably conclude that to be the kind of servitude predicted. Indeed, it appears from sacred history that fewer of the descendants of Canaan than those of Shem were reduced to individual slavery. People who are subjugated and made tributary, must labor in order to pay tribute, and, therefore, are the servants of their conquerors. This kind of servitude the Canaanites endured to a great extent. This is evidently the kind of servitude particularly predicted in Noah's curse; and our kind of servitude is not found in this ancient prediction. The Israelites were not commanded, nor even permitted, to enslave the Canaanites, but to exterminate their national existence. The curse, then, had no reference to the inhabitants of Guinea, or of Africa in general, the great slave mart of European and American Christians.

(5.) Do the slaveholders know that they are descended from Shem and Japheth? Proof is required to identify their persons. Proof can not be furnished. But, if even this could be ascertained, still it would be required to prove that *each* of the descendants of Shem and Japheth has a moral right to reduce to bondage any individual of Canaan's descendants.

(6.) The prediction of a future event is no authority for the accomplishment of that event. The profligacy and wickedness of Canaan and the Canaanites, (See Lev. xviii, 20, and Deut. ix, 4, xii, 31,) were not the *effect* of the curse, but the *cause* of it. God foretold to Abraham, "Thy seed shall be a stranger in a land that is not theirs, and they shall afflict them four hundred years," Gen. xv, 13. This actually took place in Egypt; but this prediction was not the cause of the enslavement of the Israelites, but the injustice and sinfulness of Pharoah and the Egyptians. The same may be said of the Babylonish captivity, the crucifixion of our Savior, etc. But the predictions were not the *cause* of these events. Even if it could be proved that the slaves in America are the descendants of Canaan, and suffering under the curse, it would not justify the slaveholders, any more than the predictions of murders, robberies, and oppression, would justify robbers, murderers, and oppressors. As well might the sentence of the judge condemning murder be pleaded to absolve the murderer from guilt, as the prediction of an event quoted to justify such event.

15. As a justification of American slavery, it is said that Abraham had slaves which were *born in his house, bought with money*, or *received by gift.*

(1.) It can not be proved that Abraham ever had a slave, after the manner of American slavery, or a slave in any proper sense of the word. It would be a strange sight, to see our modern slaveholders arming their slaves, going out to war with them, and becoming their captains in battle. Where do they make their slaves stewards of their household, or send them on such embassies as Abraham sent one of his servants? These facts alone prove that Abraham's servants were in no such servile condition as Egyptian, Greek, Roman, or American slavery.

(2.) Abraham was a prince possessing kingly authority. His servants were his subjects. This is the only consistent interpretation that can be given of the condition of Abraham's servants.

(3.) As to the servants *bought with money*, he, no doubt, as an honest man, paid for them. To whom did he pay the price? We answer, to the servants themselves, and not to a third person, in the character of *owner*, or *master*, as in the case of American slavery. No instance, from the Bible, can be produced, of any unoffending person being sold, with divine approbation, for a servant or slave, by a third person or owner. Joseph was sold by his brethren; the Israelites were by violence, according to Egyptian law, seized as slaves. Joseph was a *stolen* man. The Israelites were enslaved by oppressive laws. Our Africans were first *stolen* from Africa, and their children—like the descendants of Jacob in Egypt—in America are reduced to slavery, by law and superior force.

(4.) We have no account that hereditary slavery was any part of the state of Abraham's servants. We find no successive generations of slaves growing up in connection with the descendants of Abraham.

(5.) If the mere fact of *buying* infers slavery, and, of course, the right to sell as property whatever is bought, it will prove too much. Jacob bought Rachel; Hosea bought his wife; David bought his wife for the lives of two hundred Philistines. Were these wives, thus purchased, *chattels personal* in the hands of their husbands, to be sold as oxen or asses, or other vendibles? Wherever the words *bought, buy, purchased,* etc., are used in the Bible, they will never be found, when applied to persons, authorizing the fact that the persons so bought or purchased, with the approbation of God, did become marketable commodities, as other property.

(6.) As to the servants which Abraham received by gift from Abimeleck—even if they were slaves—we can not believe that, as a just man, he would retain them in slavery. He did not transmit gangs of slaves to his children. He could not be less just than his grandson, Jacob, and Jacob's sons, who, in the issue, acknowledge their great sin in selling Joseph; and could any one be better than the brethren of Joseph, who would take the stolen boy and crush him with the yoke of slavery?

(7.) But we hear of servants *born in the house* of Abraham; and who could these be other than the children of those who were the dependents of Abraham? Can we believe Abraham was a slave-raiser, like those in the grain-growing slave states, who raise slaves for market, providing that the young brood will be as white as possible, with as much skill as Isaac prepared his rods to produce the piebald flocks? He that can believe this will believe any thing.

(8.) The servants of Abraham, whether those bought with his money, born in his house, or received by gift, like the vassals under the feudal system, seem to be no other than his dependents who were protected by him.

(9.) Finally, were the servants of Abraham, to all intents and purposes, slaves, his holding them will no more prove the right of slavery than his connection with Hagar will justify concubinage. Slavery is expressly forbidden in the word of God; and whosoever enters voluntarily into its practice is a daring sinner. Such a one begins either by stealing a man, or buying or receiving a stolen man, and then treating him badly while he has him. For no man voluntarily can hold another as a slave, and treat him as a slave, without treating him badly.

16. From the permission given to the Israelites to buy servants of the nations round about them, it is argued that we have a right to buy the Africans and hold them in slavery. (Lev. xxv, 44–47.)

(1.) If this text applies to us, in the sense of those who quote it, for the purpose of supporting from it American slavery, then every nation may claim the privilege as well as ours. According to this, the Americans may buy of the English, and the English of the Americans; the English from the French, and the French from the English. If the pro-slavery argument be valid, every man has an entire right to engage in the slave-trade, and to buy and sell any other man of another nation, and any other man of another nation has an entire right to buy and sell him. Thus we establish a universal slave-trade, by which every man may become a merchant or merchandise, and may be bought and sold like a beast, or buy others in this manner.

(2.) The Israelites, by express law of God, were forbidden either to steal a man, buy, sell, or hold a stolen man, (Ex.

xxi,) and this law extended as well to other nations as to themselves. They had, therefore, no permission to buy men and hold them in the relation of slaves, but merely as servants. That is, they bought the services of men from themselves, and not from others. There were no slaves among the Hebrews, according to the meaning of the word slave in America. Nor had they any such word in their language.

(3.) At the jubilee, all servants, of every description, were set free among the Hebrews; and this law applied as well to strangers as to those born in the land. (Lev. xxv, 10.)

(4.) The words *for ever* do not mean the length of time that servants were to serve, but that *always*—a common use of the word *forever*—the permanent or household servants of the Israelites were to be of these nations. There is no hint that they were either to serve without wages, or descend as *goods* and *chattels*, an inheritance of property, like other stock.

(5.) It is a great mistake to suppose that God commanded the Israelites to kill all the Canaanites, or commute death for slavery. Because slavery was so common every-where among ancient nations, even commentators have persuaded themselves that slavery must be sanctioned in the Bible. There is, however, no such commutation of the law, or permission to change it. 1. The destruction of the Canaanites embraced the destroying of their national and political existence. 2. Their right in the soil. 3. Their worship of false gods, requiring them to conform to the worship of the God of Israel. If these things were complied with, their lives were to be spared.

(6.) Hence, they were admissible to Hebrew families as household servants, were candidates for circumcision, when circumcised to eat of the passover, and partake of all the festivals of the family, and to have their wages in advance. By this means they became incorporated into the Hebrew nation and partook of all its privileges. (On Hebrew bondage. See Record i, 123–126.)

17. It is said, "If slavery be wrong, why did not Christ testify against it?"

(1.) Christ did testify against slavery in the very first sermon which he preached, when he publicly announced his mediatorial office. Luke iv, 18, "The Spirit of the Lord *is* upon me, because he hath anointed me to preach the Gospel to the poor; he hath sent me to heal the broken-hearted, to preach deliverance to the captives, and recovering of sight to the blind, to set at liberty them that are bruised, to preach the acceptable year of the Lord." These terms, *broken-hearted, blind, bruised,* etc., represent the different degrees and kinds of misery in which men are involved by sin, from which they need deliverance through a mediator. When Christ uttered these words, about two-thirds of the Roman empire were slaves. We may conclude that one branch of his mediatorial office was the emancipation of mankind from civil and political bondage, as well as spiritual. Man's punishment for sin is just, in relation to God; but, in many instances, mankind are subject to unjust punishment in relation to one another. Christ's office as mediator was to deliver sinners from condemnation in relation to God's law, and from unjust punishment in relation to men and the power of Satan. The design of the Gospel is to proclaim deliverance from the guilt and power of sin, and to enlighten and reform the nations of the earth, so as to bring about their freedom from civil and political bondage.

(2.) Christ in proclaiming the spiritual jubilee, included in it, also, the emancipation of slaves from their bondage. He "proclaimed the acceptable year of our Lord." The jubilee proclaimed a general release of debts and obligations, of bondmen and bondwomen, of lands and possessions which had been sold from the families to which they belonged. All the contracts among the Jews were made in reference to the year of jubilee. The general release which was proclaimed in the jubilee was typical of the coming of Christ, whose office was to proclaim liberty to all that are in spiritual bondage, and to prepare and open a way for all that are unjustly detained in temporal bondage. The proclamation of the jubilee, under the Old Testament, was to the Jews—the same which the Gospel is to all nations. Hence, Christ established, in his public administrations, a foundation for the universal emancipation of slaves. "All things whatsoever ye would that men should do to you, do ye even so to them," Matt. vii, 12. Christ and his apostles declared to sinners the Gospel as the ground of salvation, and also the preceptive obligations of the moral law as a rule of duty, and so explained and enforced the authority of the moral law, as, by necessary implication, to condemn slaveholding, leaving their hearers to apply the general principles of moral justice to particular cases. But the condition of the Christian Church now is very different from that of the apostolic age, when all men were under the Roman yoke. Men under the Roman government might have been either masters or slaves without criminality, while masters were bound to pay wages to their slaves. But slavery can not be maintained under our government without great criminality; because the principles on which we maintain our own liberty and independence, and the grounds on which we make laws to promote justice and equity between man and man, strike at the root of slaveholding, and condemn it.

18. It is furthermore maintained "that the apostles did not forbid Christians to hold slaves." We answer:

(1.) They took it up just where the Old Testament left it, under the sentence of death pronounced on every person who steals, sells, or holds a man as a slave. "The law was made for man-stealers," who are classed by St. Paul with the most notorious offenders, and the law of Exodus xxi is recognized, repeated, and enforced, in all its original strictness of moral obligation; and while the temporal death is not enjoined, the eternal death is clearly threatened.

(2.) If the apostles really approved of a state of slavery, why did they not forbid their enfranchisement? And, especially, since, by so doing, they would find great favor among persons of wealth and consequence, who were the chief owners of slaves. But we find no such prohibition; and if emancipation be such a bad thing as some suppose it to be, we have a right to look for such a prohibition, so as to make the New Testament comport with the laws of slavery, which prohibit emancipation.

(3.) But the apostles do teach that liberty is better than slavery, and enjoins on all slaves to be free if they can.

(4.) All the component parts of slavery are condemned by the apostles. What is slavery but a compilation made up of theft, robbery, injustice, oppression, and the like? And what is more clearly forbidden in holy Scripture than these?

(5.) And when the apostles give directions to servants to obey their masters, and count them worthy of all honor, they teach the general duties of servants who are righteously in the state of servitude, as many are by hire, indenture, or judgment in a civil court. But they do not indorse the justice of slavery in doing so. In like manner, they give general rules of obedience to civil magistrates, without deciding on the character of the government or rules.

(6.) St. Paul does expressly enjoin on masters all unjust servitude: "Masters give to your servants that which is just and equal," Col. iv, 1. If any were unjustly reduced to servitude, as all slaves are, the text requires of masters to set them at liberty.

(7.) Besides, their argument in regard to the alleged silence of the apostles proves too much to be true. It proves that we may enslave all captives taken in war, and in unjust wars, too, as the wars of the Romans generally were. On this ground we had a right to enslave the prisoners taken from the British during the last war, and they had the same right to enslave those taken from us; and so with respect to all other nations.

CHAPTER IX.

THE DOOM OF SLAVERY IN THE UNITED STATES.

1. SLAVERY is expressly condemned by the word of God, in consequence of its inherent and incurable immorality. We have shown that it is contrary to the word of God, because it deprives men of their inalienable rights—because it inflicts innumerable wrongs on its subjects, and is contrary to many Scriptural commands, prohibitions, and principles; because it is contrary to the decalogue, and because, like a bad tree, it produces bad fruit. We have also fully shown that slavery in the United States is, in many of its leading characteristics, identical with the African slave-trade, which has been pronounced by nearly the whole civilized world to be grossly immoral. By the Bible it is, therefore, condemned as highly criminal; and those who are voluntary slaveholders or slave-dealers are, by St. Paul, ranked among the most flagitious sinners—such as lawless persons, disobedient, ungodly, sinners, unholy, profane, murderers of fathers, murderers of mothers, manslayers, whoremongers, liars, perjured persons. (1 Tim. i, 9, 10.)

2. These Scriptural principles, condemnatory of slavery, are embraced in the British Constitution, and are working the emancipation of slaves in every part of the earth. The primary rights secured by the British Constitution are "the right of personal liberty, the right of personal security, and the right of private property." And although slavery was introduced into the British dominions, yet the principles of the British Constitution, in the end, destroyed it. The famous decision of Lord Mansfield in 1772, which pronounced that the slave who touched British soil was free, carried out the teachings of the British Constitution. And the extension of the same great moral principles overturned the nefarious system in the West Indies. Indeed, this

principle of the British Constitution was borrowed from the Mosaic code. No Hebrew was allowed to be a slave within the territory of the Hebrews. Even servitude, by contract between the master and servant, was not allowed to exceed the term of six years; except in those cases where it might be renewed by the servant, and then the jubilee was to end it. Nor could the stranger be held as a slave, but as a servant, and then only till the jubilee. To secure this same state of affairs to Britain, the Magna Charta was obtained, the Bill of Rights was passed, and the succession to the throne was fixed and limited. These great principles have achieved freedom for the greater portion of the British possessions, and they will finally achieve it for the whole of them, and for the rest of the world.

3. The principles of liberty taught in the Mosaic law, and embodied in the British Constitution, were embodied with peculiar clearness in the Constitution and principles on which the American Revolution was based.

The first Congress in 1774 express themselves thus: "We will neither import nor purchase any slave imported after the first day of December next; after which time we will wholly discontinue the slave-trade, and neither be concerned in it ourselves, nor will we hire our vessels or sell our commodities or manufactures to those who may be concerned in it." This, though not intended as a formal law, was, nevertheless, a national vow and covenant against all traffic in human beings.

The Declaration of Independence in 1776 declares: "We hold these truths to be self-evident: that all men are created equal; that they are endowed by their Creator with certain inalienable rights; that among these are life, liberty, and the pursuit of happiness." This is the great basis of a moral and political faith, and is opposed to every form of despotism and oppression.

The ordinance of 1787, for the government of the North-western territory, was adopted for the purpose of "extending the fundamental principles of civil and religious liberty—to fix and establish those principles as the basis of all laws, constitutions, and governments, which forever after should be formed in said territory." Congress established certain articles of compact between the original states and the people and states in the territory, to remain forever unalterable, unless by common consent. One of these articles was, "That there should be neither slavery nor involuntary servitude in the territory, otherwise than in the punishment of crimes." This was adopted by the unanimous voice of all the states in Congress, except one member from New York.

In the Constitution of the United States, formed in 1787, the preamble states the design of the instrument; namely, "To form a more perfect union, establish justice, insure domestic tranquillity, provide for the common defense, promote the general welfare, and secure the blessings of liberty." It is clear that neither the framers of the Constitution nor the people who adopted it, intended to violate the pledges given in the covenant of 1774, in the Declaration of 1776, or in the ordinance of 1787. They do not purpose to confer on Congress or the General government any power to establish, or continue, or sanction slavery any where; indeed, it was generally expected then that the states would soon abolish it.

Thus the great fundamental principles contained in the great national, public acts of the nation, the covenant of 1774, the Declaration of Independence, the ordinance of 1787, and the Constitution of the United States, virtually reassert and adopt the principles of liberty in the British Constitution, and in the Mosaic code. These principles will overturn slavery in the United States. It can not live under them, except temporarily. And however slavery may live and flourish for a time, it has received its death-warrant from the constitutional principles which lie at the foundation of the liberties of the great American republic.

4. These principles, in the United States, have been steadily doing their work, seconded by the moral influence and the Christianity of the people.

Slavery was abolished in Vermont in 1777, as appears from the following:

"That all men are born equally free and independent, and have certain natural, inalienable rights, among which are the enjoying and defending life and liberty, acquiring, possessing, and protecting property, and in pursuing and obtaining happiness and safety. Therefore, no male person, born in this country, or brought from over the sea, ought to be holden by law to serve any person, as a servant, slave, or apprentice, after he arrives at the age of twenty-one years, nor female, in like manner, after she arrives at the age of eighteen years, unless they are bound by their own consent, after they arrive to such age, or bound by law, for the payment of debts, damages, fines, costs, or the like." (Declaration of Rights, chap. i, sec. 1.)

In New Hampshire slavery was abolished by the Constitution, which was adopted in 1783, and went into effect in June, 1784. The operation of these principles has effected emancipation in the other New England states, as well as in New York, New Jersey, and Pennsylvania, and has prevented its existence in the new states of Ohio, Indiana, Illinois, Michigan, Wisconsin, and Iowa.

Add to this, that the evils of slavery, both moral and political, are now discussed with freedom in Kentucky and Delaware, and to some degree in Virginia and Maryland, and even Missouri is beginning to consider the proper character of slavery. Indeed, through the debates in Congress, as well as the discussions in the public papers, the subject is brought before the entire southern public. Thus the principles of the Mosaic code have done much of its work in the British dominions. They have done much in the United States; and they will, through God's blessing, accomplish the design of God throughout the world, in actually proclaiming a jubilee to the whole earth, as extensive as the jubilee of the Jews was to the land of Israel, in proclaiming liberty "to all the inhabitants of the land."

5. Indeed, the statistics of slavery will show that liberty is rapidly on the advance.

In the New England states, the colored people, whether slaves or free, have never been numerous. The following are the statistics for the six New England states:

YEAR.	NUMBER.
1790	16,987
1800	18,652
1810	19,906
1820	20,942
1830	21,379

The following table will show the growth of slavery in the slaveholding states from 1790 to 1850, the latter being estimated from the best data:

YEAR.	NUMBER.
1790	561,527
1800	857,095
1810	1,163,854
1820	1,519,020
1830	1,994,765
1840	2,486,226
1850	2,957,337

6. In the West Indies the slaves decreased in ten years to the amount of fifty thousand, under the exhausting system of sugar-growing. A great decrease is also the consequence of the sugar plantations in the south. It is calculated that about one-fourth of those raised in Maryland, Virginia, and Kentucky, who are transported to Mississippi, Louisiana, and the sugar plantations of the far south, perish in the seasoning, as it is called. Still, notwithstanding the natural effects of the murderous system,

in the destruction of human life, the slaves are rapidly increasing in numbers. In the northern slave states the increase is considerable. And, notwithstanding the drain on human life on the sugar, cotton, and rice plantations, the aggregate growth of the slave population is considerable.

The Helots were frequently murdered in Greece, during the infamous institute of the crypteia. The nightly murders of Jamaica are reported to have been considerable. The United States must be virtuous enough to emancipate her slaves, or wicked enough to introduce the midwives of Egypt, the crypteia of Lacedæmon, or the night-work of Jamaica. But the latter can not, to any extent, be done; therefore, the work of emancipation must be the result.

7. The dangers arising from the continuance of slavery are neither few nor distant. Indeed, the only refuge is in freedom. We may here, on this point, quote some of the declarations of some of the wisest men of the south:

"That the dangerous consequences of this system of bondage have not as yet been felt, does not prove they never will be. At least the experiment has not been sufficiently made to preclude speculation and conjecture. To me, sir, nothing for which I have not the evidence of my senses is more clear, than that it will one day destroy that reverence for liberty, which is the vital principle of a republic.

"While a majority of your citizens are accustomed to rule with the authority of despots, within particular limits, while your youth are reared in the habit of thinking that the great rights of human nature are not so sacred but they may with innocence be trampled on, can it be expected that the public mind should glow with that generous ardor in the cause of freedom, which can alone save a government like ours from the lurking demon of usurpation? Do you not dread the contamination of principle?

"The example of Rome shows that slaves are the proper,

natural implements of usurpation, and, therefore, a serious and alarming evil in every free community. With much to hope for by a change, and nothing to lose, they have no fears of consequences. Despoiled of their rights by the acts of government and its citizens, they have no checks of pity, or of conscience, but are stimulated by the desire of revenge to spread wide the horrors of desolation, and to subvert the foundation of that liberty of which they have never participated, and which they have only been permitted to envy in others.

"But where slaves are manumitted by government, or in consequence of its provisions, the same motives which have attached them to tyrants, when the act of emancipation has flowed from them, would then attach them to government. They are then no longer the creatures of despotism. They are bound by gratitude, as well as by interest, to seek the welfare of that country from which they have derived the restoration of their plundered rights, and with whose prosperity their own is inseparably involved. All apostasy from these principles, which form the good citizen, would, under such circumstances, be next to impossible." (William Pinkney's speech in the Maryland House of Delegates, 1789.)

The following letter will speak for itself:

"*Monticello, August* 25, 1814.

"DEAR SIR,—Your favor of July 31 was duly received, and was read with particular pleasure. The sentiments breathed through the whole do honor to both the head and heart of the writer. Mine, on the subject of the slavery of negroes, have long since been in possession of the public, and time has only served to give them stronger root.

"The love of justice and the love of country plead equally the cause of these people, and it is a mortal reproach to us that they should have pleaded it so long in vain, and should have produced not a single effort—nay, I fear, not much serious willingness—to relieve them and ourselves from our present condition of moral and political reprobation. From those of the former generation who were in the fullness of age when I came into public life, which was while our controversy with England was on paper only, I soon saw that nothing was to be hoped. Nursed and educated in the daily habit of seeing the degraded condition, both bodily and mental, of these unfortunate beings, not reflecting that that degradation was very much the work of themselves and their fathers, few minds had yet doubted but that they were as legitimate subjects of property as their horses or cattle. The quiet and monotonous course of colonial life had been disturbed by no alarm and little reflection on the value of liberty; and, when alarm was taken at an enterprise on their own, it was not easy to carry them the whole length of the principles which they invoked for themselves. In the first or second session of the Legislature after I became a member, I drew to this subject the attention of Colonel Bland, one of the oldest, ablest, and most respected members, and he undertook to move for certain moderate extensions of the protection of the laws to these people. I seconded his motion, and, as a younger member, was more spared in the debate; but he was denounced as an enemy to his country, and was treated with the greatest indecorum.

"From an early stage of our Revolution, other and more distant duties were assigned me, so that from that time till my return from Europe in 1789, and, I may say, till I returned to reside at home in 1809, I had little opportunity of knowing the progress of public sentiment here on this subject. I had always hoped that the younger generation, receiving their early impressions after the flames of liberty had been kindled in every breast, and had become, as it were, the vital spirit of every American, that the generous temperament of youth, analogous to the motion of their blood, and above the suggestions of avarice, would have sympathized with oppression wherever found, and proved their love of liberty beyond their own share of it. But my intercourse with them since my return, has not been sufficient to ascertain that they had made toward this point the progress I had hoped. Your solitary but welcome voice is the first which has brought this sound to my ear, and I have considered the general silence which prevails on this subject as indicating an apathy unfavorable to our hopes. Yet the hour of emancipation is advancing in the march of time. It will come; and, whether brought on by the generous energy of our own minds or by the bloody process of St. Domingo, excited and conducted by the power of our present enemy, if once stationed permanently within our country, offering asylum and arms to the oppressed, is a leaf of our history not yet turned over.

"As to the method by which this difficult work is to be effected, if permitted to be done by ourselves, I have seen no proposition so expedient, on the whole, as that of emancipation of those born after a given day, and of their education and expatriation at a proper age. This would give time for a gradual extinction of that species of labor, and substitution of another, and lessen the severity of the shock which an operation so fundamental can not fail to produce. The idea of emancipating the whole at once, the old as well as the young, and retaining them here, is of those only who have not the guide of either knowledge or experience on the subject. For men, probably of any color, but of this color we know, brought up from their infancy without necessity for thought or forecast, are, by their habits, rendered as incapable as children of taking care of themselves, and are extinguished promptly wherever industry is necessary for raising the young. In the meantime, they are pests in society by their idleness, and the depredations to which this leads them. Their amalgamation with the other color produces a degradation to which no lover of his

country, no lover of excellence in the human character, can innocently consent.

"I am sensible of the partialities with which you have looked toward me, as the person who should undertake this salutary and arduous work; but this, my dear sir, is like bidding old Priam to buckle on the armor of Hector, '*tre-mentibus ævo humeris et inutile ferrum cingi.*' No. I have overlived the generation with which mutual labors and perils begat mutual confidence and influence. This enterprise is for the young—for those who can follow it up, and bear it through to its consummation. It shall have all my prayers, and these are the only weapons of an old man. But, in the meantime, are you right in abandoning this property, and your country with it? I think not. My opinion has ever been, that, till more can be done for them, we should endeavor, with those whom fortune has thrown on our hands, to feed and clothe them well, protect them from ill usage, and require such reasonable labor only as is performed voluntarily by freemen, and be led by no repugnances to abdicate them and our duties to them. The laws do not permit us to turn them loose, if that were for their good; and to commute them for other property is to commit them to those whose usage of them we can not control. I hope, then, my dear sir, you will reconcile yourself to your country and its unfortunate condition; that you will not lessen its stock of sound disposition by withdrawing your portion from the mass; that, on the contrary, you will come forward in the public councils, become the missionary of this doctrine truly Christian, insinuate and inculcate it softly but steadily through the medium of writing and conversation; associate others in your labors, and, when the phalanx is formed, bring on and press the proposition perseveringly till its accomplishment. It is an encouraging observation, that no good measure was ever proposed, which, if daily pursued, failed to prevail in the end. We

have proof of this in the history of the endeavors in the British Parliament to suppress that very trade which brought this evil on us. And you will be supported by the religious precept, 'Be not weary in well-doing.' That your success may be as speedy and complete as it will be honorable and immortal consolation to yourself, I shall as fervently and sincerely pray as I assure you of my great friendship and respect. THO. JEFFERSON.

"*Edward Coles, Esq.*"

8. God's judgments will be against slavery.

The judgments on Egypt for oppression are among the most prominent events of Scripture history. Multitudes of examples in the history of nations exist, in which God maintained the cause of the oppressed by the most signal judgments of his hand. Here is the standing record of God against slavery: "Woe unto him that useth his neighbor's service without wages, and giveth him not for his work."

PART VI.

OBSERVATIONS ON EMANCIPATION, ETC.

CHAPTER I.

EMANCIPATION.

1. In the foregoing chapters we have shown that every system of servitude, which has the chattel principle for an element, is sinful, however it may have originated, whatever checks it may receive by law on the power of the master, and however mildly administered by owners. This is true, in every instance, of slaveholding. It is especially true of the slavery of the United States, which originated in theft and violence, was carried on by piracy, and is perpetuated in each individual instance by depriving innocent men of their unforfeited rights, inflicts many and great wrongs on its victims, and is attended with evil consequences on the slave, the master, and the community.

Emancipation consists in restoring to slaves the absolute ownership of themselves. Emancipation from slavery does not involve the immediate investiture of the slave with political rights, as well as with self-ownership. Such investiture may attend emancipation, but is no necessary part of it. Whether it is just or wise to withhold from any class of persons, a share in the government under which they live, or whether the slaves ought to be set free and endowed at the same time with all the privileges of legal voters, or of filling civil offices, is a question perfectly distinct from the right or wrong of slavery.

Nor does emancipation release the slaves from the restraints of law. Emancipation is a recognition of the slave's manhood—of his right to himself, to his family, to his liberty, to the proceeds of his own labor. It would, also, exempt him from the cruel inflictions of the whip and of arbitrary power, so that his offenses against others should be tried and punished according to the equitable principles of courts of justice. Emancipation would not let the slave loose on society, although it would prevent society from being lawlessly let loose upon him.

2. Slavery can not be reformed by laws.

There are in the system of slavery such offenses against God and nature, that they can not be reformed but by their destruction. Yet, some think that slavery ought not to be abolished, but modified and meliorated by good laws and regulations. Mere laws, enjoining on masters to improve the condition of the slaves, can produce no effectual benefit while the slaves remain in their servile state. Indeed, it is impossible that such provisions could produce any effectual benefit. The power which is exercised over the slaves, and the severe coercion necessary to keep the many in obedience to the few, and restrain them from insurrection, are incompatible with justice or humanity, and are liable to abuses which no legal regulations can counteract. The power which a master has over his slaves, it is impossible for the generality of masters or overseers not to abuse. It is too great to be intrusted in the hands of men subject to human passions and infirmities. The best principles and the most generous natures, are perverted by the influence of passion and habit. Laws may be enacted for the better treatment of slaves; but who shall see to the execution of them? The masters will not; the slaves can not.

Besides, see how any just laws would affect slavery. Let the slave be sent to school to learn the first principles of knowledge; let the right of marriage and its accompaniments be established; let just wages be awarded, and the like; and such laws carried out would, in a few years, destroy slavery, or produce emancipation, which is the same. There are enormities in slavery which can no more be palliated or made right by laws, than murder, theft, or lying can be made right. Who can regulate the act by which a man is stolen? What law can render right the act of selling or buying the stolen man? Laws teaching how to steal, and sell, and buy, and use stolen articles, so as to render all these acts right and just, would be curious laws, indeed. They would be just such laws as would teach men to be righteous drunkards, devout swearers, godly Sabbath-breakers, chaste adulterers, and the like. The plea of Pharaoh would be the best to be used: "Ye are idle; or ye are black; or ye are the offspring of Cain or of Ham, or an inferior race."

3. Nor can any *ameliorations* of the system be a substitute for emancipation, whether the ameliorations of law or of the masters.

Some may teach that the first step is to *lighten* the chains of the slave; whereas, the first step to be taken is to *burst these chains* asunder. It may be plausible to argue, that we ought in the first place to *mitigate* the rigor of slavery, and alleviate the condition of the slave. But the right thing to be done is to resort to the eternal principles of justice, and the plain tenets of the Christian religion, both of which teach to cease to do evil, and not how to regulate matters so as to do evil, in view of lessening the evil determined to be done. It is, however, allowed, that these lauded ameliorations may produce some improvement in the condition of the slaves, or some little acceleration of the means whereby some few additional individuals may acquire their freedom. But the main mass of iniquity, the greatest evils of all, can never be removed by measures of amelioration, because these evils are, either by the blessing or curse of God, so interwoven with the system, that so long as it continues the effects must follow the cause. If, in defiance of mercy, humanity, religion, and truth, men will make slaves, they can not establish a system, by law, by which that sinful condition can be safely and effectually regulated. And though it be exceedingly difficult to get rid of slavery, when it is once established, it is but the common difficulty which attends all perpetration of crime; the greater the offense, the more difficult is the task, both of repentance and reformation. But, if men will repent of their sins, God has promised to give them power to resist temptation, and, finally, to put down the atrocities of the system.

Even though it were possible to extend Christianity through the mass of the slave population, the leading evils of slavery could not be removed. Christianity teaches honesty, industry, conscientiousness; and the best Christian feels most, and sees most clearly the sinfulness of slavery. What Christian father could endure, that his daughters, whom he had educated in virtue, should be subdued for pollution by the whip, or by the *customs* of the system? Christianity could not endure this; and, therefore, can not endure slavery.

Nor is there the least hope that the mass of slaveholders, if left to themselves, will commence and carry out such preparatory measures as will prepare the slaves better for freedom than they now are. This was fully tested in the West Indies. In 1696 an act was passed in Jamaica, in which it was declared that every slave was to be educated and was to receive instruction in the Christian religion. In 1831, after the slaveholders were pressed on the subject of emancipation, they renewed the act, but obviously intending it should be a dead letter. During a period of one hundred and thirty-five years, not only no progress was made, but things were even worse than at the beginning. (See Anti-slavery Reporter, vol. v, 57, and the authorities recited, for much information on this point.)

4. The proper principles and reasons for emancipation should be duly considered. All Christians must admit, as a preliminary basis, that no man has any moral right to make a fellow-creature, innocent of crime, his slave, or his children after him. We, or our fathers, ignorantly or sinfully, permitted the introduction of slavery. Slavery then received legislative sanction, either directly or indirectly.

But legislative enactments could not alter or supersede the decalogue. To the decalogue we must return. This is a first principle, which must not be questioned. The master and the slave are both our neighbors, and we must act toward both as the decalogue prescribes. However conflicting the details, there can be no question respecting the principle. Over the innocent slave, neither the legislator nor the citizen has any just power: we rather owe him retribution than the continuation of his wrongs. If there be any circumstances, arising out of his degraded condition, which may render it clearly not for his advantage that he should be instantly manumitted, these must be carefully inquired into, but in submission to the principle, that there is nothing right, but all wrong, in holding a slave, as such; and if any temporary restriction is laid upon him, it is to be the mildest and shortest, and the very best for the slave's welfare. This is a point of detail for serious consideration on the part of slaveholders.

And as to the slave-owner, he must no longer sanction an unjust usurpation, a palpable breach of the decalogue, or a continued act of injustice or oppression. Our laws may be repealed; but the laws of God can not. Legislators have done wrong; and citizens have done wrong to allow of the wrong. But any number of wrongs can not make a right. We are now better informed, or better disposed, and we must no longer uphold the iniquity because we upheld it in former times. We should all return to just principles, by prompt emancipation, or, in spirit, by such measures conducive thereto as we believe in our conscience best for the slave himself.

5. It is maintained by some, "that when the laws once sanction slavery, it would be a breach of faith toward those who have invested property in slaves, to wrest that property from them by an act of the legislature." We reply:

The same argument would prove that if the bodies, skins,

or bones of men were as valuable articles of commerce as furs and elephants' teeth, and a merchant were to trade in these, he ought by no means to be prevented from doing so.

The right of abolishing slavery has from time immemorial been claimed and exercised by civil governments. They have also claimed and exercised the right to correct abuses; and no abuse of legitimate servitude is greater than making one man the property of another.

Besides, all sound moral philosophers and writers on the first principles of law maintain, that none have a right to establish laws contrary to the laws of God; and all such enactments are null and void from the beginning. And no one has a right to invest property under the protection of immoral laws, directly contrary to the laws of God, such as the leading slave laws are.

If the government has the right of abolishing slavery, it is no breach of faith to exercise this right. If the government has not this right, it can not be properly a slaveholding government, and, therefore, each individual master is then the slaveholder; and certainly he will violate no right of property by manumitting his slaves.

6. A few words on *compensation* to the slaveholders for the emancipation of their slaves may here be uttered, in connection with what precedes and what follows.

The admission of the claims of slaveholders for compensation, as a matter of *right*, and granting aid and relief to them from a liberal and kind consideration of the pressure that may arise from a change of system, are very different questions. We will consider compensation as a matter of *right*, the ground on which it is mostly claimed.

(1.) The government of the United States, as it never had any control over slavery, except in the District of Columbia and territories, can only pay for those whom it has power to set free.

(2.) To make slavery profitable, the slave must generally

be overworked and underfed. But to make reparation for such acts would be the highest injustice.

(3.) Slavery is worth only its profits to the slaveholder; but as much can be made, nay, more, by free labor as by that of slaves, how, then, can the slaveholder be the loser by emancipation?

(4.) If slaveholding has been profitable, the slaveholders, having been so much profited, can afford to lose the slaves. If they are not profitable, then emancipation is no loss, and there is nothing to pay.

(5.) Paying for slaves would be paying for stolen goods, which would be encouraging theft, by paying the thief for his work.

(6.) It is very generally believed, and mostly admitted by slaveholders, that the rise of landed property, in case of emancipation, would more than equal the entire value of the slaves. This is undoubtedly true in all the border slave states; and, as the proprietors of land are mostly the owners of slaves, they would gain more in the increased value of their lands than they would lose by emancipation.

(7.) But compensation is claimed from the wrong quarter. It is the slave, and not the master, that has the right to demand recompense for the many wrongs, injuries, and robberies committed on his person, his labor, his soul and body, or his wife and children. The slave would have a heavy bill against his master, were he to be remunerated for his condition.

(8.) Slaveholders, though they should emancipate their slaves, would not then be as poor as the slaves; for, generally, the masters have lands, houses, and other wealth, besides the slaves. Therefore, after the freedom of the slaves, the poor slaves would have nothing, but must begin the world, while the masters would have their rich possessions left.

The late Mr. Vanzant, who was liable to a fine or loss of

about $1,600, for aiding runaways to escape, replied to an inquiry we put to him, as follows: "If you have this fine to pay, it will take nearly all you are worth." He answered, promptly: "Even then," said he, "I would be richer than the poor slaves whom I assisted in barely obtaining the possession of their own bodies."

As a matter of *right*, then, we contend, that the slaveholders have no right to compensation for emancipating their slaves. What may be done for them as a matter of liberality, is quite another question. And while this topic is now up, the liberality toward the slaveholder, in its claims, may be considered in comparison with the *right* which the poor, emancipated slave could set up, in reparation for the many wrongs and injuries which he sustained during his servitude. And his claim on our liberality, penniless as he is, must be greater than the claim of the slaveholder who has emancipated his slaves, as he has yet his lands, and these probably more increased in value than all his slaves would bring in the slave market. Add to all this the slave is innocent, and the slaveholder is guilty; and therefore the claim of justice on the part of the innocent slave is to be weighed against the claim of the guilty slaveholder, who has no claim of right on us, but merely a plea for the exercise of liberality toward him. If all these things are duly considered, the compensation claimed by the slaveholder for emancipating his slaves will be sustained on very slender reasons, indeed.

7. It is objected, "that others will possess slaves, if we do not; and, therefore, one may as well hold them as another." Or the objection may stand thus: "The Africans are in slavery, and will certainly remain so; and he who holds them does not take away their liberty, for this they never possessed." So, if we do not steal, rob, and murder, others will do so, and we may as well be the thieves, robbers, and murderers, as others are.

Beside, it is not true that the present race of slaves never were free, for they were all born free. The slaves taken from Africa were stolen or seized by violence. The present race were born free, but seized on at birth by the cruel slaveholders and their laws; and this certainly is the most inhuman mode of making slaves that ever existed, and branches off into regular or inevitable slave-growing, the most detestable and the most wicked course of conduct of which fallen man has ever been guilty.

Furthermore, it is far from being certain that "the Africans will continue to be slaves." A large number of those now in the United States are not slaves. The descendants of the Africans in the West Indies, Mexico, etc., have become free. And the day may not be so far distant as some suppose, when the colored people of the United States will be free. And to attempt to continue slavery on the part of individuals, because there are slaves now, is a very insufficient reason for continuing in sin, even could there be a sufficient reason found to do wrong.

8. It is also said, as an excuse for continuing slavery, "I have bought my negroes, paid a large sum for them, and can not lose the amount, as it would impoverish myself and family." Answer:

(1.) Such apologists must have very confused notions of justice. They acknowledge, in the terms of the objection, that slaves have ordinarily a right to themselves; that it would be wrong for one who has a competency to withhold from his slaves the ownership of themselves and the proceeds of his labor; but the moment he invests *all* his property in slaves, his criminality as a slaveholder ceases; or his obligation to release his slaves extends only to the luxuries and superfluities of life.

(2.) Such overlook the *rights* of the slave. They admit he is in a pitiable condition, and not that he is a wronged and injured man, unjustly held in slavery, and demanding his freedom as an inalienable *right.* And this right of the slave is the reason why the poor widow, as well as the rich man, should set the slave free. It is merely a question of title in equity. Who is the owner of the man? Is it the man himself, or some other person?

(3.) If we refuse to impoverish ourselves when called to do it in the discharge of our duty, God may impoverish us in our sins. Every demand for the surrender of property, which is made by the law and providence of God, he is able to enforce, by blessing and prospering the obedient, and by cursing and rendering unprosperous the disobedient.

9. It is objected, "If I manumit my slave, I shall be obliged to maintain him, when he shall be sick, or shall be old and decrepit." The same argument will prove, that we have a right to enslave our children or parents, because we are bound to maintain them in sickness and old age. On the ground of this argument, every county or town, obliged by law to maintain the helpless poor, may enslave all who probably may become poor. The master may free such aged slaves and still support them, or they may be supported as public paupers. Aged persons are unsafe in the hands of an irresponsible master, whose interest it is that superannuated and worthless persons should die.

It is unsafe for the orphan child to be left to the mercies of slavery. His master may now *intend* to emancipate him, as soon as he shall be able to provide for himself; but before that time arrives, the master may change his mind.

In the case in which the master, by law, provides for the emancipation of the child, at a proper age, the servant is no longer a slave. The master has surrendered the chattel principle, or the tenure of property in man, and has transmuted himself into a guardian, or the mere master of apprentices. Yet the interests of such children require, that civil government, and not an irresponsible master, should determine the period of their apprenticeship and the conditions of it.

10. And here an inquiry arises, "Is it right to hold slaves till they can emancipate themselves, by paying with their labor for their freedom, especially when bought with that understanding?" On this we remark: 1. After he had labored, as my slave, the whole period of years agreed on, I should be under no *legal* obligation to emancipate him, and my interest in retaining him in slavery would be a hazardous trial to my virtue. Promises of freedom are often made to slaves and never fulfilled. 2. I might not be able, at the close of the term, to fulfill my contract, for bankruptcy might prevent the accomplishment of my purpose. 3. It is wrong to take a man's ownership of himself for debt. 4. A man whose conscience prompts him to assist a slave to redeem himself, can do so, as he would assist a poor freeman, by loaning him the redemption money. If he is unable to run the risk, he is under no obligation to interfere.

11. Some think it right to hold slaves for life, provided they were bought at their own request, "to prevent their being sold away from their families, or to deliver them from cruel masters," or this is differently expressed, "buying slaves out of mercy to them."

(1.) The buying of slaves, to prevent the rupture of domestic ties, can accomplish only a little of what it proposes in any slaveholding country, however merciful the design may be. A demand creates supplies. If one is thus rescued, the slaveholder soon finds another to fill his place, who is separated forever from friends equally dear. Humanity gained little or nothing from the act of mercy.

(2.) The act of saving a human being from exile is no excuse for subsequently confining him to your own premises, and working him without wages. You can not be justified in robbing a man, merely because you have rescued him from the hands of a robber. An act of kindness is no apology for an act of injustice.

(3.) The motives of those who buy slaves from compassion are either not known or are soon forgotten. Their conduct is soon visible to all the world, lending the influence of their example to the reputation of slavery. Thus, for the sake of mitigating the system, they assist in continuing the system itself.

(4.) The purchasers lay snares for themselves. No one's moral principles and passions are safe, while he possesses and exercises the despotic power of a slaveholder. He is, therefore, not bound to expose himself to so fiery a trial, at the solicitation of pity.

(5.) There are thousands of slaveholders who, under the plea of "mercy to the slave," purchase, sell, and traffic in slaves without scruple or remorse. A distinguished Methodist preacher in the south-west, at the General conference of 1844, exulted in the exercise of his mercy, in the recent purchase of ten thousand dollars' worth of slaves, in addition to his former stock. Most men consider themselves more merciful than others; so that with the word "mercy" on their lips, they may be among the most unrighteous slaveholders, or rather man-stealers in the country. Hence, the plea of mercy, or of holding slaves for their good, is a mere hollow pretense for doing evil, unless the plea is followed up by emancipating the slaves, and preparing them for it, or rather in it, by intellectual, and moral, and economical instructions and trainings.

12. It is wrong to exercise the office of slaveholder, according to the existing slave laws.

(1.) Human laws do not make wrong right. The greatest crimes may be legalized, as has often been done. Thousands have suffered imprisonment, torture, confiscation of goods, exile, and even death, by due process of law. The laws of God, which prohibit such acts, are the right rule of conduct, and not these unjust laws. An apostle long since decided this question, when he said, "Whether it be right, in the sight of God, to hearken to you more than to God, judge ye." On the same principle that the three servants of God, though standing alone, refused to become idolaters, at the peril of their lives, (Daniel iii, 8–25,) they would, were they in power, have refused to support or enforce such worship. The supremacy of God and his law is the fundamental principle of correct morals.

By the law of God, it is wrong to hold men as things, because they are more than things, and have rights of personal liberty and of property, of mental and moral improvement and action, and the invasion of these rights is as truly prohibited by the law of God as any thing else is prohibited.

As the law of God must not be violated, even when the violation is positively required by human laws, and enforced by the heaviest penalties, much less may this be done when human laws merely grant *permission* and afford *authority* to the citizen to do so, if he pleases, without imposing obligation on him to do so. Permission to exercise the office of slaveholder, and support in doing it, are all that is done for slavery by the laws of the slaveholding states. No man is *compelled* by law to become a slaveholder, or to continue in this practice, contrary to his will. Legal permission to practice injustice in any department of human agency, is enough to open the floodgates of iniquity every-where. Such has been the experience of the world in respect to slavery. Permission is given to enslave all who are born in certain circumstances, and presently it is done. As matters now stand, slaveholding, in general, 1. Involves all the sin and guilt inherent in the system. 2. The man who voluntarily assumes and exercises the office of slaveholder, virtually gives his assent to the laws establishing slavery, and becomes the supporter of the institution. 3. Every slaveholder, to a great extent, is responsible for all the injustice and cruelty attending the practice of slavery.

(2.) If slaveholding is sinful when emancipation is permitted by laws, it is also sinful when emancipation is prohibited by law. Human laws may be divided into three classes: 1. Laws against crimes and immoralities. These are of absolute obligation, because they are mere recognitions of the divine laws. 2. Laws of general policy, not founded on fundamental morality, but consistent with it. The obligation to obey these laws results from their *utility* to society. Laws of this class may, in some cases, be innocently broken. Take, for an example, the law requiring certain persons to perform military duty, and imposing a fine for failure. The man who prefers to pay the fine, rather than to disobey the law, is not considered as a malefactor. 3. Laws which violate the principles of the moral law, such as laws enjoining idolatry, forbidding the worship of God, so far from being obligatory, can not innocently be obeyed. We are not only at liberty to prefer bearing the penalty, but are bound to prefer it. Such is the law forbidding emancipation, or which would require us to hold and use stolen property.

(3.) Laws against emancipation, like the bloody laws of Draco, are so inhuman and unjust, that they produce revolt in the minds of conscientious men. When the Quakers emancipated a large number of slaves in South Carolina, the government arrested and sold a few, but the greater number of them, we believe, were not molested. Were Christians generally to take this very obvious course, slavery could not exist any length of time. In Virginia, in 1782, probably through the influence of Methodists and Quakers, a law was passed authorizing manumission. In nine years about ten thousand slaves received their freedom.

Where the emancipation of slaves is prohibited by law, or frustrated by legal enactments, the exact path of duty may not be so easily ascertained. Being unable to emancipate his slaves, he seems to be a slaveholder by a kind of necessity. In such cases he ought to consult for the welfare of his slaves as he would for that of himself and children. If he can not give them *legal* emancipation on the soil, he can tell them they are free, and at liberty to pursue their freedom wherever they can find it. He may hold them as apprentices, hired servants, and objects of guardianship, in the relation of children or wards; yet he can not be justified in claiming them as his perpetual servants.

13. It is in the mouth of almost every slaveholder, "that the slaves are better off than northern laborers." Sometimes the comparison is drawn between the condition of the slaves and the laborers of Great Britain. At other times the contrast is presented between the slaves and the Irish laborers; while, in order to prove the matter conclusively, the slaves are represented as better clothed, fed, and treated than the laborers and manufacturers of the northern states.

The supporters of slavery in the West Indies employed this as a favorite argument, to show that slavery was no evil, or at least a necessary one. Mr. Clarkson, from the Jamaica Royal Gazette, of June 21, 1823, answered the argument, "that the colonial slaves are better off than the British peasantry." We have not space for the whole article of Mr. Clarkson, nor even an abridgment of it, although the facts and the reasoning on them are such as the nature of the case enforces on us. We will content ourselves with a few remarks, in the place of a long argument.

Slaves can be *sold;* but no man, woman, or child in Great Britain can be sold.

The slaves are mere property, like cattle or any inanimate creature. British laborers or servants are not placed in this degrading character.

Slaves can be sold for their master's debts. Can British laborers or servants be sold on account of the wickedness or imprudence of their employers?

Slaves, when sold, may be separated from their wives, children, families, and relatives; not so with British laborers. The British monarch can not separate the husband from the wife, the mother from the child, or the parents from the children.

Slaves are *branded* like cattle, marked on the bare skin with a heated iron, and otherwise marked with stripes. This can not be done to British laborers.

Were it even true that the slaves are better clothed and fed than the British laborers, the case would not be materially different. Neither good lodging, good eating and drinking, or fine clothing, forms the principal enjoyments of an intelligent human being. A mind undisturbed by present or apprehended evils is worth all these pleasures put together. Liberty constitutes the best part of human happiness. The enjoyment of family and home, the respect due a citizen, the freedom and enjoyment of religious liberties, and the like, form the chief happiness of human beings. We can not better conclude this head than by quoting the closing paragraph of Mr. Clarkson's triumphant pamphlet. It will apply with much more force to the American laborer; and the shade of difference among free laborers of all countries is so small, compared to the impassable gulf between them and the slaves, that we may place Mr. Clarkson's paragraph as a triumphant answer to all such pro-slavery pleas, by which the mere animal enjoyments are raised higher than the intellectual and moral.

"Tell a man that he shall be richly clothed, delightfully lodged, and luxuriantly fed, but that, in exchange for all this, he must be the absolute property of another; that he must no longer have a will of his own; that, to identify him as property, he may have to undergo the painful and degrading operation of being branded on the flesh with a hot iron; that he will be looked upon rather as a brute than as a man; that he may have to wear an iron collar or an iron chain, and may be whipped and scarred at the discretion of his master; that, if his said master should get into debt, so as not to be able to satisfy his creditors, he himself must be sold, and his wife and children also; and that they may be sold separately, by which act they may probably be separated forever from each other. Now, tell him all this—for, as far as all these points go, the Gazette will bear me out—and do you think that he would hesitate one moment as to the choice to make? Would he not instantly break out into these or similar exclamations: 'I prefer lying at my ease on a bed of straw, to lying on a bed of down, with an iron collar on my neck to grate it! I would rather forego fine clothing, than wear a chain or fetters, which would take the skin and flesh from my ankles! I would rather give up the pleasure of luxurious eating and drinking, than have a smarting back!' Try the experiment: ask any man or woman in England to serve you on these terms, and give them wages to boot. They would spurn your offer, your meat, and your drink, and your clothing, and your wages—they would spurn them all with indignation. I should be glad to know what our peasants would think or say, if they were to be informed of the wretched condition of our colonial slaves, item by item, in all the melancholy particulars, as I have extracted them from the Jamaica Gazette; or what they would think or say, if they were informed that they themselves had been classed by certain writers as below these very slaves. I doubt not that the British peasants—these lower than the lowest of the earth—would be so shocked at the sufferings of these colonial slaves, that they would consider them as the most abused of all God's creatures. Yes; they would consider their sufferings to be so great, in variety and extent, that they would absolutely lose sight of their own; and you would find them giving way to the most generous compassion, and so shocked at the barbarity of the colonial masters, that they would break out into exclamations of indignation against them. And with respect to the comparison made between their own condition and that of the colonial slaves, I am of opinion they could not be brought to believe that such a comparison could ever have been made; for they would naturally say at once, 'We know that we can not be sold. We know that we are neither looked upon nor treated as beasts. We know that no employer can brand us with a hot iron, or put an iron collar on our necks, or make us work in chains, or whip us at his pleasure. We know that our domestic endearments and enjoyments are our own, and that the king himself can not separate us from our wives and children, so long as we are obedient to the laws.' Happy, happy British peasants, who can hold such language with truth! May you always be able to hold the same language! and may you be forever exempt from the comforts of colonial slavery!" (See Negro Slavery, No. ii, p. 100.)

14. It is stoutly objected against emancipation, that the negroes, if set free, could not take care of themselves; that their idleness, vagrancy, ignorance, and want of skill in arts, sciences, and business, disqualify them for providing comfortably for themselves and families.

The source of this objection is one which throws suspicion around it. Those who make it, in general, have little sympathy for the actual poverty, degradation, hardships, miseries, and wrongs of the slaves in their present condition, nor in their future welfare, till their liberty and rights are talked of. But when these are discussed, they begin to clamor about the wants and poverty of the slaves.

But it is silly to talk about the wants and poverty of

slaves, as if they could be reduced to more poverty in a state of freedom than in a state of slavery.

The same plea of "inability to take care of themselves in a state of independence," was raised against the colonies of the United States, previous to the Revolutionary war. It is the standing objection raised by all aristocrats against equal rights. The principal troubles in the new state of things have arisen from slavery. The very same outcry was raised against emancipation in the West Indies. Almost any state can govern itself, provided it be free from slavery and slavish laws and customs. A West India slave answered the objection of starving in the following manner: "If I," said he to a naval officer, "can support my family by working one Saturday and two Sundays in a fortnight, can not I get my living in ten days, and have two Saturdays for market and two Sundays for chapel?"

As to the form of the objection, when he says, "The negroes would either starve or steal rather than work," it is well answered by Mr. Rankin, in his Letters on Slavery, p. 105, as follows: "Have not many of those who have been emancipated in America become wealthy and good citizens? And where shall we find any instances of starvation among them? Have not the poorest economists among them been able to provide something better than the few pints of corn per week in many places allowed to slaves? How many of them have gone entirely naked? And where have they committed more thefts than have been committed by the whites? And is it not well known that many of the crimes charged upon the Africans have been perpetrated by white men? It appears to me undeniable, that freedom with its worst consequences is better than slavery with its best consequences. The most miserable of those who are free are not so miserable in every respect as are some in slavery. Hence, we say that the tenderness which induces men to hold others in abject slavery, in order to save them from the ruinous effects of freedom, is but a mere palliative for a guilty conscience, and must be the offspring of blind avarice."

As to the supposed *want of employment*, in case of emancipation, there is no solid ground for its support. After emancipation, as well as before it, colored laborers will be in demand in the south; for as free labor is cheaper than slave labor, as most economists allow, the profits of southern agriculture will not be diminished.

And as to vagrancy, there is nothing in the habits or nature of the slaves to warrant any just apprehensions of this—of idleness or criminality—in the enjoyment of freedom. In Africa the negroes are stationary. They are remarkable for their gratitude and fidelity when well treated. Those in the north are in a climate incongenial to their constitutions. And were slavery done away, the emigration would doubtless be to the southern states, or probably to the West Indies, to Africa, South America, or Mexico. Their labor would find little competition in the south from the employ of white laborers. And when all reasonable motives that can induce men to pursue their own interests will be in motion, the colored people, after emancipation, will seek for the more southern latitudes.

And as to the idleness charged on the slaves, it should not be forgotten "that those who work for themselves will do double the work of slaves." In 1791 the Assembly of Grenada declared, that "though the negroes were allowed the afternoon of only one day in the week, they would do as much work in that afternoon, when employed for their own benefit, as in the whole day when employed in their master's service." The proverbial idleness of slaves, induced by the system of slavery, would, after emancipation, be done away, and the stimulus of liberty would lead the slave to the paths of industry.

15. To emancipation it is objected, that the slaves are

incompetent to enjoy liberty with advantage to themselves. We answer:

The liberty insisted on is deliverance from a state of slavery. It is compatible with a state of apprenticeship, of servitude for wages, and of guardianship. They are competent to engage as hired servants to the masters whom they now serve as slaves. They are competent to live out as servants in the same departments of industry in which they now labor. And there will certainly be as great a demand for them as hired servants as now for slaves.

It is said, however, that being accustomed to labor for a master by compulsion, they will not voluntarily labor for hire. To this it may be answered, 1. That the slaves, if liberated, would be under the necessity of laboring for their support and the support of their families. 2. Laws may be enacted enforcing habits of industry, by authorizing the civil authority to bind out, as a hired servant, any who are without employment. 3. If the natural motives to industry, and the legal enactments for the encouragement of labor, should prove insufficient, in some cases, to secure the result, the fault would be entirely the crime of the delinquent, as in many other cases of wrong acts. As the poor, the feeble, the ignorant, the young, the inexperienced, are provided for in a state of freedom, these same relations among those who are now slaves, would soon be found in the ranks of other free persons.

16. The abolition of slavery is declared to be impracticable, on the ground that the slaves are incapable of self-government in an emancipated state.

The present subjugation of slaves is an unlimited despotism. They do not enjoy the benefit of those equitable and benevolent laws which the experience of mankind has shown to be necessary, in order to secure the administration of justice. The abolition of slavery could still leave children, and others who can not take care of themselves, in the care of responsible persons, as parents, guardians, and the like. Others will be generally employed as free hired servants, in the different departments of industry to which they are accustomed. The civil authority will possess the power of enforcing order and obedience to laws. The liberated slaves will not have the means of resistance, if they were in some cases disposed, The civil and military power will be in the same hands after emancipation as before it. This power will then be as great as now, and susceptible of much greater strength by every well-disposed colored man, whose interest it will be to support government.

If the question related merely to the *capacity for self-government,* it has some considerable plausibility; for, if left unassisted to the work of erecting and sustaining civil institutions, they would be unequal to the task. But the abolition of slavery would not require this. Civil institutions, the result of the experience of ages, are already in existence around them. The question, therefore, is not whether the liberated slaves will be immediately able to construct and support a civil government, but whether it will be possible to extend over them a government already established, whose principles are founded on wisdom, justice, and benevolence. If liberated from slavery, those who are now slaves will have the greatest interest in supporting the government which liberates them. By its authority they will hold both their persons and property.

Even the ignorance of the slaves forms no insuperable barrier to their being the peaceable subjects of government, were they liberated. For multitudes of the human race, equally uninstructed, are living in peaceful subjection to civil government, as is the case of many of the peasantry of some European countries. Besides, the African race are inclined to submission, both by their great natural mildness and by long subjection to slaveholders. Add to this, that the abolition of slavery would remove the great obstacles to their improvement, and bring them under the influence of schools of every sort. Thus, the barriers to their improvement would be done away, so that the ignorance complained of would soon be removed. Let time, also, without any impeding hinderances, do its work, and two or three generations would make great changes among the colored people, as it has done among white nations. And if their color will continue to prevent their social elevation in connection with the whites, their emancipation, with its improving results, will lead to their voluntary emigration to countries further south, where their color and social and civil equality go hand in hand.

It is slavery especially that disqualifies men for freedom, by its ignorance, brutishness, and immorality. By theft, robbery, and unjust and cruel laws, men are made slaves, and thus degraded and imbruted; and then, because they are thus ignorant and inferior by this artificial and inhuman treatment, they are denied the privileges of men. This is one of the most crying sins of slavery, first to blind men, and then to punish them because they are blind. It is a most atrocious crime to turn the blind out of his way, even when the blindness is produced by the sin of the individual; but to make a man blind first, and then turn him out of his path because he is blind, is the highest degree of malicious wickedness. We make the man worthless, and then, because he is worthless, we retain him as a slave. We make him a brute, and then allege his brutality as a valid reason for withholding his rights.

17. As to the *reasons* why slavery should be *immediately* destroyed, we may, out of the many that could be adduced, present the following: 1. The institution is wrong and oppressive; and we must not do evil that good may follow. (Rom. iii, 8.) 2. Slavery ought to be destroyed immediately, or as soon as it can be done, because its injuries are immediate and immense. 3. Those who have the power

should abolish slavery, because it may not be in their power to abolish it at a future time. 4. It is likely more easy to abolish it now than at any future time. 5. The sooner it is done, the greater will be the benefit of it. 6. Delays may prepare the way for insurrections or calamities of the greatest magnitude. 7. The national honor of the United States requires the abolition of slavery. These reasons could easily be increased in number and amplified.

Nevertheless, *immediateism* has been pressed, in a certain technical form, with such pertinacity, and so much importance has been attached to this artificial formula, that, according to this theory, the soberest reasons, as well as the most successful examples of emancipation, are represented as no more than sinful expedients to avoid doing right. It would be endless to quote the formulas of expression which are constantly occurring in the writings of this class of writers. And yet, immediate *action*, in view of doing away slavery, should be the aim of every good man. An immediate beginning should be made, not in *ameliorating*, or mending slavery—for this can not be done—but in doing away the very system, which is essentially and incurably sinful. The *abuses* of slavery can not be done away; for slavery itself, in its very nature, is all an abuse or a perversion of legitimate servitude.

On the other hand, *gradualism* may be good or bad, according to the application or practical use we may make of it. The gradual process, which commences without any delay, taking the first steps in their proper order, and prosecuting them successively with all diligence, till the entire work shall be accomplished, is as sober and as Christian as the nature of the case will admit, and is as rapid as God requires. But when the plea of gradualism is taken up as a mere excuse for such instant action as can be had, or is used as a mere show in order to postpone indefinitely, or forever, the forsaking of evil, it is one of those sinful pleas which is of itself an aggravation of the sins for which it is used as an excuse. Thousands of slaveholders, under the pretense of gradualism, continue in the practice of slavery, using this false excuse as a mere cover for their sins.

The abolition of slavery may concern either a state or individuals. The destruction of slavery in the state is to be done by the enactment of new laws, and often, even, by a change in the constitution. It is an individual concern, when the slaveholder is enabled, according to law, to emancipate his slaves. Let us consider each of these.

The emancipation of slavery in the state is one, which may require more or less time to accomplish it, according to the nature of the laws and constitution of the state. When the constitution is to be changed, some time must necessarily elapse to effect this change; and, also, the enactment of laws of emancipation must necessarily cause delay. In the very act of emancipation time must elapse. And even then, the laws themselves may require freedom at a certain age, and for those to be born at a certain time. While, therefore, a strict regard is had to right, as well as to cease from wrong, with the least possible delay, the course is a right one whether it can be accomplished slowly or immediately. It is not so much the *time* taken to emancipate as the principles on which it is conducted, that are to be relied on for the moral characters of the acts of emancipation.

When emancipation depends altogether on the individual, a slow or speedy course may be pursued, according to the circumstances of the case. It is the duty of every Christian to use vigorous and *immediate* measures for the destruction of this whole system, and the removal of its effects. The most simple plan is immediate and complete emancipation. And this is certainly preferable to perpetuating bondage. There are, also, many cases in which immediate emancipation is the master's duty. The plan of the synod of Kentucky presents a gradual course, and is as follows: "The plan, then, which we propose is, for the master to retain, during a limited period, and with a regard to the real welfare of the slave, that authority which he before held in perpetuity, and solely for his own interest. Let the full future liberty of the slave be secured against all contingencies, by a recorded deed of emancipation, to take effect at a specified time. In the mean while let the servant be treated with kindness—let those things which degrade him be removed—let him enjoy means of instruction—let his moral and religious improvement be sought—let his prospects be presented before him, to stimulate him to acquire those habits of forethought, economy, industry, activity, skill, and integrity, which will fit him for using well the liberty which he is soon to enjoy. . . . .

"Neither is it true, that the gradual emancipator sins by his countenancing others in holding slaves. His example can not be appealed to by slaveholders, as a justification of their course. His system is as different from theirs as benevolence is from injustice. Let them do as he does, and slavery at once ceases. He has, by his deed of emancipation, recorded his detestation of their system, and shown that he will sacrifice his gains to his abhorrence of it. But, it is asked, what difference is there, in principle, between his holding them for life? The difference in principle is the same that exists between guardianship and slavery, or between ordinary apprenticeship and slavery. . . . .

"Brethren, there are three courses before you, one of which you must choose—either to emancipate immediately and without preparation, or to pursue some such plan of gradual emancipation as we propose, or to continue to lend your example and influence to perpetual slavery. It is improbable that you will adopt the first course. If, then, you refuse to concur in the plan of gradual emancipation and act upon it, however you may lull conscience, you are lending your aid to perpetuate a demoralizing and cruel system, which it would be an insult to God to imagine that he does not abhor—a system which exhibits power without responsibility, toil without recompense, life without liberty, law without justice, wrongs without redress, infamy without crime, punishment without guilt, and families without marriage—a system which will not only make victims of the present unhappy generation, inflicting on them the degradation, the contempt, the lassitude, and the anguish of hopeless oppression, but which even aims at transmitting this heritage of injury and woe to their children and their children's children, down to their latest posterity. Can any Christian contemplate, without trembling, his own agency in the perpetuation of such a system? And what will be the end of these scenes of misery and strife?" (Address, pp. 25, 26, 27.)

The following argument has been used in favor of immediate abolition: "Slaveholding is a sin; every sin ought to be immediately repented of and abandoned; therefore, slaveholding should be immediately abandoned." We may reply, that slaveholding, in the usual import of the word, and in the sense in which it is sinful, is immediately abandoned by the gradualist, as mentioned before. Besides, true repentance repairs the evils caused by sin. Now, if the master, after legally emancipating his slaves within a short time, and employs the space between in instructing him and preparing him for freedom, who can place such men in the list of sinners without bearing false witness against their neighbor?

But the worst kind of emancipation is infinitely better than the continuance of slavery. And those who are looking forward to sometime to come, in order to get ready for emancipation, will never be ready, but are to be set down with perpetualists.

18. We are sometimes told, "that were the slaves emancipated they would revolt and cut the throats of their masters." We answer, it is the continuance of slavery that endangers the lives of their masters. The slave, when emancipated, would as naturally become the friend of the government and of the master, as he is now the enemy of both. But if emancipated, he would be led to requite this kindness by love. They are much more likely to kill their masters, in order to obtain their liberty, or to avenge the abuse they received while in slavery, than to do it after they shall have received their liberty. And were it true, that the lives of the whites would be in danger by manumission, it is required even to sacrifice life rather than to do wrong to preserve it. But, after all, the fears professed to be entertained from emancipation, may generally be resolved into one of the false pleas so commonly made in order to sustain the system of slavery.

We give below the sentiment of one who practically carried out the lesson taught. And we are certain that, if it be duly considered, the sobriety of the measure must be approved:

"Now, to every one of you who is a slaveholder, and in whose mind exists an apprehension of the danger predicted in the objection, I am bold to offer some means of defense from all harm. Say you have become convinced that slavery, as it exists among us, is a *sin* before God, that you have repented of your own guilt in this matter, and are now anxious to show fruits that comport with true repentance: you summons before you your servants—the fathers and mothers, and such others of them as may be old enough to understand an explanation of the principles upon which you are about to act. You say to them, you have become convinced that the bonds in which you have held them are inconsistent with the laws of love to our neighbor, enjoined by God upon every man; that, moved by the sacred authority of the religion you profess, you have determined to continue the sin no longer. With this, you read and then deliver to them, accurately-authenticated deeds of manumission for themselves and their children. You further say to them: 'I have already given you the most convincing proof I can give of my friendship; it is not my intention to push you out of my doors, desiring never to see you again—exposed to the impositions of a world with whose business you are in a great measure unacquainted, or to the prejudice and scorn of such as cherish for you no kind sympathies. No; if you choose to remain in my employment, I will pay you what is just and equal—a fair equivalent for your services. I will continue to feel for you the love, and extend to you the conduct, of a Christian. I will assist you in providing the means of educating your children for usefulness in life, and should you so choose, in binding them out to profitable trades and employments, I will be your sure and steadfast friend and your protector, so long as your conduct shall not render it improper for me to be so.' I ask you, now, if, after doing this, and kneeling down with them at the footstool of God's throne to thank him for the Christian courage he has bestowed upon you, and to implore his blessing upon the down-trodden and the poor in their new estate, you would fear the flames of the incendiary or the knife of the assassin? Hateful as is to many the very name of abolition, here is its essence; and its safety is sure, because it is the offspring and the exhibition of benevolence. Well, after all this, you say, '*What can we do?*' I answer, you can rise up to-morrow and liberate all whom you hold in bondage. But you reply, 'What effect would this have upon the great body of slaveholders in this state?' I will undertake to say, that, by such a course, small as is your number, you will have crucified the giant sin of our land. His dying struggles may be fierce and long protracted, but his dissolution will be certain, because the death blow will be given. The ministry and rulers of any of the larger denominations of Christians have it in their power, to-morrow, to give the fatal word to slavery in Kentucky, and, if in Kentucky, throughout the slaveholding regions of the Union." (Birney's Letters to the Churches, pp. 22, 23.)

19. But we have many instances in which large or considerable bodies of men have obtained their liberty without any of the calamities predicted by the lovers of slavery. Thus emancipation is practicable; it is practicable, also, without danger; nay, it is advantageous to all concerned.

The slaves that fled from the United States to the British army, during the Revolution, and lived in Nova Scotia, and subsequently in Halifax, and finally in Sierra Leone, have all along manifested the kindest dispositions; so that no inconvenience arose from their emancipation.

At the close of the last war, a considerable body of refugee slaves settled in Trinidad, as free laborers, without injuring any one, or creating the least disturbance whatever.

The same may be said of the black regiments of the West Indies.

The captured negroes, amounting to fourteen thousand, in the colony of Sierra Leone, taken from captured ships, are in a state of improvement which indicates future prosperity and peace.

Nor is the case of St. Domingo an exception. The massacres which attended the revolution in that island, as Mr. Clarkson has shown, were not occasioned, originally, by the slaves themselves, but by quarrels among the white and colored planters, and between the royalists and revolutionists, who, for the purpose of wreaking their vengeance on each other, called in the aid of the slaves. And whatever may have been the disorders which since have harassed that island, they are such as have generally occurred in colonies planted by the French, Spanish, or Portuguese, which were never such as those planted by Great Britain.

In the West Indies, however, we have the matter fully tested, by the peaceable conduct of the slaves after emancipation, and their comparatively-prosperous condition since that time. Nor is it true, as the abettors of slavery say, that the scheme of freedom has failed. Their accounts are the accounts of interested enemies to freedom and to man, while the testimonies on the other side are those of impartial witnesses, and of disinterested men, except that they are philanthropists, and lovers of their race, which can not be said of slaveholders who oppress and wrong their fellow-men.

20. As to particular plans of emancipation, we leave these to those who are particularly concerned, except that we furnish a few observations of general application, leaving the details to those whose duty it is to let the oppressed go free. We remark, that no plan can be proposed, to which objections may not be raised. The position of slaveholders is an unnatural one, and it, therefore, can neither be retained nor abandoned, without great difficulties. To remain in it, however, is to continue in a state of sin; to abandon it, is to do right. No good man, therefore, should hestitate, but ought immediately to commence and follow that which is right and just.

In the first place, slaveholders should disclaim the right of property in man. Then they should act in conformity to this—cease to buy and sell human beings, set their slaves free immediately, by executing deeds of emancipation, and keeping young persons in a state of guardianship, under proper instruction, like apprentices, till they become of mature age. And where the laws will not admit of emancipation, they can, at the same time, renounce all right to the persons and services of the slaves, holding them as stolen property, till the owners can be put in possession of it. And in this case the ownership is not of a doubtful character, as in the case of the title to Indian lands, as some say; for the true owner of the slave is the *man*, who, by theft, robbery, or law, is made a slave. He was not born a slave, nor created a slave, nor redeemed to be a slave, nor made a Christian to become or remain a slave. Every man is born free, created free, redeemed free, Christianized as a free man. And if the legal owner can not restore the slave to freedom in his vicinity, there is enough of free territory to which to conduct him.

And every citizen of slave states is morally bound to exercise his power as a citizen, by his vote, his testimony, his influence, and his exertions, in order to change the constitution and laws of his state, in order that the slaves should enjoy freedom.

The rule, and the principle of the rule, should be *right*. "Do justly; love mercy." It is, therefore, mere pretext, to restrain or control justice and right by the condition of emigration or the inconveniences arising from emancipation.

21. It is stated, and objected most stoutly, by the slaveholders and their aids, "that the abolitionists [that is, those united in antislavery associations] are ranked on the side of insurrection, bloodshed, and the like." This is the customary phraseology, though often much worse, of the slaveholders. Let us see how far this heavy charge is just.

The fundamental principles of the antislavery societies contain no such principles, but those of a directly-opposite character. The convention at Philadelphia, in December, 1833, which formed the American Antislavery Society, declare:

"Our objects forbid the doing of evil, that good may come, and lead us to reject, and entreat the oppressed to reject, the use of all carnal weapons for deliverance from bondage; relying solely on those which are spiritual and mighty through God to the pulling down of strongholds: they shall be only such as the opposition of moral purity to moral corruption—the destruction of error by the potency of truth—the overthrow of prejudice by the power of love—the abolition of slavery by the spirit of repentance."

The following is the third article of the Constitution of the American Antislavery Society:

"This Society shall aim to elevate the character and condition of the people of color, by encouraging their intellectual, moral, and religious improvement, and by removing public prejudice, that they may, according to their intellectual and moral worth, share an equality with the whites of civil and religious privileges; but this Society will never, in any way, countenance the oppressed in vindicating their rights by resorting to physical force."

The American Antislavery Society addressed the public soon after, which makes a similar declaration:

"We have uniformly deprecated all forcible attempts on the part of the slaves to recover their liberty. And were it in our power to address them, we would exhort them to observe a quiet and peaceable demeanor, and would assure them that no insurrectionary movement on their part would receive from us the slightest aid and countenance. We would deplore any servile insurrection, both on account of the calamities which would attend it, and on account of the occasion which it might furnish of increased severity and opposition." (See Statement to Massachusetts Legislature, Letter A, pp. 36–38.)

We might multiply quotations from the acknowledged principles of the abolitionists, to show that they have opposed, as a whole, insurrection among the slaves, and have promoted the principles of peace and good-will. And the fact, that no insurrections have taken place, and none are likely to take place, is a proof of what we assert. Besides, the Quakers, or Friends, both in Europe and America, have been among the prominent abolitionists, and their well-known principles and practice preclude every suspicion of their encouraging insurrection or bloodshed. Nor can we suppose for a moment that they would act in concert with abolition associations, were they in any manner the promoters of evil.

Besides, the writings of abolitionists, without at all indorsing much of their reasoning on facts, and even some of their favorite positions, have brought before the public a vast amount of facts of great importance to the cause of humanity, and even to the best interests of the United States, however unpalatable these are to many or most slaveholders. The subject, too, of human freedom has been, through their means, kept before the public, after making all subtractions for the manner of their doing it.

Nevertheless, the manner of their discussions, and several of their positions, notwithstanding the solidity of their main points, have not succeeded to further the interests of human freedom, but rather to impede it. Unfortunately, Garrison, Scott, Sunderland, and others, have, by their violence and fickleness, prejudiced the cause of freedom. Hence, a large part of those who fraternized with them, becoming or continuing utterly ultra, the other abolitionists separated from them, and carried with them the most sober of the abolitionists, and a goodly, though manageable, number of the ultraists. The new society, learning experience from their failure, and the things which they suffered, have very much changed their course, and even their most exceptionable positions, and are discussing matters very much like the strong antislavery men of the present and former times. We instance the course of the National Era, at Washington, so very different from what it was when it was called the Philanthropist, and published at Cincinnati. The change is for the better, and freedom is a great gainer. Thus, while abolitionism, in its original type in this country, and as long and as far as it has retained and will retain its original characters, may be put down as a failure, the cause of freedom is becoming stronger by the growing co-operation of all good, sound, and prudent men. Nor do we wrong any one when we say, that the strongest antislavery productions are to be found among the writings of men not in the ranks of the American abolitionists of 1833, and downward. Nor do we wrong them when we say that the writings, the measures, and the characters, of the British abolitionists, are far superior to the recent American abolitionists. Clarkson, Wilberforce, Sharp, Sturge, Brougham, Buxton, Lushington, Zachariah Macaulay, will find very few of our recent American abolitionists who will compare with them. The same may be said of American abolitionists, previous to 1833, such as Franklin, Jay, etc., who will take rank in the estimation of all sober men with the Clarksons and Sharps of Britain, and not with the Fosters, Garrisons, and Gerrit Smiths of America, or the George Thompsons of England.

Any one who has perused attentively the writings of the two classes of abolitionists, and has watched their measures, we think, must agree with us in this matter, at least. These are our solemn convictions, after having perused almost every thing issued from the British and American presses on the subject of slavery, since the discussions on the slave-trade and slavery commenced. We believe that any candid person, making a similar examination, will come to the same conclusion.

But, then, there is another side to this question. The friends of slavery have nothing to gain from these facts, which, we maintain, form now a part of the history of the last seventy or eighty years. All the sober argument, and all the sound moral principles, of all classes, are against slavery, from beginning to end; while all the errors, improper agitations, uncharitableness, and even fanaticism, if they will, of all classes of abolitionists, and antislavery men, are nothing else than the fruits of the errors, sins, and inconsistencies of men, who were engaged in a good cause, but marred that cause by these means. Yet all these faults, errors, and sins, and ten times as many, are outdone by the slaveholders, in their course, with the disadvantage of having a bad, sinful cause, into the bargain. The abolitionists have erred some in *manner*, and a little in matter, but they erred in a good cause—the cause of God—the cause of freedom; while the pro-slavery theorists and practitioners have fundamentally erred in doctrine and practice—in morals—in a bad cause—the cause of bondage, ignorance, degradation, crime—of sin.

The murderous element necessarily embraced in the doings of theoretical and practical slaveholders, has fully developed itself in reference to the abolitionists, within the last sixteen years, or from 1834 to the present time. Several abolitionists have been murdered deliberately, whether the murdered men will be entitled to the claim of martyrs or not. And that this was deliberate, at least with some, who can doubt, who has been conversant with the history of the times? Their very breath "breathes out slaughter." Mr. Hammond, of South Carolina, declared: "I warn the abolitionists—ignorant, infatuated barbarians, as they are—that if chance shall throw any of them in our hands, he may expect a FELON'S DEATH."

At a public meeting, in a church, in Clinton, Mississippi, it was resolved, "That it is our decided opinion, that any individual who dares to circulate, with a view to effectuate the designs of the abolitionists, any of the incendiary tracts or newspapers now in the course of transmission to this country, is justly worthy, in the sight of God and man, of immediate death; and we doubt not that such would be the punishment of any such offender, in any part of the state of Mississippi where he may be found."

The Augusta (Georgia) Chronicle declared: "The cry of

the whole south should be death, instant death to the abolitionist, wherever he is caught."

These are mere *specimens*, from the volume which could be made up of such extracts from the southern press. By their own *mouths*, nay, from the deliberate judgments of slaveholders, *printed* in the public papers, they declare they would DELIBERATELY MURDER the men who are called abolitionists, whose principal, if not only, crime is, that they believe all men are created equal and free, and that their inalienable rights of life, liberty, personal security, and the pursuit of happiness, should not be wrested from them. Our whole work, which we are now writing, would not furnish space enough to classify the murderous announcements of the slaveholders in reference to abolitionists and antislavery men, and present the arguments on it, in order to paint it in its true, immoral, sinful, and damning colors. We cut short what might be a long discussion, by praying, "Lord, lay not these sins to their charge!"

CHAPTER II.

DUTIES OF AMERICANS.

1. THE emancipation of our slaves, with the least possible delay, is a duty which the inhabitants of the United States can neither shift nor defer, without danger and sin. It is in vain to say that there are difficulties in the way, as the utterance of this is a mere truism, which no one can deny, and which all considerate men must expect. It is God's command that the oppressed should go free. And neither national prosperity nor guiltlessness can exist, while the sinfulness of slavery remains; and as this sinfulness must remain while slavery exists, as sin is in its very being, the only remedy for this sin is to set the slaves free. The principles of freedom at the foundation of the United States government demand freedom. The moral law of God requires it, under the penalty of death to the nation or the individual who is the sinner. All the precepts of Christianity demand it. The very feelings of a Christian demand it. Even the Roman law says slavery is "contrary to nature." No man is born a slave.

2. The people of the north have very much to do with slavery, and weighty duties are imposed upon them in reference to the abolition of slavery.

In a very important sense, the question of liberty is one of *principle,* not of geography. The nations that are now free are nearly allied to the enslaved nations. And in our country the two parties are diffused all over the United States. There are, in some respects, more antislavery men at the south than at the north. In two states, South Carolina and Louisiana, they constitute a numerical majority. The slaves of the south alone are now nearly three millions. Besides, there are multitudes of white non-slaveholders in the south. The slaveholders of the south are a mere handful, compared with the free whites, the free colored people of the south, and the poor slaves, who are also men, and must sooner or later be taken into the account.

There is scarcely a family in the north, that is not connected with the ties of friendship, kindred, or peculiar interest with the south. With it we have continual commercial, political, religious, and social intercourse. In every wrong and cruel act of the Federal government in behalf of slavery, the north have been partakers, in the persons of their representatives, by votes, speeches, and other acts. The internal slave-trade, the slavery and barracoons of the District of Columbia, are chargeable principally to the north, whose dough-faced politicians have done the principal part of the evil.

If there be in the uttermost parts of the earth tribes of robbers, murderers, and cannibals, we, in America, have something to do with them. It is injurious to the human race, that there should be robbers, murderers, and cannibals, any where. As Christians, too, we are intrusted with the promulgation of the Gospel, which we are bound to promulgate among the human race. Are we bound by the Constitution of the United States, which guarantees *our* rights, to take away the rights of others? Are we called upon to give up fugitives from slavery, on the bare claim of any southern man, before any magistrate he may choose? Is slavery perpetuated in the District of Columbia, by the votes of our representatives, and have we nothing to do with it? Is slavery extended to new states, year after year, and have we nothing to do with it? Is America the breeder and nurse of slaves, and have we nothing to do with this? And who are they who ask these questions? They are the slaveholders, whose consciences and selfish interests are interfered with. They are the merchants who traffic with slaveholders, and are afraid to lose their custom. They are the politicians, who fear a change will deprive them of office. They are a certain class of preachers who have never learned, or have forgotten the ways of the Lord, and who prophesy smooth things. Those of the north have much to do with slavery, because God has given them the means to abolish it, in the right exercise of their votes, their influence, and their Christian principles.

Nor is slavery a mere *domestic* affair. The power of the master is not the power of a father over his children, but the usurped power of a tyrant over the children of other persons. Slavery is not a family government, but the destruction of families. All the families of the earth are concerned, in their proper spheres, to put it down, because it interferes with the family arrangements of the human race. The very *spirit* of slavery is the parent of the *practices* of slavery; and both are an invasion of the dearest interests of the human race. Nor is slavery a mere *southern* institution; because it ramifies throughout the whole United States, by the political, social, commercial, and religious connection of the inhabitants.

Indeed, it is the slave who has a right to complain of northern influence, which has been used so extensively in retaining him in his state of degradation.

3. The political power and influence of the free states, if properly exercised, is sufficient to remove slavery, constitutionally, legally, Scripturally, safely, and advantageously to all concerned, both master and slaves.

(1.) The free states can abolish slavery in the District of Columbia. Congress has power to do this. The moral influence of emancipation in the District would be felt against slavery throughout the Union.

(2.) Congress can prohibit the internal slave-trade. Congress has power not only to "regulate commerce with foreign nations," but also to "regulate commerce among the several states." The drainage of the extreme south in cotton and sugar growing would soon drive to their graves all the laborers, were not the supplies constantly furnished from the slave-growing states. If Congress would employ the same power in destroying the internal slave-trade that was employed in overturning the African slave-trade, slavery must soon fall. The extreme south would soon drive their slave population to the grave, and the slave-raisers would soon be glad to give up an unprofitable business.

(3.) It is in the power of the free states, through Congress, to admit no more slave states into the Union. And though much is already lost for want of exercising this lawful and humane power, during the last thirty years, even the exercise of it in future would be a serious check on oppression and wrong, as well as a support to the cause of freedom.

(4.) Without insisting on mere political equality, the rights, at least, of civil justice and humanity should be rendered to the free colored people. Let the legal disabilities on account of color be done away. Let equitable judicial decisions be awarded in the courts of justice, whether supreme or subordinate. Let the north protect her own citizens, as citizens of the United States. Let legislative remonstrance be continued in against the encroachments of the slave power, and in favor of liberty, and this, too, shall have its influence.

(5.) As a *dernier resort,* let the free states alter the Constitution of the United States, and bring slavery in the states under federal legislation, and then annihilate slavery at once and forever.

4. And the exercise of such power by freemen, in behalf of liberty, is both Christian and patriotic. We are taught in Scripture: "Let every soul be subject to the higher powers. For there is no power but of God; the powers that be are ordained of God; and they that resist shall receive to themselves damnation," Rom. xiii, 2. The people

of this country believed that despotism was wrong, notwithstanding the general obligation of subjects to obey; and whenever a whole people should so see the wrong as to demand its removal, the time for removing it had fully come. Now, who can doubt but it is the duty of these United States to do away slavery? The only difficulty is the time, and manner, and consequences. But were the subject approached under the guidance of justice, mercy, and love, there would be no difficulties in the way to prevent the speedy and advantageous destruction of slavery. But while an unscriptural expediency is the rule, in the place of the principles of right, there will never be found a right time and manner to do away slavery.

5. Duties of Christians.

Pleading the cause of the oppressed and the needy is enjoined on all men as an imperious duty: "Remember them that are in bonds, as bound with them." (See Isa. lix, 13, 15; Jer. v, 1–28; vii, 3, 5; xxi, 12; xxii, 3, 13, 17.) It becomes all Christians, in a calm and Christian manner, to endeavor to convince all men of the sin of slavery. It is important to inform the public mind, in general, on this subject. And although much outcry may be made against this course, it is, nevertheless, the duty of Christians to be on the side of righteousness, and against wrong and injustice.

It is said, however, that the business of emancipation belongs to the legislative authority, and not to the Church of God. To this we answer:

(1.) If slaves were the property of the commonwealth, as such the government might dispose of them at pleasure, and the Church could do nothing in the case. But the slaves are not public property; they are recognized by the laws of every slave state as private property, as much as houses and lands are; therefore, Christians are bound to emancipate, when the laws allow it. And where the laws do not allow it, they are bound, as Christians, to use every right of citizens to have the constitutional and statute laws repealed which give being to slavery.

(2.) Christians, through the light of the Gospel and the influences of the divine Spirit, have a more correct view of the sin of slavery than others; hence, their superior knowledge and experience lay them under peculiar obligations to use their best endeavors to have the slave emancipated. To whom much is given, much is also required.

(3.) If the Church must be governed by the legislature in the admission or non-admission of slaveholders to fellowship, she may be governed by civil determinations in all things; and this would destroy Church power and discipline. The practice of slaveholding comes under the cognizance of the Church as truly as theft does, and willful slaveholding is as truly worthy of excommunication as any other sin is.

Although Christians now may not be able to effect emancipation, they can accomplish it by persevering exertions. There are several things which Christians can do.

First. They can read on the subject of slavery. The Bible will readily show to unprejudiced minds that slavery is wrong. Other books, too, will tend to throw light on the subject. A careful study of slavery, in the light of Scripture, will eventuate in the conviction that slavery is wrong.

Second. Pray over this subject. Earnest, fervent prayer will be a sure directory in coming to a true knowledge of slavery.

Third. Speak on this subject, as witnesses for the truth and against the sinfulness of slavery.

Fourth. Act on this subject. Let those who own slaves set them at liberty. If they wish to remain, pay them wages; if not, let them go. If the laws will not allow slaves to be taught, the conduct of Shiphrah and

Puah may serve as an example: "They feared God and did not as the king of Egypt commanded them, but saved the men children alive." So did Shadrach, Meshech, and Abednego. And thus did the apostles. If the emancipated slaves are taken and sold according to law, you can testify against *man-stealing*. Such an act would be *manifest robbery*, and if exposed might, by God's blessing, do much toward the cause of emancipation.

Fifth. Let us circulate papers, tracts, and pamphlets among slaveholders, that their conscience may be awakened. Much good has been done in this way already, and much more may be expected. Public opinion has already been much changed, and there is every reason in favor of perseverance.

Christian ministers especially ought to be foremost in this good work. Sir James Mackintosh recognizes and applauds the very prominent part the Wesleyan Methodists took in the cause of West India emancipation. In his speech before the Antislavery Society, in 1831, Mr. Mackintosh said: "If the Wesleyans were at present the most conspicuous in the cause, the most sacred principles ought to excite an active rivalship among all clergymen of every denomination, to consider themselves never more effectually the advocates of Christianity, than when they were promoting the abolition of an institution which makes it impossible to observe the rules of Christian morality toward nearly a million of human beings." (See Antislavery Reporter, vol. iv, p. 263.)

Nor will the teachings of Christianity lead to insurrection. And, indeed, this point may be dismissed here, by quoting the following remark of the Duke of Gloucester in 1824, who said: "One of the most painful things that has occurred to me for a long time, is to have heard it stated that it is impossible to teach and encourage religion, for fear you should create a rebellion. Can any thing be so monstrous and so horrible as to say, that for the sake of maintaining any one system of government, you are not to inculcate into the minds of human beings the doctrines of our holy religion; that you are to refuse to give them that glorious light which would make them at once good citizens and good Christians here below, and by which alone they can hope for salvation hereafter? Can any thing be so outrageous? Can any person hear these doctrines without shuddering, and without determining to make every exertion to do away such a system?" (Report of the British Antislavery Society for 1824, p. 109.)

6. Slaveholders, too, have very serious duties imposed on them, in consequence of their participation in slavery. Let them consider what *right* they have to compel a fellow-creature to labor for them without his consent or contract. Let them also consider how many cruelties, wrongs, and acts of injustice are necessary for them either to commit or to be partakers of in enforcing the slave system. Indeed, the African slave-trade is not more atrocious than are some of the practical measures necessary to enforce the slave to submission. Will not *duty* on the part of the master call upon him to lose no time in giving liberty to the slave; and not only so, but also in remunerating him for all his unrequited labor and toil? For, in the place of seeking compensation for setting the slave at liberty, the poor slave is the person who has a right to look for compensation for the wrongs inflicted on him, his wife, and his family.

7. The women of the United States have duties to perform in the great work of human freedom.

Perhaps this can not be placed in a clearer or more forcible light, than to give an extract from the "Appeal to the Christian Women of the South, by S. E. Grimke," herself a southern lady, and well acquainted with the workings of slavery. She says:

"But you may say, 'We are *women*; how can our hearts

endure persecution?' And why not? Have not women stood up, in all the dignity and strength of moral courage, to be the leaders of the people, and to bear a faithful testimony for the truth, whenever the providence of God has called them to do so? Are there no women in that noble army of martyrs, who are now singing the song of Moses and the Lamb? Who led out the women of Israel from the house of bondage, striking the timbrel, and singing the song of deliverance, on the banks of that sea whose waters stood up like walls of crystal to open a passage for their escape? It was a *woman!*—Miriam, the prophetess, the sister of Moses and Aaron. Who went up with Barak to Kedesh to fight against Jabin, king of Canaan, into whose hand Israel had been sold because of their iniquities? It was a *woman!*—Deborah, the wife of Lapidoth, the judge as well as the prophetess of that backsliding people. (Judges iv, 9.) Into whose hands was Sisera, the captain of Jabin's host, delivered? Into the hands of a *woman!*—Jael, the wife of Heber. (Judges vi, 21.) Who dared to speak the truth concerning those judgments which were coming upon Judea, when Josiah, alarmed at finding that his people 'had not kept the word of the Lord, to do after all that was written in the book of the law,' sent to inquire of the Lord concerning these things? It was a *woman!*—Huldah, the prophetess, the wife of Shallum. (2 Chron. xxxiv, 22.) Who was chosen to deliver the whole Jewish nation from that murderous decree of Persia's king, which wicked Haman had obtained by calumny and fraud? It was a *woman!*—Esther, the queen. Yes, weak and trembling woman was the instrument appointed by God to reverse the bloody mandate of the eastern monarch, and save the whole visible Church from destruction. What human voice first proclaimed to Mary that she should be the mother of our Lord? It was a *woman!*—Elizabeth, the wife of Zacharias. (Luke i, 42, 43.) Who united with the good old Simeon, in giving thanks publicly in the temple, when the child Jesus was presented there by his parents, and 'spake of him to all them that looked for redemption in Jerusalem?' It was a *woman!*—Anna, the prophetess. Who first proclaimed Christ as the true Messiah in the streets of Samaria, once the capital of the ten tribes. It was a *woman!* Who ministered to the Son of God, while on earth a despised and persecuted reformer, in the humble garb of a carpenter. They were *women!* Who followed the rejected King of Israel, as his fainting footsteps trod the road to Calvary? 'A great company of people and *women;*' and it is remarkable that to those women alone he turned and addressed the pathetic language, 'Daughters of Jerusalem, weep not for me, but weep for yourselves and your children.' Ah! who sent to the Roman governor, when he was set down on the judgment seat, saying to him, 'Have thou nothing to do with that just man, for I have suffered many things this day in a dream because of him?' It was a *woman!*—the wife of Pilate. Although he knew that for envy the Jews had delivered Christ, yet he consented to surrender the Son of God into the hands of a brutal soldiery, after having himself scourged his naked body. Had the wife of Pilate sat upon that judgment seat, what would have been the result of the trial of this just person? And who hung round the cross of Jesus on the mountain of Golgotha? Who first visited the sepulcher early in the morning on the first day of the week, carrying sweet spice to embalm his precious body, not knowing that it was incorruptible and could not be held by the hands of death? These were *women!* To whom did he first appear after his resurrection? It was to a *woman!*—Mary Magdalene. (Mark xvi, 6.) Who gathered with the apostles to wait at Jerusalem, in prayer and supplication, for the promise of the Father; the spiritual blessing of the great High Priest of his

Church, who had entered not into the splendid temple of Solomon, there to offer the blood of bulls and of goats, and the smoking censers upon the golden altar, but to Heaven itself, there to present his intercessions, after having 'given himself for us, an offering and a sacrifice to God for a sweet smelling savor?' Women were among that holy company. (Acts i, 14.) And did *women* wait in vain? did those who had ministered to his necessities, followed in his train, and wept at his crucifixion, wait in vain? No! no! Did the cloven tongues of fire descend upon the heads of women as well as men? Yes, my friends, 'it sat upon each of them,' Acts ii, 3. Women as well as men were to be living stones in the temple of grace, and, therefore, their heads were to be consecrated by the descent of the Holy Ghost, as well as those of men. Were women recognized as fellow-laborers in the Gospel field? They were! Paul says, in his epistle to the Philippians, 'help those women who labored with me in the Gospel,' Phil. iv, 3."

8. There are also duties which the slaves owe both to their masters and to the state. A slave, while he remains under the authority of his master, is bound to honor him, not because of any moral right that the master has to hold him in bondage, but because of the benefits he receives from him, as well as to exercise the spirit and practice of a Christian. Although the master is a despot, yet, by law, he is all the protector and benefactor the slave has, to protect, feed, and clothe him. For these reasons he is as much bound to obey and honor his master as the subjects of any other tyrant are bound to obey and honor their tyrant, while they enjoy his protection. And while Providence furnishes no immediate relief to the slave, no essential difference exists between his duty and that of subjects to a despotic government. (1 Peter ii, 13–18.) So that by the same right which Roman subjects had to relieve themselves from despotism, the slaves have the same right to emanci-

pate themselves; that is, when divine Providence presents a just and fair opportunity. (See Eph. vi, 5–8; Col. iii, 22–25; 1 Tim. vi, 1–5; Tit. ii, 9, 10; 1 Pet. ii, 18–23.) These passages teach the duties of meekness, fidelity, and charity, which are obligatory on all Christians. These duties are obligatory on us toward our enemies. And these instructions, too, are appropriate to all persons doing service. The obligations to practice fidelity, honesty, and charity depend not on the claims of masters. And the inculcation of these duties does not involve the justice of the master's claims, any more than suffering under persecution justifies this sin.

The slaves in the United States are by no means justified in attempting either insurrection or insubordination, for the following reasons: 1. Their ancestors in Africa were the venders of their own people, just as the Americans and English were the more criminal actors in the slave-trade. This is one consideration why those in bonds should exercise much patience. 2. There are principles and instrumentalities at work which will, at no distant day, produce emancipation. Many millions have been emancipated during the last few years; hence, the day of visitation can not be far off. 3. The peaceable and mild way taught by the Gospel is sure to accomplish this in the best, the safest, and the most advantageous way for all concerned. Many states in the Union have entirely emancipated the slaves. In others it has never been allowed to enter, and the subject of emancipation is now advocated in several slave states, even by slaveholders themselves. Light and justice are doing the work effectually. 4. Because insurrection or unchristian means, even to promote emancipation in the United States, are both uncalled for, and could not succeed; just because the influence and working of right principles are rapidly promoting the end in the best way for all persons.

9. The free people of color, too, have duties connected

with freedom, which lay them under great obligations. The fact that many thousands of them are now free in the United States, is a good first-fruit of general freedom in the United States. The improvement of their condition by self-exertions in industry, economy, and education, is the best way to encourage, promote, and finally effect the freedom of all their colored brethren—wide fields of usefulness, too, in the countries where colored men reside, to promote among them true religion and liberty. And, whatever may be the mere political disabilities under which they now labor, there are doors opened, and about to open, under the providence of God, which will relieve them from all these. Much more is to be accomplished for the entire colored race, by the free colored people of the United States, by industry, economy, and Christianity, than by cherishing too sanguine and premature measures in accomplishing the freedom of their color. The free colored people of the United States ought to be the last either to encourage or join in any measures in behalf of freedom except those which are lawful, just, and Christian.

10. And here it is proper for us to make an appeal to the religion, justice, and humanity of the citizens of the United States. Every true citizen of the United States is bound morally to exert his full constitutional powers to abolish slavery. If the moral sentiment of the state is wrong, he is bound, by all lawful means, to correct it. If his fellow-citizens oppose him in this and oppress him, he is bound lawfully to resist this opposition and oppression. If others are oppressed, he is bound to aid them. Without this, he is guilty of the wrong which society perpetrates. So far as slavery is a wrong perpetrated by society, society is guilty; because they can, whenever they please, change their position. And for not changing it, every member of society who has not exerted his full constitutional power to remove it, must be treated as guilty before God.

It is readily allowed that the personal guilt of holding men in bondage may vary very much. The law of the state may forbid manumission, without securities for life, which the master may be unable to give. The law may require their removal from the state, and the slaves may be unwilling to be removed; or the laws may be such, as to enslave them anew when manumitted. Many such cases could be given. If manumission can not be accomplished, the master may cultivate the intellect and improve their morals, and then may emancipate them as Providence opens the way. He who acts thus, and does not hold the slave for his own benefit or convenience, but merely for the good of the slave, can not be guilty before God, while his public *testimony*, and *practice*, and *endeavors* condemn the system. Doubtless there are many such slaveholders in the south.

And here we may present the "Address to Heads of Governments," presented in 1840, by the London Anti-slavery Convention, to the kings and sovereigns of the world in behalf of freedom. Now, the "*voting citizens*" of the United States are "the kings and sovereigns" of this great country; and they have the power, had they the will, to put an end to slavery. To illustrate the primary sovereignty of the people of the Union, the following circumstance will be pertinent. A Catholic lady of the United States visited Rome, and was very desirous of having a personal interview with the Pope, and conveyed a message to him to that purpose. He sent word back, that this was conferred only on sovereign princesses. The lady replied that she, as every citizen of the United States, possessed in her person a portion of the sovereignty possessed entirely by all the people. This so pleased the Pope that he gladly admitted the American lady to the enjoyment of princely favors, and was delighted beyond measure with the intelligence of the American sovereign princess. Now, all the citizens of the Union are the kings and sovereigns;

so that the following address will be appropriate, substituting, as we will, "Citizens of the United States," to fill up the blank left for the name king, sovereign, or sultan:

"*To the Citizens of the United States:*

"MAY IT PLEASE YOUR SOVEREIGNTY,—'Righteousness exalteth a nation; but sin is a reproach to any people.' Righteousness is comprehended and enforced in this precept of our Lord Jesus Christ: 'All things whatsoever ye would that men should do to you, do ye even so to them.' God has created of one blood all nations of men that dwell upon the face of the earth. We are all, of whatever nation or clime, by nature, the children of Adam. With the great Creator of all things there is no respect of persons. All men are brethren; and, in this relation of brotherhood, they are all entitled to the equal enjoyment of personal and civil liberty.

"Slavery and the slave-trade are a violation of this great principle. The assumption by man of a right of property in man, is in open opposition to the pure and righteous law of God; and, hence, the perpetration of these crimes has ever been found to obstruct the happiness of man. Oppression and cruelty are their certain attendants; they have their origin in pride and avarice, and they foment and strengthen all the evil passions of the human heart.

"In later years the attention of the world has been increasingly directed to these enormous sins; and the Congress of the representatives of the sovereigns assembled at Verona, in November, 1822, declared that they considered the slave-trade 'as a scourge which has too long desolated Africa, degraded Europe, and afflicted humanity.' The slave-trade continues to exist in an aggravated form. It is estimated that upward of three hundred thousand human beings are annually sacrificed on the continent of Africa in the prosecution of this wicked traffic. In addition, upward of seventy thousand are annually transferred from the older to the more newly-settled slave states in the United States of North America. Millions of the human race are also still retained in unrighteous and cruel bondage.

"This convention, therefore, being solemnly impressed with a sense of the national sin of slavery and the slave-trade, and under a settled conviction that the only effectual means to put an end to the slave-trade is to abolish slavery, does most earnestly and respectfully appeal to the citizens of the United States to employ all that influence and power with which divine Providence has intrusted them to secure immediate and unconditional liberty to the slave.

"It is high time that the civilized world, and more especially those nations which bear the Christian name, should purge themselves from these foul abominations. We open our mouth for the dumb and plead for brethren who can not plead for themselves. The Lord Jesus Christ died upon the cross for them equally as for us.

"Great Britain has at length manumitted the slaves in the West India and in other colonies. Since it has been declared by the law of the British government that slavery shall forever cease in those colonies, the happiest results have ensued." (Proceedings of the Antislavery Convention of 1840, pp. 520, 521.)

11. And here we may remark, that while slavery exists among us, we, as a people, are subject to and must receive the just scoffs of the enlightened, the civilized, and Christian world. A writer in the Edinburg Review writes as follows:

"The great curse of America is the institution of slavery, of itself far more than the foulest blot upon the national character, and an evil which counterbalances all the excisemen, licensers, and tax-gatherers of England. No virtuous man ought to trust his own character, or the character of his children, to the demoralizing effects produced by commanding slaves. Justice, gentleness, pity, and humility, soon give way before them. Conscience suspends its functions. The love of command, the impatience of restraint, get the better of every other feeling; and cruelty has no other limit than fear. That such feelings and such practices should exist among men who know the value of liberty, and profess to understand its principles, is the consummation of wickedness. Every American who loves his country should dedicate his whole life, and every faculty of his soul, to efface the foul stain from its character. If nations rank according to their wisdom and their virtue, what right has the American, a scourger and murderer of slaves, to compare himself with the least and lowest of the European nations—much more, of this great and humane country, where the greatest lord dares not lay a finger upon the meanest peasant? What is freedom, where all are not free; where the greatest of God's blessings is limited with impious caprice, to the color of the body? And these are the men who taunt the English with their corrupt Parliament—with their buying and selling votes. Let the world judge which is the most liable to censure: we who, in the midst of our rottenness, have torn off the manacles of the slaves all over the world, or they who, with their idle purity and useless perfection, have remained mute and careless, while groans echoed and chains clanked round the walls of Congress? We wish well to America, we rejoice in her prosperity, and are delighted to resist the absurd impertinence with which the character of her people is often treated in this country; but the existence of slavery in America is an atrocious crime, with which no measures can be kept, for which her situation affords no sort of apology, which makes liberty itself distrusted, and the boast of it disgusting." (Edinburg Review, No. lxi, pp. 146–148.)

CHAPTER III.

PROSPECTS OF FREEDOM.

1. It may not now be amiss to take a survey of the prospects for human liberty in our country, so as to have some tolerably-accurate idea of what awaits us. Are we to have slavery continued among us till it shall be done away by revolution and bloodshed, under the judgments of God? Or may we look forward to the operation of Christian principles, and the Christian spirit, for its annihilation, constitutionally, legally, peaceably, advantageously, and shortly? It is our confirmed persuasion, that, through God's mercy, the latter will be the mode of deliverance, so that principle and the right spirit will counteract the wrong, and save this great nation from bloodshed or anarchy. The following are our reasons for this opinion.

2. The principles of the holy Scriptures, in regard to slavery, as well as other topics, are so diffused in the community as to undermine the system. We allow there is much of wrong Scriptural exegesis afloat in regard to slavery. Commentators for three hundred years, many divines, and others, have found slavery every-where lurking under the Hebrew name, *obed*, a *servant*, or *husbandman*, and the Greek word *doulos*, a *servant.* But these words only rarely mean slaves, and when slavery is meant it is wholly condemned, the same as murder or the most atrocious crimes are condemned. Slavery is condemned in the patriarchal ages in the cases of Joseph and the Egyptians; and among the Hebrews, by limiting the time even of service, so as to prevent it from running into slavery. And so all the teachings of the New Testament, on the subject, reaffirm the Mosaic code, and regulate servitude so as to prevent it from running into slavery, and thus correct the evil principles of slavery, so as to do them away, and bring slavery back to

lawful and righteous servitude. And the spirit of Christianity is molding the public mind, north and south, into this Scriptural form. The fact that some attempt to justify slavery from the Bible is no argument against our position, any more than the teachings of Miller, and such, can claim Scriptural authority. The principles and spirit of Scripture will do their work, and destroy slavery.

3. The embodiment of these truths in the fundamental, constitutional principles of the country, form a bulwark against the continuance of slavery. The Declaration of Independence asserts: "We hold these truths to be self-evident: that all men are created EQUAL; that they are endowed by their Creator with certain inalienable rights; and that among these are LIFE, LIBERTY, and THE PURSUIT OF HAPPINESS." The Constitution of the United States uses similar language.

These great principles of the Constitution and the Declaration are fundamental. They are at war with slavery, and the victory must be on their side, to the final extinction of slavery.

4. Besides, the power of Congress, constitutionally, legally, and influentially, is such as to carry out practically, in the end, the principles against slavery. It is true, there may be some more corrupt political compromises among statesmen, in addition to the many that have already taken place. But the prospect is now, that such bartering of truth, in this matter, has nearly come to an end, and the principle and right will prevail against the atrocious slave code.

5. Slavery, too, is now principally in the power of the free, states. The whole north are antislavery at heart. According to Mr. Calhoun, only about five per cent. of the north are sympathizers even with southern slavery, and even this, we are of opinion, is more than the truth. The northern people are the freest in the world; they, generally, have no

pecuniary interest that binds them to slavery; they inherit the principles of English liberty; they have lived these last seventy-five years under the incessant teachings that all men are born free and equal; they are, therefore, opposed to slavery. They are prepared to do every thing they constitutionally can against slavery; and it is a fair question to ask, Is slavery at all constitutional? Be this question decided as it may, either way, the *moral power* of the free states, united against slavery, would and will end it. There are other kinds of power besides physical and legislative power, and of far more efficacy and efficiency. The moral power of the truth, which is the power of God, is the most potent to effect great changes in society. It precedes, regulates, and controls all other kinds of power. (2 Cor. x, 4, 5.) It overthrew the heathen corruptions of the Roman empire. It overthrew the corruptions of Christianity at the Reformation. It overthrew slavery in the West Indies, and in the greater part of Europe; and it will overturn it also in due time in America. Yet it will proclaim and bring to pass a jubilee for the whole earth which will free all its inhabitants from slavery.

6. Truth is mighty, and will prevail. There is nothing like Christian truth, in its simplicity, to remove error and promote righteousness and justice. Witness the heathen reformations, the Protestant reformation, the temperance reformation, and many others. All the genuine liberty in the world sprung from the Scripture, and has been supported by it. In modern times, wherever liberty has been lost, it has been for the want of the light and influence of true Christianity. Human oppression may spring up under impure Christianity; but the genuine sort will overturn slavery. It did so in the primitive Church. And when the tares of slavery grew up, under corrupt Christianity, in modern times, true Christianity, in principle and spirit, continued its appropriate work of setting at liberty the captives.

In the British colonies, the work is either done or nearly finished. In the United States, it is more than half done.

7. Nor are we to overlook the *power* of God. This has always been exercised, according to wisdom, goodness, justice, and righteousness, in behalf of the oppressed, especially slaves. It delivered the slave Joseph from bondage, and made him governor of Egypt. It delivered the Israelites and punished severely their oppressors. It brought down the haughty power of Spain and Portugal, the modern Pharaohs who opened the slave-trade, so that they are become a reproach to the nations. This same power is still at work on the behalf of the downtrodden slave.

8. But let us especially survey what Christianity is doing for the slave in the United States. According to a certain class of persons, Christianity in the United States has been the bulwark of American slavery. It is true, the phrase used is, "The American Churches are the bulwarks of slavery." Nay, gentlemen, disguise aside, and using words in their right meaning, and considering all things, your charge is, that the Christianity of the United States is the bulwark of slavery. The press has been long, loud, and even pertinacious in maintaining this charge. It has been proclaimed, even by Americans, in speeches, letters, pamphlets, before the British public, and American Christianity has been accused, condemned, and excommunicated, in the mother-land. It is useless here to give names. The thing is so notorious that we may omit further identification.

In the origin of African slavery, by the Popish nations of Spain and Portugal, there were enough of corrupt elements in their religion to carry on the slave-trade and to establish slavery. Indeed, their treatment of the Mexicans and South Americans was identical, in spirit and practice, with the subsequent doings in the introduction of the African slave-trade and slavery, as all know who have considered the subject.

The introduction of slavery into the British colonies was in downright antagonism with Protestant Christianity, and the principles of Christianity embraced in the British Constitution and the British common law. Individuals and companies, influenced by the vile spirit of gain, commenced slavery under the British flag, in contradiction to its Christianity; and yet these same individuals and companies had the address to obtain, for a time, not only the sanction but the support of the government. But the principles of Christianity in the British Constitution, and the spirit of Christianity in the British people, overturned slavery in the British colonies.

The same Christian influence in America has been at work in doing away slavery. One half of the states are already free, some of them by emancipation, as the old states, and some by carrying out Christian, antislavery principles, as the new free states. The present slave states, too, are deeply imbued with the antislavery element, which, in its time, we trust, will work out its results. The principles of action in all these movements were Christian principles, or, in other words, the principles of the American Churches. And leading members and ministers in the Churches were the active agents in this great moral or religious movement. We may now say a few things in regard to some of the Churches, especially those which have spread in the south.

The Quakers have all along been antislavery, yet they generally, in the south, became slaveholders; and for fifty years or more they contended against it, so as to exclude it from their societies. But, then, as they did not act aggressively among slaveholders, to any great extent, their example is not such as to form the complete standard in regard to the disciplinary course to be pursued by a Church, which, like the Methodist Episcopal Church, is diffused both among masters and slaves. The Presbyterian and Baptist Churches took but little part in the assertion of antislavery principles, in the exercise of discipline, in the slave states, in regard to slavery; and yet the address of the Kentucky synod is one of the strongest and most correct antislavery arguments ever issued from the American press. We find no such thing from any of the Baptist bodies or Churches in the south.

The Methodist Episcopal Church, ever since its organization as a whole, has been the faithful witness and actor against slavery; and that, too, we contend, on sound Christian principles. Their rule in their moral code—called the "General Rules"—prohibits any purchase or sale of slaves which either originates or perpetuates slavery. It is as follows: In 1789, "The buying or selling the bodies and souls of men, women, or children, with an intention to enslave them." In 1792 the rule reads, "The buying and selling of men, women, or children, with an intention to enslave them." In 1808, and ever since, the rule reads, "The buying and selling of men, women, and children, with an intention to enslave them."

The declaration, "We are as much as ever convinced of the great evil of slavery," has been, and now is, the avowed doctrine of the Methodist Episcopal Church on this subject. Disciplinary regulations, from time to time, were enacted, requiring emancipation where it was possible. State laws were constantly coming in direct opposition to the salutary exercise of this discipline, which often baffled all the endeavors of the Church to execute the Discipline. Non-slaveholding was a condition required of all office-holders, whenever this could be done. In many portions of the slaveholding states little could be done other than to maintain the testimony of the Church against slavery, and to preach the Gospel to master and slave, instructing the slaves in the best way they could, by preaching, Sunday schools, and catechising the young, planting missions among the slaves, etc. The results of these labors have been very salutary in improving the morals and enlightening the minds of the slaves, notwithstanding all the adverse influences which slavery has thrown in the way.

Ever since the organization of the Methodist Episcopal Church the slaves have been cared for in regard to their spiritual interests. The following statistical survey will show the progress of the Church in this important though neglected department of the population. The number of members, both whites and colored, will be seen at a glance.

YEARS.	WHITES.	COLORED.
1790	45,947	11,682
1800	51,442	13,452
1810	139,336	34,724
1820	217,628	38,753
1830	402,561	69,383
1840	745,534	96,983
1845	985,698	150,120

According to the Minutes of 1845, the Methodist Episcopal Church, just previous to the formation of the Methodist Episcopal Church South, had 150,120 colored members in her communion, and nearly all in the slaveholding states. In the year 1847 the Methodist Episcopal Church South had 124,961 colored members, the white members being 327,284; so that the colored members were more than one-fourth of the entire membership. In 1848 there were 29,254 colored members in the Methodist Episcopal Church. And in both Churches in 1848—allowing a trivial difference between the year 1847 and 1848—the number of colored members was 154,215. We may, while I write—in 1850—rejecting the odd thousands, say the whole number of colored people in the slave states, in both Churches, to be 150,000.

During the last twenty years, or over, many missionaries were devoted to the instruction of the colored people and slaves, although the greater number was connected with circuits and stations of white members. The children, and sometimes old persons, were catechised from a catechism prepared by Dr. Capers for the purpose. The result was a very general improvement in morals and knowledge. Hence, Methodism has contributed largely toward the elevation of the colored people, in spite of the impediments of slavery.

The Baptists of the south have been for many years laboring among the slaves, and many of them became members of their Churches; so that their entire colored membership is calculated to be 100,000.

The Presbyterian synod of South Carolina and Georgia turned their attention to the condition of the colored people in 1835, and pronounced them generally in a state of heathenism. In the year 1835 the Methodist Episcopal Church had 83,135 colored Church members; the Baptists then had probably 70,000; and both together about 153,000. So that the report of the synod was certainly incorrect, doing great injustice to the character of the religious colored people of the south. It is true, as far as slavery was concerned, nothing short of heathenism, or something worse, could exist under its disabilities. But the religious culture of the slaves did not depend on slavery, but was carried on without it, or in spite of it, or at least by its mere tolerance, and that with unwillingness. The statements of the synod, and others of similar character, were taken up at the north by a certain class, and trumpeted over Europe, so that the religious state of the colored professors was considered no Christianity at all. It is most true, that under the regime of slavery true Christianity, to its fullest extent, can scarcely exist. Yet it can, and does exist in much vigor among some, though greatly vitiated in regard to others.

We are glad to learn that since the Methodists took up the subject of catechising, instructing, and preaching to the slaves, other Churches in the south have followed their example with great success, and to great advantage. We find a meeting convened in Charleston, South Carolina, in May, 1845, composed of delegates from South Carolina and Georgia, in reference to the religious instruction of the negroes. The proceedings of the meeting are of the most gratifying character, and fill a pamphlet of seventy-two pages.

The following points were presented in the call for the meeting inviting members, and answers were asked, either in writing or orally:

"1. The number of negroes in your parish or district; and of these, the number that belong to the Church in which you worship, and the number that belong to any other Church?

"2. The number of ministers or religious teachers who labor among them, and the denominations to which the ministers or teachers belong—whether any of them are persons of color, and, if so, under what regulations their teaching is admitted, and what is its practical result?

"3. The number of times and the specific plan under which this instruction is given, and the number of children who are catechised?

"4. The different comparative results observable in those who have grown up under religious training, and in those who have only received instruction as adults?

"5. The degree of benefit apparently derived by the negroes, generally, from the instruction imparted, and particularly as it regards their morals—their tempers, and their conduct in the relation of parent and child, and husband and wife—their chastity—their regard to truth—to the rights of property—and their observance of the Sabbath?

"6. The influence of this instruction upon the discipline of plantations, and the spirit and subordination of the negroes." (See proceedings of the meeting in Charleston, S. C., on the Religious Instruction of Negroes, p. 14.)

There are many points made prominent in the report, which go to show that a course is taken which will, in the end, go far to overturn slavery.

Instruction is communicated orally by the aid of books. The next step will be that the negroes will learn to read, and that they will have books.

Marriage, and the duties of husband and wife, parent and child, are inculcated.

Regard to truth is enjoined.

The rights of property are to be respected.

The Sabbath is to be observed.

These, and many more points inculcated, are truly anti-slavery—they are truly abolition, taking the word in its literal meaning. The Episcopalians have entered on the work of instructing the negroes. The Baptists are supposed to have one hundred thousand Church members among the colored people of the south. In the ten years previous to 1845, the Presbyterians had labored diligently in instructing the slaves.

The following is the award which this report gives to the Methodist Episcopal Church:

"This branch of the Church of Christ has advanced beyond all others, in direct and well-sustained efforts in the colored field. It is the only denomination which furnishes statistical information respecting its colored membership and missionary efforts for that class of our population. The present number of colored communicants can not be less than one hundred and sixty thousand in the slave-holding states. Besides the attention paid by the traveling and local preachers to the negroes in their regular administrations, there are between eighty and ninety missionaries to them, who have under their charge over eighteen thousand Church members and one hundred thousand in attendance on their services. Over one thousand negroes are in connection with the Methodist Church in Texas. The *South*

Carolina conference has sixteen missions to the negroes; the *Georgia conference twelve, Tennessee five, Alabama seven, Memphis nine, Arkansas one, Mississippi seven, North Carolina two, Virginia two.* The catechising of the children and youth is a prominent part of their labor. Dr. Capers' catechism, prepared expressly for the purpose, is extensively used. Four thousand, three hundred and eighty children are catechised in the missions of South Carolina conference, and the expenses of these missions are over $11,000 annually." (Proceedings on the Religious Instruction of Slaves, p. 69.)

9. The great object of Christian missionaries is to instruct men in the truths of religion, and lead them to a saving knowledge of it. This will always lead to freedom sooner or later. So the missionaries in the West Indies taught. In this manner have the ministers of the Methodist Episcopal Church taught; and hence the colored people of the south are advancing under their instructions and the instructions of the other Churches, which prepares the way for freedom. We can not deny our readers the following testimony from Sir Lionel Smith, in behalf of the West India missionaries, who were principally Methodists. He says:

"On my assuming the government of this colony, I strongly expressed my reliance on the whole body of missionaries, in their high integrity of purpose and in their loyal principles. You more than realized all the benefits I expected from your ministry, by raising the negroes from the mental degradation of slavery to the cheering obligations of Christianity; and they were thus taught that patient endurance of evil which has so materially contributed to the general tranquillity. Even with the aid of a vicious and well-paid press, both in England and Jamaica, and, it may be presumed, some habitual confidence in Jamaica juries, the enemies of your religion have never dared to go to the proof of their audacious accusations against you. Gentlemen, the first year of general freedom has passed away. What were the forebodings of its enemies? Where are the vagrants? Where the squatters? Where the injuries against properties or the persons of white men? Out of the three hundred thousand oppressed slaves let loose in one day to equal rights and liberty, not a human being of that mass has committed himself in any of those dreaded offenses. The admirable conduct of the peasantry in such a crisis has constituted a proud triumph to the cause of religion, and those who contributed to enlighten them in their moral duties, through persecutions, insults, and dangers, have deserved the regard and esteem of the good and the just in all Christian countries. The people of England have a right to demand, and will still insist, that the liberty of the negroes purchased by them at such a heavy cost, should be perfectly secured to them, and much remains to be done for them. You may feel assured, however, that the same power which achieved such a glorious national honor as the destruction of slavery in all its dependencies, will ultimately put down the bad laws of petty tyrannies by which the peasantry are still harassed and oppressed." (Proceedings of the London Antislavery Convention of June, 1840, pp. 364, 365.)

The following is the charge of Mr. James G. Birney, in his address to the British public, in his pamphlet entitled "The American Churches the bulwarks of American Slavery." He declares, "There is no systematic instruction of the slave-members of Churches, either orally or in any other way." This is not true. The Church members have preaching, exhortation, and catechising, and other means of improvement.

10. It is readily allowed, that while the slaves are taught much truth, they are also taught much error. But, as truth is great and must prevail, the truth will finally triumph. While it is proper that the slaves should be taught submission to their lot, though a hard one, the state of slavery

seems to be officiously obtruded on them as one which God himself approves of or rather ordains. Bishop Meade, who is not placed in the rank of pro-slavery men, in one of his sermons for slaves, says: "Almighty God hath been pleased to make you slaves here, and to give you nothing but labor and poverty in this world, which you are obliged to submit to, as it is his will that it should be so." This is but a bare specimen of the teachings of error which are mingled with the truth, but altogether gratuitously on the part of the teachers, though this conciliates the slaveholders. But though the slaveholders and their teachers may believe, or affect to believe, that "God makes men slaves," and that "it is his will that it should be so," no slave believes any such doctrine. They will believe that the preacher lies outright, or believe he is greatly mistaken, rather than believe that God makes men slaves. They know enough of Scripture to know that the Bible neither ordains nor sanctions slavery. It is right that the slaves should be taught by the minister to submit to their masters, and that no encouragement should be given them to insubordination, insurrection, or the like. But while they are taught this, they should also be taught to submit for conscience sake, and to bear slavery as a burden, till God's providence makes a way for their deliverance; while their masters, also, for their own good, are to be taught that they owe equivalency for labor, and justice to the slave.

11. We have said it is not proper nor Scriptural for ministers to teach insubordination or insurrection to the slaves, but, on the contrary, to instruct them in the duties of patience, meekness, forgiveness of injuries, etc. And so all the missionaries of the Churches among the slaves, both in the West Indies and America, have taught. The Baptists, Methodists, and Moravian missionaries, in the West Indies, taught in this way the slaves; and when the day of freedom came, in a legal way, by the providence of God,

the slaves, on account of their Christian teaching, were prepared to receive the boon of freedom so as to avoid the evils which were connected with freedom in other places. So the southern ministers and missionaries all along have taught in the United States; and hence the progress that is already made through their instrumentality for freedom. And as to false teachings, so courteously volunteered to please the masters, the masters in many cases give them no thanks for this, and in the end they will all despise this foolish tampering with truth, as many of them even now do. And as to the slaves, no conviction can be fastened on their minds that slavery is right; though they can be convinced that it is best to bear its heavy yoke for conscience sake. And though the *design* of the missionary in preaching the Gospel is not to emancipate, but to save men's souls, by holiness and obedience to God here, yet they must have known that the *consequence* of true Christianity will be that slavery will perish under its influence.

A correspondent of the New York Observer, in writing from Georgia, has high hopes of the plan pursued by the Methodist Episcopal Church, and now carried on by the Methodist Episcopal Church South. May the pro-slavery tendencies of the new Church not mar the work in their hands!

"The most sure and certain means, in my judgment, to elevate the slaves, is through the agency of missionaries, as now pursued by the Methodist Episcopal Church South; and it is to be regretted that the body of Christians throughout the Union can not unite and redeem, by mild means and efforts, the black population from the thralldom of ignorance and superstition.

"The reports of these missions furnish the most abundant proof that the plan will succeed. The Alabama Missionary Society, which is connected with the state conference, sends out twenty-five missionaries into as many different circuits, each one of whom has ten or twelve appointments per month. It appears that eighteen to twenty of these missionaries labor almost exclusively with the blacks. The number of members under the care of twenty-two of these missionaries is three thousand, six hundred, and the number of the blacks who are catechised by them is four thousand, two hundred. Most of the latter are children. Nearly every missionary in his report speaks of the interest manifested by the negroes, and the willingness of the planters to sustain the missionaries. Some speak in stronger terms, and wish for their 'perpetuation.'

"But Alabama is not alone; South Carolina and Georgia are equally liberal. The minute statistics are not before me, but the aggregate number of members in Georgia is forty-three thousand whites and seventeen thousand blacks. There is one county that employs its own missionary, and he has collected six hundred and forty-seven members, and catechises eight hundred individuals.

"At the late Georgia annual conference resolutions were passed, the substance of which is as follows:

"1. The preachers in charge of circuits, stations, and missions, within its bounds, are instructed to require the colored members under their charge, who may hereafter take husband or wife, to be married in due form by an ordained preacher or authorized officer of law, provided the masters do not object.

"2. The performance of the ceremony by any unauthorized person is discountenanced.

"3. Preachers in charge are instructed to pay special attention to this subject in future; and when Church members have heretofore agreed to be man and wife, or may hereafter be married, they are not to be allowed, voluntarily, to separate, except for Scriptural causes.

"Other interesting facts could be adduced, but it is not deemed necessary for my present purpose.

"The spirit of *missions* is in the Churches. The importance and duty of affording religious instruction to the black population, is acknowledged and deeply felt by the mass of Christians. Many at the south are beginning to ask themselves if they have the MORAL RIGHT to withhold from two-fifths of their number the revealed will of God. And, if the fanaticism of the north will allow this leaven to work, we may, in a few years, see its happy effects.

"Let Christians of every name and section unite in permitting and promoting the redemption of the negroes by the mild influence of the Gospel."

3. The controlling providence of God, not only in the working of the moral principles of his word, and the diffusing spirit of Christianity, is at work in producing freedom.

The constant drain in the sale of slaves in Virginia, Maryland, and Kentucky for the more southern states, is an element in the emancipating processes of the times. An Alabama paper, on this subject, speaking in reference to these states says: "Emancipation, however, can not be helped, for such is the inevitable destiny of these states." Another southern paper says:

"A number of the southern states—among them Georgia, Alabama, and, we believe, South Carolina—have severe penal laws prohibiting the introduction of slaves from the adjacent states for sale. By the penal code of Georgia, the introduction of slaves from other states is strictly prohibited, except to residents domiciliated, or those who move in, with the expectation of becoming residents; the penalty is $500, with imprisonment in the penitentiary. The laws are evaded in many ingenious ways, and slaves are daily imported into those states for sale with perfect impunity. We notice that the press in Georgia has taken the subject in hand, and that one of the judges of the Superior Court of the state has called the attention of the grand iurors of his court to the repeated and flagrant violations of the law. The judge held the following positions:

"That the large influx of negroes from other states tended to the depreciation of value of the negroes already in the state, and to the over-production of cotton—thereby lessening the price of the staple.

"That the encouragement of negro-trading was holding out a premium to the states of Virginia, Maryland, and Kentucky, to emancipate their slaves. That they were, under the existing state of things, sending off their young negroes to the south, and only retaining their old ones; thus contributing to the overthrow of slavery in those states.

"That this practice of the introduction of slaves, as before alluded to, was gradually, but effectually, tending to the ultimate destruction of our slave institutions." (New Orleans Bulletin.)

"In all the slave states bordering on the free states there is a growing indifference to the institutions of slavery. This results from a variety of reasons. The land in those states, under the system of agriculture prevailing in the south, is becoming exhausted, and there is every inducement for the planters there to move further south. Slave property in those states is insecure, because of the enticements for slaves to make their escape into free territory. This keeps the planter constantly uneasy and insecure in his possessions. Delaware is about to abolish slavery, Kentucky is growing ripe for a similar movement, and in western Virginia proposals have been made for issuing an antislavery paper. These things point inevitably to the time when these states will be free states; and we imagine that when that shall be consummated, Tennessee and North Carolina will soon follow in the same path. The result will be that slavery will come down further south. The natural tendency of the slaves, under humane policy, is to increase.

The effect follows, that if we have no outlet for them, no soil to put them in, they will be huddled within the extreme southern limits of the Union, and two consequences may follow: by their numbers and the temptations of abolitionism they will be rendered insubordinate, and the result will be too terrible for contemplation; or their excess may make them profitless, and those who own them be obliged to set them free voluntarily, or to submit to any plan for the purpose which may be proposed by the government. These evils may be avoided by taking new territory adapted to slave labor, or, indeed, by taking any kind of territory in the direction of Mexico. The profitable existence of slavery is by no means incompatible with a more temperate region, but is incompatible with a very dense population. We need plenty of soil to render it valuable.

"These are the more obvious reflections which occur in thinking on this subject. A hundred inferior ones might be suggested, and, indeed, volumes of the most momentous matter might be written on it. Our object, however, is, within our usual brief limits for an article, to suggest, with as few words as possible, something which every southern reader, and, indeed, every patriotic man in the Union, should seriously ponder on." (Mobile Herald.)

Robert J. Breckenridge speaks thus: "We utter but the common sentiment of mankind when we say, none ever continue slaves a moment after they are conscious of their ability to retrieve their freedom. The constant tendency for fifty years has been to accumulate the black population upon the southern states; already in some of them the blacks exceed the whites, and in most of them increase above the increase of the whites in the same state with a ratio that is absolutely startling; [the annual increase in the United States is sixty thousand;] the slave population could bring into action a larger portion of efficient men, perfectly inured to hardships, to the climate, and privations, than any other population in the world; and they have, in distant sections, and on various occasions, manifested already a desperate purpose to shake off the yoke. In such an event we ask not any heart to decide where would human sympathy and earthly glory stand; we ask not, in the fearful words of Jefferson, what attribute of Jehovah would allow him to take part with us; we ask only—and the answer settles the argument—which is like to be the stronger side?" (African Repository, January, 1834.)

CHAPTER IV.

CONCLUDING AND PRACTICAL REFLECTIONS.

1. After presenting to our readers the foregoing chapters on the sinfulness of slavery, it now remains to conclude this subject with some appropriate remarks.

We have seen what slavery is. It deprives a man of his liberty, prevents him from acquiring property, compels him to work without wages, deprives him of the right of marriage, of education, and religion, inflicts on him numerous and grievous wrongs, and leaves the slave without redress, as he is subject to the will of his master. We need not here give a more full enumeration of the character of slavery, as this has already been done.

2. We have also presented our readers with the proofs of the sinfulness of slavery. We have proved it to be wrong in its origin, and that it possesses all the moral evils of the African slave-trade. It was shown that slavery is sinful from its injustice, or its depriving men of their natural rights—such as liberty, the right of property, the right of personal security, the benefits of education, religious privileges, marriage, and civil disabilities which involve injustice. The sinfulness of slavery was shown from the wrongs which it inflicts, its punishments, and cruelties. It was shown to be contrary to many Scriptural prohibitions and commands, Scriptural principles and privileges, as well as the decalogue itself, and the very spirit of Christianity. From its effects on masters, slaves, and all concerned in it, it was shown to be sinful.

3. Our hereditary slavery, or the enslavement of infants, is monstrously unjust and inhuman. Every just and liberal mind must revolt at hereditary slavery, independently of the crimes found in its origin, or in the abuses of the master's powers. And this cruel privation of freedom, and

of almost every civil and human right, is the punishment of no crime, nor the consequence of hostility in war, but imposed on the innocent and helpless by violence alone, and maintained for no other object than the master's profit or convenience. Were our merchants to buy captives from the pirates who carry on the slave-trade, and sell them here to work for farmers and manufacturers, and were the purchasers to hold them and their children forever in bondage, and take their work without wages, the case would be morally the same. Yet the pirates are hanged, because they bring the slaves from Africa; while those who do the very same wrong here—that is, make a slave of a free person—escape the halter. For it must not now be a mooted question in the United States, that all men are "born free and equal," and that no one is born a slave. Indeed, the Roman law declared that slavery was *contra naturam—contrary to nature.* We sin because our fathers sinned, and because multitudes of our own generation sin in the same way without discredit. When slavery shall cease to be tolerated by human laws, and live in history alone, men will look back on it with horror, and wonder at the darkness and depravity of the times.

4. We know the claim of *compensation* is set up on the part of the master as a condition of emancipation. But the slave is the person who is wronged, and no such plea can be a just bar against his enjoyment of freedom. The slaveholders and the civil powers may settle their business as they think best, or as they can, as to claims of indemnity for manumission; but the slave should have his freedom. And if he is content to let the masters and government off without damages for the high criminal and civil wrongs committed against him, the act is a generous one. We care little how this matter be disposed of between the civil powers. But we claim that mere injustice in reference to the slave might cease by granting him his freedom;

especially as he is willing to relinquish claims for the assault and battery, and false imprisonment, by which he was unnaturally, nay, contrary to nature, made a slave as soon as he was born, though born free, just as all other men are born free.

5. The judgments of God must sooner or later overtake those who are engaged in the sin of slavery. "The people of the land have used oppression, and have vexed the poor and needy; yea, they have oppressed the stranger wrongfully. Therefore have I poured out my indignation upon them: I have consumed them with the fire of my wrath. Their own way have I recompensed upon their heads, saith the Lord God," Ezekiel xxii, 29, 31. We must here repeat and adopt a sentiment of the Edinburg Review, that "every American who loves his country should dedicate his whole life, and every faculty of his soul, to efface the foul stain of slavery from its character."

6. How clearly was the sin of slavery punished or visited on the brethren of Joseph! They sold their brother, or they made a slave of him. They were grievously harassed with adverse providences till they repented of their sin. In their penitence they cried, "And they said one to another, we are verily guilty concerning our brother, in that we saw the anguish of his soul, when he besought us, and we would not hear! Therefore is this distress come upon us. And Reuben answered them, saying, Spake I not unto you, saying, do not sin against the child, and ye would not hear? Therefore, behold, also his blood is required," Genesis xlii, 21, 22. Twenty-two years previous to this time they sold their brother, and conscience seems to have been asleep all that time, till the prospective judgments of God awakened them. Never was there a truer picture of slavery. It hardens the heart, and it is only when genuine repentance fills the soul that slaveholders cry out, "We are verily guilty."

7. The judgments of God on Egypt, so circumstantially narrated in Scripture, may serve as an example of what may be expected from a course of enslaving mankind. As the moral principles of the Divine government can not change, every nation following the example of the Egyptians, must, without repentance and reformation, be punished in like manner.

8. The kingdoms of France, Spain, Portugal, and Holland, are also examples of the retributive justice of God visiting for the sin of slavery, on the African coast and in their distant colonies. The infidel or profane may join the slaveholder and scoff at this view of the subject; but we must insist that there are plain indications of wrath manifested against these nations. The fate of the Bourbon kings are sufficiently clear examples. Portugal is no longer a slave mistress. Spain has Cuba alone remaining, and it seems to be on the eve of retreat from the Spanish crown.

9. It were easy to show what calamities and threatened judgments were impending over England while she supported or tolerated slavery. It would be equally easy to show, that since she has acknowledged and carried into practical effect the principles of justice and right, in the good work of emancipation, that a manifest change for the better has taken place in her national affairs.

10. Few can be so blind as not to see, that in the United States the nation has greatly suffered, and is still suffering, on account of the sins of slavery. Ignorance, immorality, and degradation, are manifest on the one hand, and pride, reckless sinning, and Lynch law on the other hand. And should the spirit of slavery prevail, what could follow less than the destruction of American liberties, and anarchy such as now reigns in Mexico and the South American states? But the knowledge of the truth, a deep conviction of the wrongs of slavery, and a partial reformation, give omens of a thorough repentance, and an entire abandonment of the

system of slavery. And the day is not far distant, we trust, when slavery shall cease to exist in the land of equal rights.

11. The duty of the United States, and of every citizen in it, is clear; namely, to use all constitutional, lawful, and just measures to put an end to slavery. Much is done, much remains to be done by every one who loves the best interests of this great country. In no country under heaven were there or are there more favorable circumstances to encourage emancipation. In the event of freedom, there is ample room and need for the free services of every liberated man. And on the increase of population, or any serious difficulties arising on account of color, whether real or imaginary, there are vast regions in Africa where the colored man can find a congenial home, with far less and fewer difficulties than those accompanying the voluntary emigrations from Europe. Truly, God hath opened a door of escape from all serious difficulties, so that the work of freedom may go on without let or hinderance, without commotion or insurrection, while all the departments of agriculture, commerce, manufactures, etc., may proceed with great ease, peace, and prosperity.

12. In this great and good work every citizen and inhabitant of the United States may take a part. Slaveholders may unite in it—as many of them have done—and be great gainers, temporally and spiritually, in the end, and their posterity after them. Non-slaveholders, as members of the great American confederacy, and, therefore, more or less participants in the evils of slavery, are called upon to unite in the most liberal measures to free the country from the curses of slavery. The bondman, too, is called on to wait patiently and suffer on, till principle can work out its theorems, and practice solve the problem of deliverance. We conclude by saying, let every man do his duty to the utmost; let him do justly, love mercy, and walk humbly

with his God. When that shall be the case, the jubilee of freedom shall be proclaimed throughout the land; and then the banners of American liberty will cease to wave over slaves, because all shall be free.

LIST OF BOOKS AND PAMPHLETS,

CONTAINING THE TITLES OF THE PRINCIPAL AUTHORS CONSULTED, CITED, OR QUOTED IN THIS WORK.

This list does not include Weekly Periodicals, all of which, of any importance, have been read, considered, or quoted, and referred to when necessary.

ANTISLAVERY RECORD, 3 vols., 12 mo. New York, 1836.

AXSON, REV. J. S. K. Association for the Religious Instruction of the Negroes, in Liberty County, Georgia. Savannah, 1843.

APPEAL against the American Antislavery Society, by a citizen of New York: [D. M. Reese.]

ADDRESS to the Ladies of Ohio.

ADDRESS to the Churches, in relation to Slavery.

AMERICAN ANTISLAVERY SOCIETY:
- Fourth Annual Report. New York, 1837.
- Sixth Annual Report. New York, 1839.
- Report of 1847.
- Report of 1848.
- Constitution, Declaration, and Address of. N. York, 1838.

AFRICANS TAKEN IN THE AMISTAD: a Congressional Document. New York, 1840.

ADDRESS to the Friends of Constitutional Liberty on the Violation of the U. S. House of Representatives of the Right of Petition. New York, 1840.

ANCIENT LANDMARKS, or the Essential Elements of Civil and Religious Liberty. Dedicated to the Young Men of New England. By a Pastor. Middletown, 1838.

ADDRESS to the Senators and Representatives of the Free States in the Congress of the United States, by the Convention of American Women. Philadelphia, 1838.

ACCOUNT of the Receipts and Disbursements of the Antislavery Society for the years 1823–1826.

ANTISLAVERY SOCIETY, British, First Annual Report of. London, 1824.
- Second do. do., London, 1825.
- Third do. do., London, 1826.
- Ninth do do., London, 1848.

ABSTRACT of the Acts of Parliament for abolishing the Slave-Trade, and the Orders in Council for them. London, 1810.

ACCOUNT of a Shooting Excursion in Jamaica. London, 1824.

ADDRESS to the People of Britain and Ireland, April, 1831.

ANTISLAVERY REPORTER, from June, 1825, to February, 1833, in 5 vols., 8vo., Ed. Z. Macaulay. London, 1825–1833.

ADDRESS of Congregational Union to Christians in America. New York, 1840.

AMERICAN S. S. UNION. Letters on a Book dropped from the Catalogue. New York, 1848.

AMERICAN MISSIONARY ASSOCIATION, Second Annual Report. New York, 1848.

ADDRESS of the Liberty Convention of Cincinnati, held June, 1845, to the People of the United States. Cincinnati, 1845.

ABOLITION TRACT, by Solemn Truth. New York, 1845.

ADDRESS to the Office-Bearers and Members of the Free Church of Scotland, on her present connection with the slaveholding Churches of America. Edinburg, 1847.

ADDRESS to the same, by the Committee of the British Antislavery Society. London, 1846.

ADAMS, REV. C. An Address to Abolitionists of the Methodist Episcopal Church. Boston, 1843.

ARMISTEAD, WILSON. A Tribute for the Negro. Manchester, 1848.

AMERICAN SLAVERY AS IT IS, or a Thousand Witnesses, by Theodore D. Weld. New York, 1839.

ANTISLAVERY ALMANACS, from 1836 to 1849.

ANTISLAVERY REPORTER, New Series, from 1846 to 1849.

APPEAL of Southern Commissioners.

BIBLICAL REPERTORY, for April, 1836. VIEW on the subject of Slavery. Pittsburg, 1836.

BIRNEY, J. G. Letter to the Churches.

BLACK, REV. JOHN, D. D. Slavery Contrary to the Bible. Pittsburg, 1839.

BALDWIN, ROGER S. Argument before the Supreme Court of the United States, in the case of the United States appellants *vs.* Cinque, and others, Africans of the Amistad. New York, 1841.

BROOKE, SAMUEL. Slavery and the Slaveholder's Religion, as opposed to Christianity. Cincinnati, 1846.

BROWN, JAMES. American Slavery in its Moral and Physical Aspects; also, an Epitome, showing the mutilated state of Modern Christianity. Oswego, 1840.

BENEZET, ANTHONY. A Caution to Great Britain and her Colonies, in a short representation of the Calamitous State of the Enslaved Negroes in the British Dominions. London, 1785.

BRIEF VIEW of the Nature and Effects of Slavery. London, 1830.

BROWN, WILLIAM W., Narrative of, written by himself. Boston, 1848.

BIBLE, shall we give it to slaves?

BIRNEY, J. G. The American Churches the Bulwarks of American Slavery. Newburyport, 1842.

BURCHARD, REV. SAM'L. D. Causes of National Solicitude: a Sermon preached on Thanksgiving Day, November 25, 1847. New York, 1848.

BUSHNEL, REV. HORACE. The Evangelical Alliance. New York, 1847.

BRISBANE, REV. W. H., D. D. Slaveholding Examined in the Light of the Holy Bible. Philadelphia, 1847.
Eulogium of Hon. Thomas Morris. Cincinnati, 1843.

BUXTON, CHARLES, ESQ. Memoirs of Sir J. F. Buxton, with Selections from his Correspondence. Philadelphia, 1849.

BIBLE AGAINST SLAVERY. New York.

BACON, REV. LEONARD, D. D. Slavery Discussed, in Occasional Essays, from 1833 to 1846. New York, 1846.

BARNES, REV. ALBERT. An Inquiry into the Scripture Views of Slavery. Philadelphia, 1846.

BLANCHARD AND RICE. Debate on Slavery. Cincinnati, 1846.

BUXTON, J. F. The African Slave-Trade. Philadelphia, 1839.

BEECHER, REV. EDWARD, D. D. Narrative of Riots at Alton, in connection with the death of Elijah P. Lovejoy. Alton, 1838.

CHURCH ABOLITIONISM, or the Legitimate Tendency of the Doctrine of Modern Abolitionism, Practically Illustrated in the recent disruption of the First Baptist Church of Cincinnati, being an answer to Dr. Brisbane. Cincinnati, 1841.

Constitution of the Pittsburg Antislavery Society. Pittsburg, 1833.

Channing, W. E., Dr. Slavery. Boston, 1835.

Colored People of Cincinnati, Annual Report of the Educational Condition of the; including the Sentiment in Mercer County, O. Cincinnati, 1847.

Constitution, the: a Pro-Slavery Compact, or Selections from the Madison Papers. New York, 1845.

Child's, Mrs., Antislavery Catechism. Newburyport, 1839.

Cropper, James. Relief for West India Distress, showing the Inefficiency of Protecting Duties on East India Sugar, and pointing out other modes of Certain Relief. London, 1823.

Cooper, Thomas. Facts illustrative of the Condition of the Negro Slaves in Jamaica, with Notes and an Appendix. London, 1824.

Correspondence between Geo. Hibbert, Esq., and the Rev. T. Cooper, etc. London, 1824.

Conder, Josiah. Wages, or the Whip. London, 1833.

Catechism of the Mexican War, by a Farmer.

Channing, W. E. Letter to Hon. Henry Clay. Boston, 1837.

Crummell, Rev. A. Eulogy on T. Clarkson. New York, 1847.

Condensed Antislavery Argument, by a Citizen of Virginia. New York, 1843.

Clarkson, Thomas, A. M. History of the Rise, Progress, and Accomplishment of the Abolition of the African Slave-Trade, by the British Parliament. London, 1839.

Copley, Esther. History of Slavery and its Abolition. London, 1839.

Duncan, Rev. James. Treatise on Slavery, 12mo. Vevay, 1824; New York, 1840.

Douglass, Frederick, Narrative of the Life of. 12mo. Boston, 1845.

Does the Bible Sanction Slavery?

Dialogue, on Slavery, by a Lady.

Despotism in America, by the author of Archy Moore. Boston, 1846.

Debates in Congress, on the subject of Slavery, in 1848.

Emancipation in the West Indies. By Thome & Kimball. New York, 1838.

Edwards, Rev. Jonathan, D. D. The Injustice and Impolicy of the Slave-Trade, and of the Slavery of the Africans. Preached, September, 1791. Newburyport, 1834.

Elmore, Hon. F. H. and J. G. Birney, Correspondence of. New York, 1838.

Exposure of an Attempt to Mislead Parliament. London, 1831.

Edmondson Sisters. New York, 1848.

England, Bishop. Letters of, to Hon. John Forsyth, from the Catholic Miscellany of December 9, 1843. Baltimore, 1844.

Fuller and Wayland's Letters. 18mo. Boston, 1845.

Featherstonhaugh, G. W. Excursion through the Slave States. New York, 1844.

Foster, Stephen S. The Brotherhood of Thieves; or a True Picture of the American Church and Clergy. Boston.

Facts for the People of the Free States.

Fanatic, the, or the Perils of Peter Pliant, the Poor Pedagogue, by the author of Winnona. Philadelphia, 1846.

Garrison, Wm. Lloyd. Thoughts on African Colonization. Boston, 1832.

Green, Rev. Beriah. The Chattel Principle the abhorrence of Jesus Christ and his Apostles, or no Refuge for American Slavery in the New Testament. New York, 1839.

GRIMKE, A. E. Appeal to the Christian Women of the United States. New York, 1836.

GODWIN, REV. BENJAMIN. Lectures on Slavery. London, 1830.

GREEN, REV. BERIAH. Sketches of the Life and Writings of James G. Birney.

GARDINER, O. C. The Great Issue; or, The Three Presidential Candidates; being a Brief Sketch of the Question of Freedom in the Congresses of 1774 and 1787 to the present. New York, 1848.

GROSVENOR, CYRUS PITT. Review of Fuller and Wayland. Utica, N. Y., 1847.

HODGSON, ADAM. A Letter to M. Jean-Baptiste Say, on the Comparative Expense of Free and Slave Labor. Liverpool, 1823.

HISTORY of Mary Prince and Asa-Asa. London, 1831.

HALLEY, ROBERT. Sinfulness of Slavery. London, 1833.

HARVEY, SYLVESTER. Letters from the West Indies. N. York, 1838.

HISTORY of the Organization of the Methodist Episcopal Church South.

IMMEDIATE, NOT GRADUAL ABOLITION; or, An Inquiry into the Shortest, Safest, and Most Effectual Means of getting rid of West India Slavery. London, 1824.

IRVING, REV. JOSEPH. Lecture on the Extinction of Slavery, as an object of Scripture Prophecy. London, 1832.

JAY, HON. WM. View of the Action of the Federal Government in behalf of Slavery. New York, 1839.

Inquiry. New York, 1835.

An Antidote, etc., in reply to Dr. Reese. New York.

Letter to Bishop Ives. New York, 1848.

Letter to Hon. Theodore Frelinghuysen. N. York, 1844.

Review of the Causes and Consequences of the Mexican War. Boston, 1849.

JOHNSTON, HON. WM. Plea before the Franklin Circuit Court, Ky., April 10, 1846, on Slavery, Kidnapping, Fugitives from Justice. Cincinnati, 1846.

JOHNSON, REV. EVAN M. Discourse on the Communion of Saints. Brooklyn, 1848.

JEFFREY, REV. GEORGE. A Lecture on Pro-Slavery, Character of the American Churches, and the Sin of holding Christian Communion with them. Edinburg, 1847.

KINGSBURY, HARMAN. Law and Government: the Origin, Nature, Extent, and Necessity of Divine and Human Government, and of Religious Liberty. New York, 1849.

LEWIS, JUDGE SETH. Review of Abolitionism.

LETTER to John Bull; to which is added, the Sketch of a Plan for the Safe, Speedy, and Effectual Abolition of Slavery. By a freeborn Englishman. London, 1832.

from Legion; being an Exposure of the Evidence before the House of Lords, on the Colonial side. London, 1832.

SECOND LETTER from Legion; being an Analysis of the Antislavery Evidence before the Committee of the House of Lords. London, 1833.

LEGION OF LIBERTY. New York, 1847.

LLOYD, ELIZABETH. Appeal for the Bond Woman to her own sex. Philadelphia, 1846.

LONGSTREET, AUGUSTUS B. Letters on the Epistle of Paul to Philemon, on the Connection of Apostolic Christianity with Slavery, addressed to Drs. Durbin, Bangs, Peck, and Elliott. Charleston, S. C., 1845.

LEVERING, ROBERT E. H. The Kingdom of Slavery. Circleville, 1844.

LOVEJOY, J. C. Memoir of Rev. Charles T. Torry, who died in the Penitentiary of Maryland, where he was confined for showing mercy to the poor. Boston, 1847.

LETTERS of the late Ignatius Sancho, an African, with Memoirs of his Life. 2 vols. London, 1782.

LUNDY, BENJAMIN. Life, Travels, and Opinions of. Philadelphia, 1847.

LEE, REV. LEROY M., D. D. Life and Times of Rev. Jesse Lee.

MATLACK, REV. LUCIUS C. Life of Rev. Orange Scott. New York, 1847.

History of American Slavery and Methodism from 1780 to 1848, and History of the Wesleyan Connection in America from 1843 to 1848. Boston, 1849.

MEMORIAL of the Ohio Antislavery Society to the General Assembly of the State of Ohio. Cincinnati, 1838.

MORRIS, HON. THOMAS. Speech of, in reply to Henry Clay, February 9, 1839. New York, 1839.

M'KEEN, REV. SILAS. Scriptural Argument in favor of Withdrawing Fellowship from Churches tolerating Slavery among them. New York, 1848.

MOODY, LORING. History of the Mexican War; or, Facts for the People. Boston, 1848.

MAY, REV. SAMUEL J. Discourse on the Life and Character of Dr. Fuller. Boston, 1840.

MARPLE, REV. PERRY B. Funeral Address, on the Execution of Peter, slave of James Douglass, who murdered three of his own children, attempted suicide, by cutting his throat, feloniously assaulted his master, and murdered his mistress. Springfield, Mo., 1848.

MARTINEAU, HARRIET. Views of Slavery and Emancipation from Society in America. New York, 1837.

MELLEN, G. W. F. Argument on the Unconstitutionality of Slavery. Boston, 1841.

MOTT, A. Biographical Sketch and Interesting Narratives of the People of Color. New York, 1825.

MOORE, ARCHY. Memoirs of. 2 vols. Boston, 1848.

METHODISM AND SLAVERY. By Rev. H. B. Bascom.

NEGRO PEW, the. 12mo. Boston, 1837.

NOURSE, REV. JAS., A. M. Views of Colonization. New York, 1839.

NEGRO SLAVERY; or, a View of Slavery as it exists in the United States and the West Indies, especially in Jamaica. London, 1824.

NEEDLES, EDWARD. Historical Memoir of the Pennsylvania Antislavery Society. Philadelphia, 1848.

NELSON, REV. ISAAC. A Lecture showing that Slavery is supported by the American Churches, and countenanced by the Free Church of Scotland. Edinburg, 1847.

OHIO ANTISLAVERY SOCIETY. Report of the Third Anniversary of. Cincinnati, 1838.

Fourth Anniversary. Cincinnati, 1839.

O'KELLY, REV. JAMES. Essay on Negro Slavery; also, Essay on Slavery, by another hand—Othello. Philadelphia, 1789.

O'CONNEL, DANIEL. Appeal to Irishmen in America. 1843.

OLCOTT, CHARLES. Two Lectures on the subjects of Slavery and Abolition. Massillon, O., 1838.

PHELPS, REV. AMOS A. Letters to Professor Stowe and Dr. Bacon. 12mo. New York, 1848.

Lectures on Slavery and its Remedy. Boston, 1834.

PROCEEDINGS of the Session of Broadway Tabernacle against Lewis Tappan, with the action of the Presbytery and General Assembly. New York, 1839.

PROCEEDINGS of the meeting in Charleston, S. C., May 13–15, 1845, on the Religious Instruction of the Negroes, together with the Report of the Committee, and the Address to the Public. Charleston, S. C., 1845.

PEABODY, ANDREW P. Position and Duties of the North, with regard to Slavery. Newburyport, 1847.

Do. do. Newburyport, 1843.

POWER OF CONGRESS in the District of Columbia. New York, 1838.

PICTURE of Colonial Slavery, in the year 1828, addressed especially to the Ladies of Great Britain.

PHILLIPS, JOSEPH. Outline of a Plan for the Abolition of Slavery. London, 1833.

PROCEEDINGS of the General Antislavery Convention, held in London, June, 1840. 8vo. London, 1841.

for 1843. 8vo. London, 1843.

PATTON, WM. W. Pro-Slavery Interpretations of the Bible productive of Infidelity. Hartford, 1847.

PILLSBURY, PARKER. The Church As It Is; or, the Forlorn Hope of Slavery. Boston, 1847.

PERKINS, REV. G. W. Scriptural Missions: a Sermon. New York, 1848.

PALFREY, JOHN G. Papers on the Slave Power. Boston, 1846.

PROCEEDINGS of the Second Convention for Bible Missions, held in Albany. New York, 1846.

PROTEST and Remonstrance against the Evangelical Alliance. 1846.

PARKER, THEODORE. Discourse on the death of J. Q. Adams. Boston, 1848.

A Letter to the People of the United States, touching the matter of Slavery. Boston, 1847.

PAULDING, J. K. Slavery in the United States. New York, 1836.

PECK, REV. GEORGE, D. D. Answer to Dr. Bascom.

QUARTERLY ANTISLAVERY MAGAZINE: edited by Elizur Wright, jr. 2 vols., 8vo. New York, 1836–37.

RANKIN, REV. JOHN. Letters on American Slavery. Fifth edition. Boston, 1838.

REESE, D. M. Letters to Hon. Wm. Jay. 12mo. New York.

REVIEW, a, of some of the arguments against Parliamentary Interference in behalf of the Negro Slaves; with a statement of the Opinions of the most distinguished Statesmen. London, 1823.

REPORT of the Debate in the House of Commons, June 16, 1825, on the deportation of Lecesne and Escoffery.

REVIEW of the Slave-Trade and Slavery; also, on Free Labor. Birmingham, 1827.

RILAND, REV. JOHN, A. M. Two Letters on the Slave-Cultured Estates of the Society for the Propagation of the Gospel. London, 1828.

Letters on the Codrington Estates, to the Archbishop of Canterbury. London, 1830.

REMARKS on the demoralizing influence of Slavery. By a resident of the Cape of Good Hope. London, 1828.

REVIEW of the Rev. Dr. Henry Duncan's Letters to Sir George Murray. Edinburg, 1831.

REPORT of the Agency Committee of the Antislavery Society.

REVIEW of the Committee of the House of Commons. Liverpool, 1833.

REASON, CHARLES L. Poem on T. Clarkson. New York, 1847.

SUNDERLAND, REV. LE ROY. Testimony of God against Slavery. Boston, 1835.

SMYLIE, REV. JAMES. Review of the Chilicothe Letter to the Presbytery of Mississippi.

SHARP, GRANVILLE. Life of, by C. Stewart. 12mo. New York, 1836.

SCOTT, REV. ORANGE. Address to the General conference of 1836.
Appeal to the Methodist Episcopal Church. Boston, 1838.

STATEMENT, a full, to the Committee of the Legislature of Massachusetts, respecting Abolitionists and Antislavery Societies. Boston, 1836.

SYNOD OF KENTUCKY. Address to the Presbyterians of Kentucky. Cincinnati, 1835.

SLAVERY IN AMERICA, for 1836. 8vo. London, 1836.

SMITH, GERRITT. Letter to Rev. James Smylie, of the state of Mississippi. New York, 1837.

SLAVERY ILLUSTRATED, in its effects upon Woman and Domestic Society. Boston, 1837.

SAWYER, LEICESTER A., A. M. A Dissertation on Servitude, embracing an examination of the Scriptural Doctrines on the subject, and an Inquiry into the Character and Relations of Slavery. New Haven, 1837.

SUBSTANCE of the Debate in the House of Commons, on the 15th of May, 1823, on a motion for the Gradual Abolition of Slavery throughout the British dominions, with preface and appendices. London, 1823.

SLAVE COLONIES of Great Britain; or, a Picture of Negro Slavery, drawn by the Colonists themselves. London, 1826.

STEVENS, JAMES, ESQ. Slavery of the British West India Colonies Delineated, as it exists both in Law and Practice, and compared with the Slavery of other countries, ancient and modern. Vol. 2, 8vo. London, 1830.
England Enslaved by her own Colonies: an Address to the Electors and People of the United Kingdom. London, 1826.

SPOONER, LYSANDER. Unconstitutionality of Slavery. Boston, 1847.

SLAVERY AND THE SLAVE-TRADE at the Capital. New York, 1848.

SNETHEN, W. G. Black Code of the District of Columbia. New York, 1848.

SUMNER, CHARLES. White Slavery in the Barbary States. Boston, 1847.

SLADE, GOVERNOR. Speech before the House, Dec. 20, 1837.

STEWART, ALVAN. Legal Argument before the Supreme Court of New Jersey, May term, 1845. New York, 1845.

STARR, TIMOTHY. National Responsibility, and the Duty of the Ministry in relation to Politics. Rochester, 1846.

STRICTURES on the Proceedings of the last General Assembly of the Free Church of Scotland. Edinburg, 1847.

SLAVERY. A Treatise, showing that Slavery is neither a Moral, Political, nor Social Evil. By a Baptist Minister. Penfield, Georgia, 1844.

STROUD, GEORGE M. Sketch of the Laws relating to Slavery in the several states of the United States. Philadelphia, 1827.

THOMSON, REV. ANDREW, D. D. Slavery condemned by Christianity. Edinburg, 1847.
Speech on the Abolition of Slavery.

THOME AND KIMBALL. Emancipation in the West Indies. New York, 1838.

TAPPAN, LEWIS. Address to the

Non-Slaveholders of the South. New York, 1843.

THOMAS, REV. ——. A Review of the Rev. Dr. Junkins' Synodical Speech in defense of American Slavery, published December, 1843, with an outline of the Bible Argument against Slavery. Cincinnati, 1844.

TYLER, E. R. Slaveholding a *malum in se*, or invariably sinful. Hartford, 1839.

TEXAS. Address of J. Q. Adams on. Washington, 1842.

TAYLOR, JOHN. De L'Emancipation des Noirs, et d'independence des Indes-occidentales, consideres comme etant dans l'interet bien entendre de la Grande Bretagne. London, 1824.

THOUGHTS on the Abolition of Slavery, humbly submitted in a Letter to the King. London, 1824.

TRIAL OF JOHN MURRAY, for libel on Lecesne and Escoffery. London, 1830.

THOMPSON, JOSEPH P. Duties of the Christian Citizen. New York, 1848.

TREADWELL, S. B. American Liberties and American Slavery Morally and Politically Considered. New York, 1838.

THOMPSON, GEORGE. Prison Life. New York, 1848.

Prison Bard; or, Poems on various subjects, written in Prison. Hartford, 1848.

WAYLAND AND FULLER'S LETTERS. Boston, 1845.

WHITTIER, JOHN G. Voices of Freedom. Philadelphia, 1846.

WILSON, REV. J. L., D. D. Relations and Duties of Servants and Masters. Cincinnati, 1839.

WRIGHT, REV. ELIZUR. The Sin of Slavery and its Remedy. New York, 1833.

WESLEY. Thoughts on Slavery.

WILBERFORCE, WILLIAM, ESQ., M. P. An Appeal to the Religion, Justice, and Humanity of the Inhabitants of the British Empire, in behalf of the Negro Slaves of the West Indies. London, 1823.

WIN, T. S., formerly resident in the West Indies. Emancipation; or, Practical Advice to British Slaveholders, with suggestions for the improvement of West India Affairs. London, 1824.

WEST INDIA SUGAR.

WILSON, REV. D. Thoughts on British Colonial Slavery.

Sermon on Slavery. London, 1830.

WILKS, REV. SAMUEL C. Sermon on the Abolition of Slavery. London, 1830.

WHITELEY, HENRY. Three months in Jamaica, in 1832. London, 1833.

WELD, THEODORE D. On Fugitive Slaves.

American Slavery As It Is, or a Thousand Witnesses. New York, 1839.

WATSON, HENRY. Narrative of. By himself. Boston, 1848.

WILLIAM, JAMES. Narrative of Events. London, 1837.

WINONA, THE BROWN MAID OF THE SOUTH. By a Citizen of the South. Philadelphia, 1846.

WHEELER, JACOB D. Practical Treatise on the Law of Slavery. New York, 1837.

WILBERFORCE, SAMUEL, BP. Report of the American Church. New York, 1846.

WILSON, JAMES N. Address on Slavery, delivered in Fayetteville, Sept. 14, 1837.

YOUNG, REV. J. C., D. D. The doctrine of Immediate Emancipation unsound. Cincinnati, 1835.

The Duties of Masters. A sermon. Danville, Kentucky, 1846.

YOUNG, REV. DAVID. Lecture on Slavery: forbidden in the word of God. Edinburg, 1847.

INDEX.

THE END.